I WAS WITH
PATTON

★ ★ ★

FIRST-PERSON ACCOUNTS OF WWII
IN GEORGE S. PATTON'S COMMAND

D.A. LANDE

MBI Publishing Company

Dedication

This book is dedicated to Martin Blumenson who, more than anyone, has perpetuated the fascination in Patton and his armies.

First published in 2002 by MBI Publishing Company, Galtier Plaza, Suite 200, 380 Jackson Street, St. Paul, MN 55101-3885 USA

MBI Publishing Company books are also available at discounts in bulk quantity for industrial or sales-promotional use. For details write to Special Sales Manager at Motorbooks International Wholesalers & Distributors, Galtier Plaza, Suite 200, 380 Jackson Street, St. Paul, MN 55101-3885 USA.

Library of Congress Cataloging-in-Publication Data Available
ISBN 0-7603-1071-8

Edited by Ronald Klug
Designed by LeAnn Kuhlmann

Printed in China

Contents

Acknowledgments

I am grateful to the following people and organizations for contributing to this project:

- Dr. Richard Sommers, Pamela Cheney, and Michael Monahan at the U.S. Army Military History Institute at Carlisle Barracks, Pennsylvania
- Ivan Hannibal and Richard Harrison at the Wisconsin Veterans Museum Archives
- Charles Lemmons at the Patton Museum of Armor, Fort Knox, Kentucky
- D. Chris Cottrill, reference librarian at the Smithsonian Libraries, National Museum of American History
- The Library of Congress. Most of the Patton quotations in this book come from his collection of papers housed there.
- The Dwight D. Eisenhower Library
- Margit Chiriaco-Rusche at the General Patton Memorial Museum, Chiriaco Summit, California
- The always helpful staff of *VFW* and *The Retired Officer* magazines
- Catherine Schenker, editor of *Rolling Together*, the 4th Armored Division Association newsletter, and William C. Young of *Golden Acorn News*, the 87th Infantry Division Association newsletter
- Last but certainly not least, Ron Klug and Sara Perfetti for their editing expertise and support, and to Michael Haenggi, who had the idea that launched this book

I am also grateful for permission to quote from the following sources:
- The Vanguard Press for Robert S. Allen quotations from his book *Lucky Forward* © 1947. Used with the permission of Adeline Sunday Allen.
- Little, Brown and Company, division of Time Warner, Inc., for Charles R. Codman quotations from his book *Drive* © 1957. Used with permission of the publisher.
- Doubleday, a division of Random House, Inc., for Dwight D. Eisenhower quotations from his book *At Ease: Stories I Tell My Friends* © 1967. Used with the permission of the publisher. (Eisenhower's last letter to Patton is courtesy of the Dwight D. Eisenhower Library.)

Introduction

Ask a silver-haired GI what he did during World War II and he'll tell you his branch of service and where he served: "Navy's Atlantic Fleet." "Marine in the South Pacific." "Army Air Force based in Italy." Unless he's a veteran of North Africa, Sicily, or the Third Army in Europe. Then you'll hear a terse "I was with Patton."

Why would these veterans—from unit commanders down to the lowliest private in a rifle squad—identify themselves with General George S. Patton Jr.? How does an Army general have such a far-reaching effect on his troops?

In war, a GI's entire reach of consciousness might extend only as far as his 40-man platoon. In the words of W. King Pound, private in the 4th Armored Division, "The 'doggies' didn't have any real idea of what was going on at the top. Even at the company level. Your whole world was your immediate unit, your platoon." So a typical GI would certainly know his squad leader, he'd remotely know his platoon leader, and he might know his company commander's name. The strata of division commanders and corps commanders, let alone the commanding general above all of them, was a world away.

But the GIs *would* come to know the soldier's general, Patton. He demanded they know. He wanted each of them, down to the lowliest private, to be shaped in his image—infused with his aggressiveness, his sense of destiny, and his pride.

What Patton demanded of his troops—and got from them—goes beyond rational explanation. But his extraordinary demands and their extraordinary performance in response set them apart, and they knew it. They relished it. Coy Eklund of Third Army headquarters finds a way to put it simply: "We knew he was a winner. And with him, *we would win.*"

That's not to say that his soldiers always appreciated the aggressiveness and headline-grabbing flamboyance of their commander. They referred to him as "Ol' Blood and Guts," and under their breaths muttered: "Our blood and his guts." Despite the grousing among the ranks, to have been in Patton's command is a point of pride. There is distinction in being part of Patton's hell-for-leather drive that finally impaled Hitler's Germany with a spearhead of armor. Chesterfield Smith, artillery officer in the 94th Infantry Division, recalls letters written in

Patton at the peak of glory during his rampage across France. "I'm proud to be here to fight beside you," Patton said to a small gathering of GIs. "Now let's cut the guts out of those Krauts and get the hell on to Berlin. And when we get to Berlin, I am going to personally shoot that paper-hanging goddamned son of a bitch just like I would a snake."
U.S. Army photo courtesy of the Patton Museum, Fort Knox, Kentucky

the field that he reviewed as a censor: "Sometimes people that'd write those letters saying how wonderful Patton is would go outside and bitch about him to each other. Didn't like him. They'd say, 'He's not looking out for us. He's giving us too much risk.' But when they'd write home, they'd brag, brag, brag. They'd say, 'I'm a Patton man!' "

Patton was a larger-than-life figure whose genius for mechanized warfare and relentless pursuit of the enemy made him one of the great commanders of World War II. Combine this with *color*—swaggering self-confidence, insufferable brashness, a penchant for profanity, an explosive temperament, eccentricities, and a talent for exasperating his superiors—and you have a legend.

His *modus operandi* of "attack, and keep on attacking, and after you have done that, keep attacking some more" drew the undivided attention of the Wehrmacht and singled him out personally by name. As

Introduction

Supreme Allied Commander Dwight D. Eisenhower phrased it, "It's no exaggeration to say that Patton's name struck terror in the hearts of the enemy."

His name could strike terror in the hearts of his own troops, too. Patton's motivational techniques often included foaming-at-the-mouth tirades. Harry H. Semmes, one of Patton's armored commanders, writes in his book *Portrait of Patton*, "It is noteworthy that in two World Wars, the soldiers and the officers who served under Patton always bragged about the 'bawlings out' that they had received from him. They took pride in having been [bawled] out so wholeheartedly—with such enthusiasm and energy. Instead of resentment, there were many tales about how tough the reprimand was [for] the storyteller."

Of course, the tirades featured a liberal dose of swearing. Those within earshot say that his language sometimes amounted to nothing more than a staccato of four-letter expletives. Upon overhearing a tirade aboard ship after Patton slipped and fell on a wet deck, Navy Petty Officer Lewis C. Moorman assessed that the man was capable of "profanity . . . no one has ever heard or witnessed before." Patton's words may not have been original, but his arsenal of obscenities and profanities spewed out in endless and amazing variety. Rivaling the best top kicks, Patton's swear words took the form of nouns, verbs, adjectives, adverbs, and even a part of speech—yet unnamed by grammarians—that served as a bridge between two syllables of the same word. Swearing was not only reserved for tirades and speeches to masses of men, but was present in his normal everyday speech. Patton's personal driver, Horace Woodring, remembers: "We had conversations. He cursed with every breath. . . . Nothing serious, you know. That's just the way he talked."

It was all part of the image. All part of bullying the best out of his men by "making them fear me more than the enemy." But it was more than fear that moved them. Even if he didn't yell—even if he didn't say a thing—his presence was motivation enough. After all, if the Old Man was up at the front lines eating the same food, putting up with the lousy weather, and facing the same dangers of combat, then the GIs could do it, too. George Davis, who won the Silver Star in Brittany, comments: "I see Patton in my mind as clear as the first time I saw him at St. Lô. . . . He stood so straight—the picture of the perfect soldier. It was inspiring to us. We thought, *Here's a leader—up here with us and he's not afraid. If he can do it, I can do it.*"

Ask what else kept the "dogfaces" going, and many will give an answer similar to William Kunz's, who fought through 10 campaigns on the Continent and in the Mediterranean: "The civilian homefront fades out of your mind. . . . It isn't real anymore. What's real is the war, and the homefront is a reverie. You live only in the here-and-now, and what you have here and now are your buddies. So you live for them. You want to be there when the guy next to you needs it. That's all you can think about."

After these desperate times, the GIs returned home with a horrible imprint of brutality, carnage, and death. But they also brought back an understanding rarely grasped in the human condition—discernment of what is truly important in life and a conviction about what is worth fighting for. "The experience makes you grow up," utters Lewis Ingalls, a captain in the field artillery. "Having been in the Army and in the war, it hardens you to some things and softens you to others. You have a better understanding of life." Carl Ulsaker, referring to two particularly harrowing weeks of combat in Germany as an infantry company commander, adds, "It provided me early in life with the nadir of my existence, enabling me to cope calmly with all subsequent crises; for nothing I have since faced has proved to be worse than that experience."

Most didn't talk about the experience after they came back. For them, too, it was the "nadir of their existence," and they tried hard to forget it. But as the decades passed and maturity called attention to the most influential times of life, great floodgates of memories opened. What had floated in the backwaters of the mind spilled forth, and they realized they really could talk about it with pride. It was as Patton once said: "When you are sitting by the fireplace with your grandson on your knee and he asks you what you did in the great World War II, you won't have to cough, shift him to the other knee and say, 'Well, your granddaddy shoveled shit in Louisiana.' No sir, you can look him straight in the eye and say, 'Son, your granddaddy rode with the great . . . Army and a son-of-a-goddamned-bitch named Georgie Patton.' " The stories they lived to tell are spoken with awe, tears, pride, and sometimes even joy and laughter.

So, the stories here range from the humorous to the horrific; from the extraordinary to the everyday common GI's experience. The composite includes GIs of all ranks and roles who experienced the relentless drive under Patton's command. Many of them encountered Patton personally on the front lines. It includes those on the headquarters staff, who had constant contact with him and can offer more intimate insights, and also those outside the command who were left with indelible memories. Certainly not all aspects of Patton's commands are encompassed, but what's here is representative. Collectively, their quotes serve to paint what could be called an impressionistic picture of service with Patton throughout World War II.

Since this is a memory book that asked many to reach back to a distant and cataclysmic past, those quoted are honest in their recollections, but in a few cases may have misrecollected details. I've included bracketed clarification to explain what might be sketchy or obscure, or misremembered. The memories are certainly colored by each person's predilections and by the many experiences that have shaped his or her life.

The anecdotes and reflections are organized into 10 chapters that follow the highlights of Patton's World War II commands: his rigorous training of troops stateside, the campaigns in Africa and Sicily, preparations for the Continent, and his astonishing rampage across France and finally into Germany.

The memories are drawn from about a hundred personal interviews, oral histories, collections of letters and notes, and memoirs written for the family, such as that of Garrison H. Davidson, a retired lieutenant general who titled his unpublished memoir "Grandpa Gar: The Saga of One Soldier as Told to His Grandchildren," in the spirit of Patton's vision of a fireplace and grandson on a knee. Select excerpts also come from published books, but only when quotations were available in no other way.

The form of medium from which the quote is drawn (that is, personal interview, letter to the author, wartime letter, memoir, and so on) is noted in the "Sources of Quotations" at the end of the book. Paragraphs preceding each quotation provide pertinent information, such as division, location, and other items if not explicit in the quote. When rank is stated, it reflects the timeframe of the action remembered (some of these GIs later retired as first sergeants, master sergeants, colonels, and generals).

It was my great pleasure and privilege to interview, correspond with, and get to know so many who can say, "I was with Patton."

—D. A. Lande

Chapter 1

Training for "A Nice Juicy War"

April 1941–July 1942

G eorge S. Patton Jr. was ready for war—"a nice juicy war" in his phrasing. But his government and Army were not, even when Nazi aggression threatened to erupt into global war in 1939.

During the two decades of peace after World War I, America's armed forces had atrophied. Despite threats overseas in both Asia and Europe, America's Congress was pacifist and isolationist. The U.S. Army remained underfunded; troop strength had dwindled dangerously; and equipment rusted its way to obsolescence. In training exercises, armored units pretended that canvas-covered trucks with telephone poles were tanks, broomsticks were machine guns, and rain pipes were mortars.

All this needed to change quickly as America teetered on the brink of war—and Patton would play a key role in whipping the feeble prewar Army into fighting trim.

In April 1941, Patton was officially appointed commander of the 2nd Armored Division (he had been acting commander since November 1940) at Fort Benning, Georgia, and was promoted to the rank of major general.

Training became Patton's top priority. As a decorated combat veteran of World War I, he knew the need for conditioning that would cause a soldier to "react automatically when the bullets were flying."

He exhorted his troops to take the training seriously, despite the makeshift props for weapons. "Think this is war," Patton told his soldiers on maneuvers, six months before Japan's attack on Pearl Harbor. "That is the only chance, men, that you are going to have to practice. The next time, maybe, there will be no umpires, and the bullets will be very real—both yours and the enemy's."

He loved to deliver such addresses to the great masses of troops, forever prodding, taunting, teaching, and driving them with the zeal of a young Napoleon. One of his first acts as commander was to create what came to be called the "Patton Bowl," a natural amphitheater in the wooded hills of Fort Benning. It was large enough to accommodate his entire division. It was in gathering places such as this that seeds for the will to win World War II were first planted among the troops. And it was the place where many of them got their first startled taste of the patented Patton persona. Vincent Hooper, then a private in the 2nd Armored Division, heard Patton speak there. Hooper remembers this amphitheater, home to the famous "blood and guts" speeches that would lend Patton the nickname he would carry throughout the war:

> God made a natural bowl formation in the woods at Fort Benning just for General Patton. Patton ordered it made into a half shell or amphitheater that would hold the entire division of 15,000 men. It was appropriately called Patton Bowl. . . . He had a photographer take our picture on our first assembly and made it available as a five-foot long photo that we could send home. Anyone who had his picture taken that day can point to the face among the other 14,999 men in the sea of faces and say that is his picture at Patton's first assembly. . . .
>
> [After the photo was taken,] Patton himself took the stand for one of his well-known orations. His voice wasn't actually rough, but making it sound that way was part of his act to scare the hell out of his men. It was his plan not only to make the men as he said, more afraid of him than of the enemy, but to inure them to the horrors of battle.
>
> I am positive the Patton image was born on the first day he spoke in that bowl. Following an old cavalry credo to the effect you should always "Hit 'em where they ain't," he said to us: "You have to grab 'em by the [censured] and kick 'em in the [censured]." . . . At the end of the speech he said, "I am taking this division into Berlin and when I do, I want every one of your tracks to be carrying the stench of German blood and guts."

Leon Luttrell, also a private in the 2nd Armored Division, heard a similar message, but in a different setting. At the age of 16, he had enlisted in the Army and joined the division just after Patton took command. In a letter to the author, Luttrell relates his memory of assemblies and a slightly different rendition of the "Old Blood and Guts" moniker that would follow Patton into legend:

> I was assigned to C Company, 41st Armored Infantry, 2nd Armored Division, Harmony Church area at Fort Benning, Georgia. General Patton was the division commander. He trained us hard in order to prepare us for what was waiting in our future—and was well liked by all the troops.

> It's true that he used profanity in his talks and at our division assemblies. However, he used it to express his feelings for the enemy we were preparing to meet. At our last division assembly at Fort Bragg, North Carolina, where we were field training before going to Fort Dix, New Jersey, to embark for Europe, he told us that " . . . we would use their blood and guts to grease the wheels of our vehicles and tracks of our tanks." This is where he got the name "Old Blood and Guts," and that's a fact!

First Lieutenant Ralph Luman joined the 2nd Armored Division when Patton was just beginning to shape the troops into the blood-and-guts unit he wanted. He remembers the start of training under an impatient Patton:

> After New Years (1941), I received orders assigning me to the 1st Armored Brigade of the 2nd Armored Division under Major General Patton commanding. When I went to report in I found the Brigade orders were rescinded, and I got new orders to the 41st Infantry Regiment (Armored), then to Company E, under Captain Baker.

> We moved into newly built barracks and began to receive draftees, nearly all of whom were from New York City. All were high school graduates, but none had driven a car! We trained these men in everything!

> About 10 January 1941, General Scott [previous 2nd Armored Division commander] was moved to Fort Knox to establish the Armored Force Training Center to train all personnel for the new armored divisions. General Patton became the [acting] commanding general. We found we had to train every draftee, because the center at Knox couldn't get going.

> General Patton was not the kind to wait. Within a few weeks, our training units were turning out men with two or three military specialties. Every man could drive any truck, half-track, or tank in his own unit. Each officer was taught to drive every vehicle, from motorcycle up through medium tank. Only the 70-foot-long tractor-trailer pontoon bridge truck was excepted—that was engineer equipment.

Chapter One

Luman also remembers the day he witnessed the dubiously famous "green hornet" outfit (designed personally by Patton), which Luman was invited to photograph:

On the day we were "graduated" from our orientation course on vehicles and weapons, General Patton showed up in his new uniform. General officers could specify their own uniforms, and Patton felt that the Army had no satisfactory uniform for the armored units. So he was wearing a two-piece dark green corduroy outfit with the trouser legs fitted into his laced field boots. The jacket was waist length and buttoned up the right side, brass buttons polished. On his head was a close-fitting leather helmet with goggles on the top. Those present immediately dubbed him "the green hornet."

By March, we held the first full division parade: 17 tanks abreast (one company) followed another till all three tank regiments passed, followed by the eight companies of armored infantry regiments' half-tracks, then the engineers, medical, signal, ordnance and quarter-master battalions. It was really impressive!

While on a [training exercise], General Patton sat down [near me]. I had a camera with me and I asked him if I might take a photo of him. He smiled and said, "Certainly." Since I was only a first lieu-tenant, I had to work up courage, but he was as gracious as anyone I have ever met.

Harry H. Semmes, one of Patton's armored commanders, took note of Patton's uniforms as always sporting that "personal touch" or, in the case of the tanker outfit, being completely self-designed, as he relates in his book *Portrait of Patton*:

He always dressed immaculately and expensively. His combina-tion riding breeches and jodhpurs, with a specially made English combat boot, were distinctive. His famous glistening helmet liner was the result of literally dozens of coats of varnish by ordnance per-sonnel. Around this shinning halo were the insignias of all his former commands, like a garish chaplet. When he traveled he carried an arse-nal of guns and an extensive wardrobe in several traveling bags, packed by his loyal . . . orderly, Sergeant George Meeks.

Of all his amazing costumes, none approached the green dragon outfit that he designed and wore for a while. It was his glorified idea of what a proud unit like his 2d Armored Division should wear. Basically it was along practical lines because it fitted snug for tank use and was made of lasting material. But when he had added his own sartorial whims, it became a sight to behold.

A short cadet jacket of soft green leather was resplendent with two long rows of gold buttons, slanting downward toward his golden belt buckle. Tight jodhpur breeches carried this green ensemble on down to his short, soft boots. His heavy pearl-handled revolver was carried in a shoulder holster under his left arm.

To crown this already amazing uniform, he had obtained from the Washington professional football team an almost-luminous plastic helmet in a golden color.

Soldiers stopped short in amazement when they saw him. The fame of this startling getup spread throughout the Army and was featured in the press. All of this publicity Patton thoroughly enjoyed.

Once as the division was maneuvering around Fort Benning, a visiting staff officer from Washington went down to the C.P. [command post] to observe. An eager staff officer offered to outline the maneuver and situation on the map. "No, don't bother about that," said the visiting general. "We just came down to have a look at Georgie's uniform."

But this splendid uniform was discarded as the division training went on. One last remembrance of it was in the first Carolina maneuver. It was in the late fall, and the dust from the country roads was blinding. As day was breaking, two tank columns converged on a dusty crossroad. The traffic snarl was being handled by a tired tank captain, with bloodshot eyes glaring from his dirt-gray face. Tempers were short everywhere as idling tanks backed up, and the night had been long and rough.

Out early to lead his troops, General Patton came onto this scene of temporary confusion. He was in his full green dragon uniform, complete with golden helmet. His scout car, with his own special Gabriel horn on it, pulled up to the crossroad. This horn was another specialty of his, listed as a "a steamboat trombone, that can be heard eight miles on a clear day." With the general standing up beside the driver and towering over the scene, he let forth a shattering blast from this horn to clear the road.

This was too much for the captain's frayed nerves. Without turning his head, he shouted back, "Shut up there, you son of a bitch."

Then he turned around and saw the apparition above him. This was enough to startle anyone, and the general's face completed the terrifying picture. The horrified captain took off, crashing through the sumac bushes as he disappeared from the scene.

Patton addresses troops of the 2nd Armored Division about the Louisiana maneuvers. At a May 1941 division assembly, he spoke: "There are no bullets in maneuvers, and things sometimes get a little dull. But play the game. . . . Try, above all things, to use your imagination. Think this is war. 'What would I do if that man were really shooting at me?' "
U.S. Army

Good combat training called for "maneuvers"—war games in which a unit's performance in simulated combat was judged by umpires. Patton wanted maneuvers to be hard. He wanted them to be realistic. He wanted natural conditions that matched what his troops would be facing. There would be maneuvers in Tennessee, Texas, and the Carolinas, but the biggest and most memorable were the Louisiana maneuvers.

Training for "A Nice Juicy War"

Colonel Paul Harkins, who would later become Patton's deputy chief of staff, recalls the early maneuvers and how they improved as America geared up for war:

I was there with the 2nd Armored [in] Louisiana. It was the first time armor had been used in the maneuvers. We didn't have all the vehicles. We had 2-1/2-ton trucks with trees on them for cannons and things like that, but [at least commanders] learned to handle big units. General Patton commanded the 2nd Armored, and he'd do a hundred-mile night march to get to the place to attack the next day. It was fascinating to see how well we did.

I think his concept of training was something. It had to be realistic. He said you have to repeat and repeat and repeat and repeat training, because when you're being shot at you just do things automatically, and that's the purpose of training and why there is so much repetition and it seems boring to people. But he said once you've been hearing the whine of bullets around you, you automatically take cover or shoot at the other guy. I think he thought a lot of discipline and attention to duty.

Vincent Hooper of the 2nd Armored Division describes the Louisiana maneuvers—and the complications of using pretend guns:

Most of the western part of Louisiana was divided into two halves like a football field. One half was RED territory and one half was BLUE territory. And as in football, we would reverse or trade places after each phase (we would change ends).

There had to be a lot of umpires, and so I was assigned to ride in a jeep behind a captain and operate a tiny CW radio while bouncing around the scroungy back roads amidst the Spanish moss-covered oak trees. The captain wore a prominent white armband to show he was neutral. Without umpires, you might expect every battle to end up in a fistfight, because there was nearly always an argument as to whether or not the one side had made a legitimate conquest.

In one instance, the captain spotted a crew of men using a tree branch as what would be considered a 37-mm antitank gun. When the captain saw it was located down in the bottom of a creek bed and that the road over which a tank could have been expected to have approached went high up on the hill, he knew there would be some argument as to whether a gun in this position could knock out a tank. . . . After about a half-hour, a light tank came rolling along the road. The gun crew, rather than trying to shoot the tank from the creek bed, picked up the tree branch and hauled it up onto the road where it claimed to have fired at the tank and knocked it out. The captain drove up and the tank crew . . . dismounted to accept the decision of the captain, thinking it would be that the tank had been knocked out.

The captain asked the sergeant in charge of the crew if he thought his men could have hand-carried a 37-mm antitank [gun] up the steep embankment from the creek to the road. The sergeant of course claimed that was what they had done. It didn't matter that it was made of wood. It was a 37-mm antitank gun. The tank crew was beginning to see where the umpire was going and began to grin. "I don't think it would be possible," the captain began, "to carry a real 37-mm antitank gun up the slope and I am directing that you carry it back down. If you want to bring the tree branch up to this road, you will have to go get a jeep and have the gun towed down the creek bed to the road and then back up to this spot. But even if you do, I doubt it will do you any good because since the tank isn't really knocked out, it will radio back for mortar or artillery fire, so my advice to you is to clear out of this area." The sergeant uttered a barely audible "Damn!" but followed up with a clearly spoken, "Yes, sir."

◆

Ubiquitous to Army life was guard duty. During maneuvers, guard duty meant standing in the woods at a lonely outpost, where you hoped you'd encounter no one. Angelo Peter Rosato, one of Patton's tankmen in Louisiana maneuvers and later on, had to challenge someone he recognized—namely, his company commander, who evidently had been cast in the Patton mold.

I was assigned as the lone guard for the first shift of the night-long post. Suddenly, a peep, normally referred to as jeep by civilians, came roaring along that scrubby trail out of nowhere and heading straight for my post. I stood slightly to the side as I yelled, "Halt, who goes there?" So far, so good. . . . I recognized my own company commander returning from wherever.

Having been taken by surprise, I forgot the rules of guard duty. It had been a while since I did the same back in the barracks villages, so I blurted out, "Oh, Captain Kelly," while forgetting to ask for the password and some form of identification. Captain Kelly stepped casually out of the peep and came to face me. Next he said, "Let me see your weapon." I dutifully obeyed and in my naiveté, I handed my Thompson submachine gun over to him. Big, big, big mistake. He examined it rather casually. Then the fireworks began.

Training for "A Nice Juicy War"

"Rosato! When you are on guard duty you are in absolute command of your assigned post. You recognize no one . . . until they prove to you who they are and why they are there. Furthermore, only the O.D. [officer of the day], who assigned you to this post, can take the weapon from you, and only with good reason. No one, but *no one*, can take it from you under any other pretense."

His voice rose as he spoke: "No one, do you understand? Even if General Patton were here and attempted to pass during wartime without identifying himself, you shoot him!" His voice rising still further: "You are the sole commander of this post. Not even the Pope can pass through here except by your permission." Then his voice rang out in crescendo: "So long as you are here on duty you are in supreme command! You are not the general of the Army! You are not the pope! You are *God*! God! Gaawd! *You—are—God!*"

. . . references to Patton, the Pope, Jesus Christ and others are still ringing in my ears, especially his repeated reference to my temporary, ultimate eminence. To say that I was rather uncomfortable during his recitation is an understatement, but I must admit that for the first time in my military career I knew how vital a role it was . . . on a guard post. That knowledge stood me in good stead during my combat career.

◆

During maneuvers, Patton was a relentlessly hard driver. A long-time proponent and armor authority from World War I, Patton was known for his innovations and for shaping doctrines in this new thing called mechanized warfare. He had very firm beliefs about how mechanized warfare should be waged. Above all, he demanded that the armor keep rolling, no matter what—as he would demonstrate so boldly in his Third Army's drive across France. But even while training in the States, he did not tolerate delays. Numerous encounters with slow-moving vehicles, usually mule carts obstructing movement, resulted in drastic solutions that would become part of Patton lore. Captain Dupré Sassard describes one such instance:

In 1941, I commanded an infantry company on maneuvers in Louisiana. We were marching on a small country road when a section of armed half-tracks came past, but came to a stop at a small bridge just ahead of us. A farmer in a wagon drawn by a mule was in the middle of the bridge, stopped by a wheel broken off. This stopped our march and the half-tracks. After a few brief moments, another half-track came crashing up on the right side of the road. In it was General Patton, screaming his head off at the delay. When he saw the wagon, he ordered the mule unhitched and taken off the road. He then ordered the half-tracks forward, crashing over the disabled wagon. My company followed. When we passed the farmer and his mule, an officer of General Patton's command was buying him a new wagon.

As hard-driving as Patton was on maneuvers, he was known to give individuals a break from the heat and dust as long as it wasn't *too* obvious, as Leon Luttrell appreciated:

I was a motorcyclist on the Louisiana and Tennessee maneuvers, after being assigned to an I&R platoon [intelligence and reconnaissance] and was liaison between regiment and division. I personally delivered numerous messages directly to General Patton, who was in his personal tank. He never failed to offer me a cold drink of water, a Bull Durham cigarette, and a 10-minute break in the shade.

James Moncrief, later G-1 (personnel) officer for the 6th Armored Division, served as a liaison officer during maneuvers and, like Luttrell, traveled regularly by motorcycle to Patton's command post.

As a lieutenant in Patton's 2nd Armored Division, I made all the maneuvers in 1941: The Carolina maneuvers, the Tennessee maneuvers, and the big Louisiana maneuvers. I was my regiment's liaison officer with the division headquarters in most of those maneuvers. So I had several personal "encounters" with General Patton—that's the best way to say it.

On maneuvers, I saw him almost every day, me being the liaison officer. He was not in headquarters all the time, just as I was not always there, because I was off shuttling back and forth with regiment. But I saw him daily on normal maneuvers.

While on the Louisiana maneuvers, General Patton had dispatched me on motorcycle to take a message to a colonel in the 41st Infantry Regiment. I had to make this U-turn on the gravel road to get back on the highway. I had been checked out [on motorcycles], so I had some experience riding them.

On this particular occasion, the back end started passing the front wheel. I spilled. Took an awful spill. I took a hell of a spill. Blood was streaming down my boot. I had just left the CP [command post], so General Patton was still within sight.

"Get me another one! Get me another one!" Patton was yelling in his high-pitched voice. "And I don't mean another motorcycle! I mean another *lieutenant!*"

Training for "A Nice Juicy War"

Moncrief was at the scene of another accident a few months later, at the Carolina maneuvers, although he was not a victim of the crash this time. Patton happened upon the scene and his reaction—both immediately and on the next day—shows some of the capriciousness of Patton's character.

The SOP, standard operating procedure, was that the first officer who came upon an accident immediately took charge to get it squared away for the traffic en route. He was to take immediate action. Whatever was necessary. I was the unfortunate officer who happened to be the first to come upon an accident where a tank had been going over a bridge during blackout and had tied into the back end of a two-and-a-half truck. The truck and tank had become intertwined on the bridge, and traffic couldn't proceed either way.

Being the first officer on the scene, it was my unfortunate task to try to get it squared away. I did the best I could. I posted two guards, one at each end of the bridge. It had been raining and pavement was still a little wet—dangerous for skidding. I didn't want any other vehicles pushing through and adding to the accident. So I posted two guards up on the hill to stop oncoming traffic. And I radioed and sent my motorcyclist to get a winch truck from the maintenance battalion, because we had no equipment to yank the tank or truck off that bridge. That's all the action I had taken.

Coming down the hill was a quartermaster truck that ignored my guard, bearing down on the bridge. He tried to stop, skidded off just before the bridge, and ended up going off the road into the creek. So here was my second accident. I dashed over to see if anyone was hurt, and to find out what action was needed with that truck.

Remember this is blackout. While I was over there, all of a sudden, sirens started blowing, lights flashing, and all kinds of lights were shining over on the accident.

It was then I knew my third "accident" had occurred: General Patton was on the scene.

I dashed over to report in the usual fashion. "Sir, Lieutenant Moncrief—"

"I don't give a damn who you are. What the hell is going on?"

He started right away chewing me out. I thought he was so mad he was going to lift up that tank and throw it off the bridge. In a few minutes, he left in a huff.

I stayed there the rest of the night, wrestling with that situation until it was cleared up in the morning. I went on to my CP [command post] and saw Colonel Green, my boss. I went in to report about the activities of the night.

21

I explained that this wasn't a regimental accident. It was some-body else's [truck and tank], but I just happened to be the first officer on the scene.

Then I told him about General Patton. He became more inter-ested in General Patton than anything else. So I relayed in great detail all that General Patton had to say about it. Finally, the colonel said, "Go on home and get some rest, lieutenant." I went in and hit the bunk about 10 in the morning. I hadn't had any sleep.

They had a unit commanders' meeting later that afternoon, and Colonel Green told me later what General Patton said there. I thought I'd hear a lot of remarks about how inadequate lieutenants were—Patton always had a few choice words to say about things like that.

General Patton had gotten up on the platform and said in his high voice, "Green, you got a lieutenant in your outfit named Moncrief?"

"Yes, sir. He's my liaison officer." Since Colonel Green had already heard all the details from me about how mad the general was, he thought Patton was going to [direct him to] court-martial me. I expected it.

But from the platform, General Patton started telling what a wonderful job this lieutenant had done with the accident on the bridge. "I want to you to convey my respects and regards to Lieutenant Moncrief and tell him what a great job he did."

Hell, I really thought I was going to be court-martialed. Really.

On the Texas maneuvers, a young assistant battalion surgeon named John Erbes had his first encounter with Patton in the field.

One of our medium tanks got too close to the edge of a new road with a six-foot-deep ditch at the side and rolled off onto its back. I was called from the rear of the column and came up with my ambu-lance. There was no way to get the ambulance off the road, so I parked it and went to treat the injured men in the tank. Suddenly a Piper Cub observation plane came over and this "celestial voice from the heavens" said, "This is General Patton. Get that goddamned ambulance off the road or I'll have a tank push it off." My ambulance driver had to drive up the road for about a half a mile to a crossroad and come back cross-country to get the injured.

In January 1942, only a month after Pearl Harbor and the United States' formal declaration of war, German and Italian troops under the command of General Erwin Rommel pushed toward Egypt. Rommel, soon to be promoted to field marshal, had set his sights on the Suez Canal. As British troops were reeling eastward, it became clear that the U.S. Army would have to join the Allied desert campaign.

One problem: The U.S. Army had no experience in desert warfare. It had no desert training program and no adequate training grounds to simulate conditions. On January 31, 1942, Lieutenant General Lesley J. McNair, head of the Army Ground Forces, turned to Patton (now commanding I Armored Corps) to quickly establish desert training grounds. Patton selected a region of the American Southwest that most closely matched the harsh desert conditions of Africa. The region was immense—350 miles by 250 miles—stretching from the westernmost region at Indio, California; east to Aguila, Arizona; from the northernmost region at Searchlight, Nevada; and south to Yuma, Arizona. It was by far the biggest training area for maneuvers in the history of the United States. Much of the land was government-owned and the rest was sparsely populated.

Margit Chiriaco-Rusche remembers the stories of her late father, Joe Chiriaco, who owned much of the land in the vicinity of Chiriaco Summit, near what would become Camp Young, in California. He also owned a restaurant that became the local hangout for off-duty soldiers. Chiriaco struck up a friendship with Patton. Chiriaco's daughter remembers her father's introduction to Patton.

My dad was at the counter with his back to the customers and someone came in and asked him if he was Joe Chiriaco and how long he had been here. Without looking around, my dad quipped, "I'm Joe Chiriaco. And see those mountains over there? They were this high when I came here." And he held his hand about two feet from the floor.

Then my dad looked up and saw all the gold on this general's jacket, and he knew he was in the presence of someone very important. Realizing this was the General Patton, he again introduced himself, and they began an acquaintance that would last the whole time General Patton was in the desert near Chiriaco Summit.

General Patton made the Chiriaco Restaurant on limits to the camp men so that they could come in casual clothes.

He also was a careful protector of civilian rights. More than once his tank maneuvers cut off the water supply to Chiriaco Summit and Patton immediately had the men fix it. My father remembers him as a gentleman and a person who greatly respected the rights of others.

My father wanted badly to go to war, but he had four children and his wife, Ruth, and the business here at Chiriaco. On more than one occasion he mentioned his desire to go to war.

Finally, after discussing this one more time, General Patton said to him: "Joe, you let me take care of the war, and you stay here and take care of the business."

Chiriaco stayed and served thousands of servicemen in his restaurant. As Vince Gish of the 6th Armored remembers: "We were in the middle of the desert, close to Desert Center. That was near Chiriaco Summit. Joe Chiriaco opened a hot dog stand up there. He had said, 'Those soldiers need a beer and a hot dog.' And it's been there ever since."

◆

Over the next 2-1/2 years, more than a million GIs in 7 armored divisions and 13 infantry divisions would train in the desert area. It is plain to see why Patton chose the area. Remote and desolate, there were wide-open spaces for every form of training. There were mountains, gorges, and great salt lake beds—and no civilians to get in the way. James Moncrief adds:

> There were no farmers' fences, and you could just walk out of your tent and you were on any kind of range you wanted to be on. Pistol range, rifle range. Walk a hundred yards more, and you were on a tank range. Ideal training for an armored division.

While there wasn't an actual human adversary present, the environment in its own way was a real-life adversary. It hardened the GIs, developed self-reliance, and prepared them to live and function in harsh conditions (even if the combat they would face was not in the North African desert). Vince Gish remembers the conditions.

> What I remember most was the heat of the desert. The winds at night. The elements. Even rain, hard rain, sometimes. You had to put up with the snakes and the scorpions, and the flies. Remember we were in tents, not barracks there. It reached somewhere around 120 degrees. There was no shade in the desert, only cacti, and there's very little shade from cacti. They never called off training because it got too hot. They actually *wanted* that. The tougher, the better, because it toughened us.

Private Charlie Markovitz of the 6th Armored Division remembers the "good news" that they were going to California for training. He tells how this wasn't the side of California they envisioned:

Training for "A Nice Juicy War"

When they told us we were leaving Camp Chaffee to go out to California for training, we were all pretty happy about that. It sounded good! Most of us were from cities out east, including me. I was from the Buffalo, New York, area. When we thought of California, we thought of beaches and glamour.

Then our train stopped—in the desert.

We were pulled off onto a railroad siding at Rice, California. It was one building in the middle of the desert. We disembarked and got on trucks to go out to our supposed "camp."

We drove a little while into even more barren territory—if that were possible. All of sudden, whoever was in charge said, "Men, this is your camp." We all looked out of the truck and didn't see anything but desert. The railroad siding had seemed like a metropolis compared to this!

The area was marked off with something like lime to outline company streets. So we marched down those [imaginary] streets, until the guy showed us to our tents. He points to a pile—a bunch of tents all folded up in a pile. Pretty soon we realized we didn't even know how to put up these six-man tents. *This* would be our home for the next five months.

Markovitz remembers the good, the bad, and the routine of the Desert Training Center. Daily life included:

. . . washing up with cold water from the tanks. We had a cold shower, maybe once a week. There was a pot-bellied stove in each tent. We burned wood that was rationed. When we ran out of wood, we'd go out in the desert and pick up mesquite or anything else that would burn. When we were out on maneuvers, you didn't have toilet facilities. You had to go out with your little folding shovel, dig a hole, do your business, and cover it up.

Every day we would be in the tanks training, practicing. When you're in tank, there was always a vehicle in front of you. And *every* vehicle there had tracks. Even the half-tracks. So every vehicle churned up so much dust and the exhaust blew it back toward you. Choking dust. You had goggles on, but the rest of your face just got covered with dirt, and you'd breathe it in. When you got out of that tank, you were just covered.

But we had some fun times, too. Kay Kyser and his Musical College or whatever his band was called. Ish Kabibble was his singer. Other entertainers came out from Hollywood, which wasn't all that far away. Red Skelton came there. Rosalyn Russell, too. Rosalyn Russell's brother was in the 6th Armored, so that may have had something to do with it. A lot of big stars came out, especially around Christmastime.

For Christmas, they had big meal for us—turkey and all the trimmings. The kitchen was set up at the base camp, outside of course. Then a big windstorm came up. The cooks set up a canvas windbreak so they could serve the food. But the wind was blowing all the sand around and we ran back to our tent to eat it, but the food got all full of sand. Gritty sand and dirt.

Then, the wind was so strong it started to blow the tents down! While we were eating, the corners started getting pulled up. When the stakes let loose, then it would fall down in the middle. Everybody ran around trying to keep it up. But the tent was collapsing. What a Christmas dinner!

The conditions helped prepare us for battle though. Just *being* in those conditions. About the time we got to the Desert Training Center was when the battle for Africa ended, so the 6th Armored didn't go there. But it got us prepared for the hardships to come in Europe.

Vince Gish adds his memories of the routine:

A typical day included battle scrimmages and planning out mock attacks. I was dumbfounded that, at the same time we were there, the Army Air Force was flying overhead and dropping large sackfuls of flour [instead of actual bombs]. But the first one that landed close scared me to death! When those big flour sacks hit the sand they exploded in a great puff of white smoke. They could easily see if they hit [their target]. I guess they didn't want actual explosions, because they were landing right around us. The Army Air Force was learning to do their thing, too.

Typical days were maneuvers with the tanks, the infantry and the artillery. I was in the armored engineers. But if we had to build a river bridge, we had to go clear to the Colorado River to do it.

After I got overseas, I was a demolition specialist. But we didn't have much training for that in California. We practiced laying mines, and picking up mines. What we practiced most of all in California was using mine detectors and your best buddy, the M-1 rifle.

Usually, we were up at the crack of dawn, with mess kits, eating sand for breakfast, along with our pancakes. At least we had hot meals.

There were night maneuvers. The nights get really cold, winter or summer. But the days got really hot.

It was just about unbearable in the tents out there, but you got used to it. The tents were small. You had to park your boots outside.

Things happened to people. Guys would get up in the morning and get out of their tent to put their boots on, and all of a sudden a little lizard or scorpion would come flying out of the boot. That would scare you to death. More than getting flour sacks dropped on you! You learned to dump out your shoes and be ready to stomp on anything that fell out. Or, the next night you kept the boots in the tent, even though there wasn't much room in a two-man pup tent.

Stan Wolczyk, a young officer in the 7th Motorized Division, was given an unenviable assignment as umpire to judge the mock battles for Patton's desert maneuvers.

My experience with General George Patton was not with any unit under his command, but as an umpire during desert maneuvers in 1942 in the Mojave Desert. I was a second lieutenant in G Company of the 7th Motorized Division. During the maneuvers, I was stuck with the job as an umpire.

I was assigned to follow a column of Patton's tanks during an evening and night problem. We were required to use only blackout lights. Couldn't see a thing. All you could hear were tanks moving during the night.

I was situated in the middle of a column of tanks. When morning came, there wasn't a single tank or other vehicle to be seen to our front. But there were at least 30 tanks behind, and we found ourselves to be the leading vehicle!

Soon a command car with some stars waving in the breeze stopped abruptly in front of my vehicle. It was General Patton with his holstered six-guns. He demanded to know what I intended to do with all his tanks. And if I wasn't using them he would like to have them back!

I received the worst chewing out anybody ever had. "No more umpire in the middle of any column!" he said. "I want all umpires to situate themselves at the *tail end* of all vehicles engaged in any exercise."

That evening during a critique of the exercise, the general repeated his instructions on where the umpires should be stationed.

Not long after Patton established the Desert Training Center, he was called away to lead the Western Task Force that would invade North Africa. By July 30, 1942, the men were left to carry on training without him. Many would rejoin him with the Third Army in Europe. Although Patton was gone, he had left his mark and the hard-driving tempo of training was set.

Chapter One

By the time he left the States for the North African campaign, Patton was pleased with the progression and rehabilitation of the Army, which only a year before had been in a deplorable shape. He wrote a letter to retired General John "Blackjack" Pershing, whom he admired and had known for years, beginning with his time as Pershing's aide-de-camp for the 1916–1917 Punitive Expedition into Mexico. Pershing had led U.S. Army troops into Mexico to hunt down a band of bandits who had harassed and killed American citizens. "Our equipment is coming along splendidly," Patton wrote, "and I believe that the troops throughout the Army, and particularly in the armored force, have attained a very high standard of proficiency."

Chapter 2

Dueling in the Desert

November 1942–June 1943

North Africa was the scene of a fierce seesaw battle. Beginning in February 1941, British Commonwealth forces had a series of sweeping victories that won great expanses of land, but they were hurled back repeatedly by Germany and Italian forces. Always spoken in the same breath with Axis victories was the name Erwin Rommel, the vaunted German field marshal. By early 1942, when the Suez Canal was threatened, the United States committed itself to the desert war. And Patton was spoiling for a showdown with the star of the desert show, Field Marshal Rommel.

"I should like particularly to be in a position to beat Marshal Rommel, because . . . no one has licked him yet," Patton said. News magazines of the day played up the personal showdown by suggesting that Patton wanted to meet Rommel man-to-man for a "duel," with each wielding a tank instead of dueling pistols. Patton loved colorful portrayals of himself, but he denied that particularly wistful proposition in private correspondence.

Before any kind of German-American showdown was a possibility, Allied forces had the mission of seizing French North Africa—the colonial holdings of the French government to the west of Rommel's position. Under the aegis of Operation Torch, three separate task forces would invade Algeria, Tunisia, and Morocco. Patton was assigned command of the westernmost forces, set to invade Morocco.

29

Chapter Two

French forces, under control of the German-puppet government of France, defended the North African coast. Unofficially, many French soldiers supported the Allied cause. But the situation became complicated by several factors: The Germans had occupied only part of France during the blitzkrieg of 1940 and left the other part to be governed by puppet French leaders. The French didn't want to give the Germans a reason to occupy the rest of their homeland, as well as the far-flung colonies. So that served as coercion to push the French soldiers into a fight against an Allied invasion of the colonies. Add to that the French Army's already bruised pride after a humiliating defeat by the Germans in the blitzkrieg, and Patton's men in the Higgins landing boats faced an unpredictable welcome on the beach.

Regardless of the French attitude, a determined Patton prepared for all-out battle. While planning the operation in Washington, he announced to President Franklin D. Roosevelt, "I will leave the beaches either a conqueror or a corpse." He thought the sentence catchy enough that he shared it again later that day with General George C. Marshall. Patton expected similar resolve in his troops, green as they were.

Early on the morning of November 8, 1942, Patton's invasion troops went ashore in three separate landings focused around Morocco's main port of Casablanca: at Safi, 150 miles south; at Port Lyautey, 90 miles north; and the main landing at Fédala, 18 miles north. A firsthand account of each of the three landings follows.

Taking part in the main landing at Fédala was T/5 John A. Watters in the 10th Combat Engineer Battalion of the 3rd Infantry Division. Watters writes about being among the first troops ashore in the first major American ground action of the war, in his words, "to knock off Hitler's thousand-year Reich":

> My squad's mission, in brief, was to land ahead of the main assault waves before daylight. We were to make our way inland a short distance (a mile or less), and blow up a section of the railroad that ran parallel to the beach. The purpose of this was to intercept and prevent any reinforcements from coming to help the enemy troops at Fédala, either from the north or the south, and either German or French.

At midnight Watters' squad clambered down the sides of the transport ship into the Higgins boat that would take them to shore:

> It's [a different] experience to climb down a net and try to get into a little boat that is bobbing up and down, somewhat comparable to a yo-yo, especially when you are trying this little stunt 10 miles

out at sea, with a pretty good surf running. Black as pitch, full field pack, rifle slung over your shoulder, cartridge belt full of heavy ammunition, scared as hell for what lay before you in your first taste of combat, in an assault landing on a foreign shore, 3,000 miles from home.

The trick of course was in the timing, when a heavy surf was running. The landing craft was bobbing up and down against the side of the ship, and you had to gauge it just right, and step or jump from the net into the boat, just as it reached its highest point. If you jumped too soon, you landed with a terrific thud and could break a leg, or even miss the cotton-picking boat altogether. If you didn't jump or step soon enough, it was possible that the boat could come up and knock you off the net or even crush you against the side of the ship. I heard of this happening several times, but it never happened to anyone in our squad.

Watters' squad was not to land until daybreak, which meant bobbing around like corks in the landing boats on open sea for hours before beginning their mission on land. Watters continues:

We cruised around from about midnight until just before daylight. The sailor boys certainly knew what they were doing, and as events proved, they put us right where we were supposed to land. To start out 10 miles at sea, cruise around over four hours, and hit a small beach at the correct point is, to me, almost incredible. My hat is off to our particular boat crew. Unfortunately, everyone wasn't so fortunate. Some boats were scattered up and down the coast for 30 miles.

The Coast Guard coxswain put the prow of the boat up on a pretty nice beach. . . . We were the first on the beach, with not a soul in sight anywhere and not a shot had been fired by anyone, friend or foe.

The next step was to find that railroad we were supposed to blow up, so Sergeant Wayne Kesterson from Fort Wayne, Indiana, sent out some scouts to find it. It was imperative that we find our objective as soon as possible, and if the scouts could locate the railroad and then lead us to it, we could go and blow it up and not roam around willy-nilly and get knocked off.

As Watters' squad waited outside a small seaside village for the scouts to return, shooting erupted.

Supposedly, there had been a prearranged signal that if the French shined their search light up into the air there would be no shooting. If they shined it out to sea they would resist. As the story goes, the French turned the light on before they had it pointed upward, and some trigger happy GIs shot the searchlight out. Some said this act started the fireworks.

Whatever the reason, all hell broke loose. A hail of rifle and machine gun fire began singing over our heads, seemingly from every direction.

We wasted no time vacating that spot, and headed right down the one street of the native village . . . Everything was pandemonium. All the shooting and a bunch of wild-eyed dogfaces riding down a street was enough to send anyone into shock. Every soul in the village was in the street, and running frantically to get away from the shooting.

After escaping the bullets, his squad soon found the objective: the railroad tracks they were to destroy with explosives.

We were almost [ready to lay our charges] when a passenger train came around a curve. It was going at a pretty good clip, and it was evident that it had no intention of stopping. The engineer was really pouring on the steam.

I had been around trains all my life and at the age of 15 had hoboed and rode freight trains all through the southern United States. I had seen dozens of hobos riding on one train, but I had never seen anything like I now saw.

This passenger train was speeding along, and out of every window were hanging two or three people. People were all over the roof, jammed between the cars, and even on the coal tender. Someone was standing or hanging on every conceivable place. It was a veritable anthill in motion. We just stared in amazed wonder at this mass of humanity going by. It soon passed out of sight to the north.

We laid our charge on the rails. We then withdrew to where a high, thick, stone wall ran at right angles to the railroad. I was always thankful that we hadn't found the railroad and blown it up before the train came. If we had done so, the train would have surely been wrecked, and perhaps hundreds of people would have been killed and injured.

Concurrent with the Fédala landing were the landings to both the north and south. Lieutenant James M. Burt, who would later win the Medal of Honor for action in Germany, landed near Port Lyautey in the dim light of predawn with an armored landing team. He tells of the unique scenario that lessened resistance in their area.

In Morocco we had apparently planted advance men who helped us. The French Foreign Legion here did not wish to fight us. By some manner, word went to them that we were the outfit of Leonard H. "Steamer" Nason, of Norwich. They had old-timers who remembered and revered "Steamer" Nason. I think he was an honorary corporal in the French Foreign Legion and had been decorated by the Sultan with the Star of Islam. They weren't too keen to tangle with "Steamer" Nason's boys. I'm sure that helped minimize our invasion's resistance.

We were met with no fire as we landed on the beach. But we were ready for whatever would come. It's not something you think about it too much ahead of time. Your attitude has to be *whatever comes, we'll be ready for it.*

The saddest thing was what happened to one tank. This crew had driven their tank all the way up on the beach the way they were supposed to. Normally, everyone threw open their hatches at that point, as soon as they were on the beach. The rest had. But that didn't get done in this tank.

I watched this tank as it U-turned after it got up on the beach. It was on the sand and then turned right around and went back into the sea and submerged. All drowned. They apparently didn't have enough oxygen inside the tank. See, we were equipped to go right up to the turret in water. Hatches all had to be down and sealed with a goo, because we were prepared for driving off the landing craft into the water. Normally a hatch isn't sealed like that, but we put on goo that would withstand salt water. We didn't know how we would hit the beach. We thought we might have to drive in through fairly deep water. This crew passed out for lack of oxygen and they all drowned.

There was another [mishap] before we could leave the beach, but nothing so serious. I was a tank company maintenance officer and, as needed, a tank platoon leader. One tank was almost on its side. It made a bad turn coming out of the water and hit soft sand on a high sand dune, and threw a track by going sideways. My mechanics had a lot of ideas and didn't care for mine, which was a pick-and-shovel brigade. After trying all their ideas they reluctantly tried mine. There was room for about six men with shovels, so we shoveled away the uphill "mountain" so that the tank was able to tip into the uphill side of the sand dune. Lo and behold, the track popped back into place. It really didn't take very long, a couple of hours, because the soft sand was easy to dig. During the course of the whole war, I think that was the only time we put on a tank track with a shovel!

Facing no resistance, Burt's unit wheeled around the southern end of a lagoon and raced inland to take positions on the French flanks.

Chapter Two

There had been no shots on the beach. The defenders were back a bit and didn't know we were coming. Or if they did, I think they had no awareness of *who* we were.

We opened fire before they knew what was happening. There was some shooting, some fighting, some casualties. The French had a few. The Arabs had a few. But not massive.

The French forces had a squat World War I tank—or an interim period tank with small caliber gun—so squat it could go under the fig trees. And its round was probably 35 or 40 millimeters. One of these tanks had put one of ours out of action by a round that stuck in the turret track. Using our Marine amphibious vehicle, we went back to the ship and they sent a crew with a torch and we were able to get the stuck turret back into action.

Once past the light resistance, Burt's unit and other landing forces at Port Lyautey turned toward the main objective of Casablanca.

The third landing, at Safi, was different for Lieutenant John Erbes of the 2nd Armored Division. The first wave had gone ashore simultaneously with those at Port Lyautey and Fédala and, as Patton journaled, "The landing at Safi . . . went as planned . . . [and the troops] captured the harbor at 0515." So the remaining forces aboard ship did not have to shuttle ashore on landing craft, but instead simply shuffled down the gangplank after docking in a harbor, untouched by combat.

The landing was unique for an invasion force, as was Erbes' perspective as a battalion surgeon. And he himself was unique among surgeons—according to the 2nd Armored Division Association, Erbes became the most decorated surgeon in the European Theater of Operations during World War II. He writes:

> On November 8, at about 3 a.m. we approached the port of Safi. We hesitated, offshore, until daylight, when several lone scouting planes flew over us, but our antiaircraft guns encouraged them to stay up plenty high. They soon withdrew with no damage to either side.
>
> Shortly thereafter the large naval guns of our escorts began to bombard several isolated gun emplacements surrounding the city and port. The enemy guns were soon put out of action, and we sailed into the harbor. We began to unload immediately at the undamaged docks.
>
> We did not expect much opposition from the French defenders of Morocco. However, we were prepared to deal with any resistance that they might show.

Dueling in the Desert

Captain Sutter, the assistant battalion surgeon, and I were standing on the deck that morning, watching the unloading of our vehicles when we noticed a twin-engine bomber take off just beyond the city. It returned at once and swung low over the city, evidently on an observation flight. We recognized it as an enemy plane because we had been informed that all twin-engine bombers that we might see on the first day would be hostile.

The bomber went out of sight and we had all but forgotten about it when it suddenly came over the horizon following the coastline and flying directly at our ship. Captain Sutter and I began to shout to the antiaircraft (ack-ack) gunners aboard the half-tracks on the top deck of our ship, but they evidently did not hear us, because they paid no attention until the plane was nearly upon us.

They opened fire just as the plane reached the ship. Their target was quite obscure because of the ship's hoists and riggings, but nevertheless, they fired with great gusto shooting up the deck crane and the dock warehouses.

The plane came over very low, about 25 yards to the port side and 40 yards high. His nose guns were blazing and raking everything in sight. The tracer bullets made him seem to be spitting fire in our direction. The .50-caliber tracers from our deck guns, as they ripped through the cranes and warehouse, ricocheted and glanced off the metal of the cranes like a welder's torch, with sparks flying in all directions. Finally the Navy antiaircraft gunners began to shoot as the plane banked to go over the hill. We learned later that one of our own half-track antiaircraft vehicles, which had been the first vehicle ashore and had been sent to guard us from the top of the hill, had opened fire on the exposed belly of the plane just as the plane had banked to go over the hill, and shot him down about 40 yards beyond his position. The total result of the encounter was one twin-engine French bomber shot down with the entire crew killed, no casualties on our side, and plenty of scared soldiers.

Erbes would see his first battle wounds that day, as his unit began its mission on land:

There was considerable fighting between our infantry and enemy snipers, principally the French Foreign Legion. From the ship we could see quite a bit of the skirmishing. I went ashore with two Medical Corpsmen that afternoon to investigate the local water facilities and the shore medical aid station that had been set up by the infantry division in one of the dock buildings.

I had no sooner gotten back about the ship when they brought news of four infantrymen in critical condition. We took the most seriously injured man to the operating room first. We cleaned up the knee wound, tying off bleeders and debriding obviously destroyed tissue, and then applied a traction splint. We closed what tissue was viable and put Penrose drains into the badly contaminated and bruised areas. Before closing, we applied sulfanilamide powder. (We had not heard of penicillin at that time, and it wasn't available to us for about another year.)

All four of the patients had several bullet wounds each. Later a sergeant told us the story of the shootout. His platoon had come ashore early that morning to scout a certain French barrack. On the way they had met an Arab who spoke a little French. One man in the platoon also spoke a little French and they asked the Arab if he would lead them to the barrack, and he agreed.

Instead of leading them to the barrack, he led them into a trap where the French had several machine guns mounted on a wall. Every man in the platoon was either wounded or killed. The Arab was shot up beyond recognition.

◆

Even as the U.S. seaborne assault forces were landing along the Moroccan coast, American leaders still hoped that diplomacy would prevail, and the French would cooperate. That hope continued even after the hostilities began. Early afternoon on the first day, Patton sent two of his officers to negotiate with the French. Hap Gay, Patton's trusted chief of staff, was one of the two men chosen to go to Casablanca.

When we landed in Africa in 1942, they sent a lieutenant colonel and me in to see the French and tell them we had come not as enemies, but as friends. We went into Casablanca. They stood him up, my partner, against a well and shot him. They stood him up and killed him. They took me down into the basement, stood me against the wall and had me put up both hands above my head. He took out his gun. Thank goodness he didn't use it for some reason or another. I don't know.

But, he then let me go down and see the admiral there and I told him we had come as friends, not as enemies, and just then our Air Force bombed the ship. As near as I could understand his French, he said, "Your actions belie your words." They considered us the enemy.

Dueling in the Desert

We went through the battle lines, and when I got back and told this to General Patton, he went right after them.

According to the plan, Patton sent another wave of soldiers to hit the beaches. That evening, Corporal William J. Kunz also climbed into a Higgins boat and headed toward Fédala. As a soldier in the 3rd Infantry Division, Kunz would participate in 10 campaigns during World War II. This would be the first of his five landings on hostile shores. He had been "assigned to a radio section as an extra man," he notes, "part of the 20 percent overstrength that they booked into the division anticipating that percentage of casualties."

At first, it was kind of like a big adventure. A big parade. They brought flags up the beach, and carried them as they went. Fédala was the easiest of all five landings I made during the war. We came ashore late in the evening of the first day. We sat around all day on the transports, went down and got into the Higgins boats and floated around all day until dark. It was about 11 p.m. or midnight when we finally landed.

It was not a *Private Ryan* type of deal. Not this time. They didn't hammer with machine gun fire on the front. This was relatively mild. We lost a couple hundred people on other parts of the beach. It was a cakewalk where we were.

We were in Higgins boats, about 25 or 30 of us. This was before the DUKWs [amphibious 6-by-6 trucks] were being used. There was a lot of gunfire from the French Navy, and the French Air Force was flying. Some German submarines came up from Dakar and sank some transports not long after we had left them. A lot of the Higgins boats were beached, with the bow up on the sand. In our case, we tied up at a pier. It was pitch dark and we stepped up on the pier and walked right on in. I didn't know war would be so easy!

There was some strafing from the French Air Force. When they flew over we didn't run for cover. This was regular Army stuff. They drilled this sort of thing—when they blew a whistle, you stood up and fired. When they blew the whistle again, you stopped. We were still fresh from the States and ready to go at 'em. Our attitude was: "Let's get this thing over with and get back home"—which took three years.

During the first night of the invasion, Kunz's unit moved into the dark streets of Fédala, where his platoon was told to take cover until morning.

We started walking down the streets of Fédala. We could hear gunfire and shells exploding but nothing immediately where we

William Kunz, 3rd Infantry Division, about landing on the Moroccan coast: "At first, it was kind of like a big adventure. A big parade. They brought flags up the beach, and carried them as they went. Fédala was the easiest of all five landings I made during the war. It was not a *Private Ryan* type of deal. Not this time. This was relatively mild. We lost a couple hundred people on other parts of the beach. It was a cakewalk where we were." (This photo was taken late in the war when his division had moved into Austria.)

were. We found a big hole, shell hole, right in the middle of the street, and the order was for us to bed down and stay in it until daylight.

When daylight came, I stuck my nose up over the edge of the hole, I was 3 feet away from a dead Frenchman. I didn't even realize he was there. He looked like he had been killed by a shell explosion—maybe the one that made the hole we spent the night in.

As it got lighter, I could see that we had camped out right by a Texaco gas station sign. The station had pumps and everything still. The next morning, we could hear small arms fire maybe at a quarter-mile distance. The infantry a couple blocks ahead of us did engage some French soldiers. Shot some of them. In my case, the platoon didn't have to exchange small arms fire with anyone.

[On the voyage,] we had all heard George Patton's speech that "we're going to fight the French and then they're going to be on our side." They broadcast it over the loudspeaker of the transport ship, although it wasn't his voice. Somebody else read what they said was Patton's speech on the ship. But I don't know, we weren't paying very much attention, because there were some very important crap games going on. At our level, the dogfaces, the grunts, it didn't mean much. You didn't get much information on anything.

Patton had written a letter distributed to each ship that read in part: ". . . all resistance by whomever offered must be destroyed. However, when any of the French soldiers seek to surrender, you will accept it and treat them with the respect due a brave opponent and future ally. Remember, the French are not Nazis or Japs." As it turned out, resistance was light in Fédala. Casualties were also light, and the 20 percent overstrength was unnecessary for the landing.

◆

The next morning, November 9, Watters' unit reached Casablanca on foot and witnessed the resistance put up by the French Navy, particularly by the battleship *Jean Bart.*

One of the largest battleships in the world, the *Jean Bart*, lay at anchor in the harbor of Casablanca. It was unfinished, but its 16-inch guns were able to fire, and it was doing so. All night long its big shells were whooshing over, making the darnedest racket. Luckily the shells did not land near us. They were firing at Fédala, and even the ships at sea. I heard later that the *Jean Bart* almost sank the light cruiser *Augusta*, General Patton's command ship.

Chapter Two

Commanding Watters' unit of combat engineers, Colonel Garrison Davidson was on a transport ship near the *Augusta* and saw the *Jean Bart* from the seaward point of view.

We on the staff could not get ashore on Sunday, but we had a grandstand seat for the duel between the shore batteries and the unfinished grounded battleship *Jean Bart* in Casablanca harbor and the [U.S.] cruiser *Augusta*. General Patton and his key staff officers were on the *Augusta*. Our transport was close by.

Toward the end of the morning the shore batteries got a perfect bracket on the *Augusta*. The next salvoes would have spelled disaster but the cruiser *Brooklyn* steamed in hell bent for leather between the *Augusta* and the shore. Its main armament was 15 8-inch guns in five turrets. These were all turned toward shore, and the guns were spewing out shells like I've never seen them shot before or since. They smothered the shore batteries until the *Augusta* could pull out of effective range. The rate of expenditure of ammunition must have set some sort of record.

Yet the *Jean Bart* persevered. Navy air support was needed to knock her out of commission, but there was none. A captured airfield was necessary, and the all-weather airfield at Port Lyautey was made to order. It was up to Patton's ground troops to capture it, but resistance inland was stiff, and the field wouldn't be taken for two days.

◆

On November 11, the 2nd Armored Division, which landed at Safi, was on the move 150 miles up the coast to attack Casablanca from the south. John Erbes writes:

Everyone was excited and on edge. Our orders were to attack and capture Mazagan, seize a river bridge at Azemmour, and then attack Casablanca.

We traveled all night with everyone on the alert and all guns ready to fight. At dawn on November 12, we stopped just 7 miles out of Mazagan. There was a last-minute briefing, which I attended. It was decided that we must take the Azemmour bridge intact at all cost, because it was the only place that the tanks could cross the river. If we failed, the bridge company of the engineers would have to build us a bridge, and this would cost us from four to six valuable hours. Such a delay might result in losing the attack on Casablanca.

Dueling in the Desert

Lieutenant Colonel Stokes was to storm Mazagan with the 1st Battalion, while Lieutenant Colonel Hillyard was to take advantage of the confusion by bypassing the city and taking the bridge that was about 8 miles out of the city. Lieutenant James R. McCartney was to take his platoon of tanks and form the point of the attack on the bridge. He was told that it would probably be protected by antitank artillery, antitank mines, and barbed wire. The barbed wire was intended to "keep off" the foot troops and wouldn't hinder the movements of his tanks. Everyone was in dead earnest. Mac's [McCartney's] face was a slate gray color, but determination was written all over it. As I looked at him I wondered how badly mangled he would be when I got to him. We lived three years during the three-hour wait until "H" hour—the time of the attack.

Many thoughts flashed through my mind. My mother and dad were probably busy with preparations for the Thanksgiving holidays. Two of my sisters were busy helping my other sister, Rose, who would have a baby. Many other thoughts flashed through my mind. I tried to make jokes to keep the medical corpsmen from thinking of what was to come. I watched an Arab trying to make a camel named Schultz go where he didn't want to go. I laughed, but only a few others thought it was funny. T/5 Henry L. Miller, our conscientious objector, frequently put his hands to his forehead and said a short prayer, and nobody commented. I think that we were all quietly doing the same thing, even Charles Shelly, our self-proclaimed agnostic.

Finally, Lieutenant Colonel Stokes's tanks clattered into Mazagan and found the streets lined with civilians and soldiers waving and cheering them on. The town surrendered without a shot being fired. Lieutenant Colonel Stokes's tanks continued on toward the bridge. When we of the 3rd Battalion got to Azemmour, we were astounded to see the French soldiers standing on the streets, still armed and acting friendly, and we remembered the wondrous ways of the military and continued taking the bridge.

Meanwhile, Patton's troops finally captured the airfield at Port Lyautey to provide a runway for U.S. aircraft. High on the Navy air wing's target list was the French battleship *Jean Bart*, which had continued blasting away at U.S. ships outside the port of Casablanca. When Navy planes took to the skies at last, Watters witnessed the demise of the great ship.

As soon as the 9th Infantry Division had accomplished capturing the airfield the Navy could land its planes, and promptly proceeded to knock out the *Jean Bart*.

Chapter Two

I stood on a hill outside of Casablanca and watched them peel off and dive straight down on the *Jean Bart*. There were seven or eight planes, and a couple of dives finished the *Jean Bart's* firing. Funny how you can stand and watch people being blown to smithereens and not give a thought to them. War brutalizes one unbelievably.

With the newly acquired airfield, all pieces were in place for Patton. He planned a massive pounding that coordinated a naval, air, and ground attack on Casablanca that would finish off French defenses. All was set for November 11, his birthday. It was to be a birthday bash worthy of a fighting general, with emphasis on *bash*, as Patton planned to throw everything he had against the French strongholds. But just before he unleashed the attack, the French surrendered. Watters recalls hearing the news.

The 3rd Division had Casablanca surrounded, and every unit was scheduled to attack the city at 7:30 a.m. I don't know exactly what time it was when Paul Schneidt woke me up. He was pretty excited. He said he had heard bugles blowing from Casablanca, and he thought the French had surrendered. We certainly hoped so.

Sure enough, at about 7 a.m. word came through that the attack had been called off. The sense of relief that swept over us was just as intense as if we had been fighting for three months instead of three days.

And John Erbes, awaiting the inevitable wounded of a tank battle, heard the news by radio:

At 11 a.m. on November 12, the news that an armistice had been signed came over our FM 528 radios. We were all excited and ecstatically happy that Mac didn't have to attack the bridge, because when we finally got there, we saw the barbed wire, of which the tankers were not afraid, but also the antitank mines and antitank artillery and even a few small French tanks on the other side of the river.

Lieutenant Colonel Charles R. Codman was a "retread"—a combat flyer in World War I accepted for service again in World War II—who became Patton's aide. Codman writes about what he saw behind the scenes of the French cease-fire:

Shortly before three o'clock [November 11, 1942] General Patton ordered a guard of honor drawn up before the hotel entrance. At the prescribed hour, a black limousine with motorcycle outriders swept up the drive. Out of it got General Nogués, trim, erect, ascetic, rather Spanish in appearance. He walked smartly up the steps, followed by

General Lascroux, the compact, stoutish commander of ground forces, and General Houlle, chief of the French air forces, whose genial, forthright aspect made an immediately favorable impression.

At the top of the steps they were met by General Keyes, who escorted them to the smoking room, where General Patton received them.

A preliminary conference attended by Admirals Hewitt and Hall had taken place with the French admirals, Michelier and Ronarch, who had arrived from Casablanca an hour earlier. Matters concerning the ports had been discussed. Michelier had been *pincé* and difficult, but thawed out more or less when Admiral Hewitt offered to shake hands.

General Patton now opened the full séance by expressing his admiration for the courage and skill shown by the French armed forces during the three days of battle.

"We are now met to come to terms," he said. "Here they are."

As the conditions of Treaty C were read aloud and the full import of their stringency began to sink in, the faces of the French grew more and more somber. At the end there was a strained silence, then General Nogués arose. "Permit me to point out," he said, "that if these terms are enforced it means the end of the French Protectorate in Morocco."

Rising to his full height, Patton picked up the familiar typescript of Treaty C and tore it into small strips.

"Gentlemen," he said, "I had the pleasure of serving with your armed forces throughout two years of World War I. Needless to say, I have implicit faith in the word of honor of a French officer. If each of you in this room gives me his word of honor that there will be no further firing on American troops and ships, you may retain your Army and carry on as before—but under my orders. Agreed?"

It was.

"There is, however, an additional condition upon which I must insist."

The faces of the French delegation, which had brightened considerably, lengthened.

"It is this," General Patton said, signaling one of his aides, "that you join me in a glass of champagne."

Garrison Davidson writes about the other reason to celebrate on November 11:

November 11 was General Patton's birthday. To celebrate that event and at the same time the French decision to no longer oppose the landing, the staff had a little dinner for General Patton in a blacked out hotel near the shore. About halfway through the proceedings a German submarine, which had been lying on the bottom under the transport fleet, started to sea, firing torpedoes right and left as it went. It hit several transports which went up like the Fourth of July. Their cargoes of ammunition and gasoline kept the pyrotechnics going for hours. The balance of the night was spent hauling burned GIs and sailors out of the surf and to the hospital improvised in one of the hotels.

The U-boat attack reminded everyone there that, although a celebration for the French cease-fire came after three days, a celebration for victory over the Germans and Italians in North Africa could very well be a long way off. In fact, overall victory in North Africa would not come for another six months. But the shooting in Morocco was over.

◆

While Patton was in Morocco, American forces to the east in Tunisia had suffered a terrible defeat. At a desolate place called Kasserine Pass, Major General Lloyd Fredendall's II Corps was humiliated by Rommel's *Panzerarmee*, the augmented juggernaut once known as the Afrika Korps. American casualties exceeded 3,000; Americans taken prisoner numbered 3,700; and tanks destroyed were nearly 200. Some blamed the inexperience of the American newcomers. Others blamed the leadership.

Eisenhower stepped in to remedy the situation. He concluded that no one but Patton could infuse the kind of discipline and fighting spirit so sorely needed.

"The troops had to be picked up quickly," Eisenhower later wrote. "For such a job Patton has no superior in the Army. General Patton's buoyant leadership and strict insistence upon discipline rapidly rejuvenated II Corps and brought it up to fighting pitch."

Patton was promoted to lieutenant general and appointed commander of II Corps on March 6, 1943.

A change was perceptible immediately. Patton's top priority was to bolster morale and discipline—a mission he seized ferociously. He wasted no time in distributing a message that diagnosed the failure. First Lieutenant Nathan A. Allen Jr. received a copy of Patton's message. A supply officer for 109th Ordnance Company (part of the II

Corps that landed originally in Algeria), Allen copied the message into his journal as his entry for March 12:

> I saved Patton's first order to us. He wrote: ". . . we are not ruth-less, and not vicious, not aggressive, therein lies our weakness. Children of a free and sheltered people who have lived a generous life, we have not the pugnacious disposition of those oppressed beasts, our enemies who must fight or starve. Our bravery is too negative. We talk too much of sacrifice, of the glory of dying that freedom may live. Of course we are willing to die but that is not enough, we must be eager to kill, to inflict on the enemy—the hated enemy—wounds, death and destruction. If we die killing, well and good, but if we fight hard enough, viciously enough, we will kill and live. Live to return to our family and our girl as conquering heroes—men of Mars. The rep-utation of our Army, the future of our race, your own glory rests in your hands. I know you will be worthy."

Allen later learned about the "bunker mentality" and the underly-ing reasons for the shakeup at the top of the command chain:

> A delegate of General Dwight D. Eisenhower visited the front during the attack and found General Fredendall (commander of II Corps) "80 miles back of the front line and everything in chaos." He was relieved by Major General George S. Patton Jr., who brought additional troops with him. Patton resulted in a complete change. We suffered no more setbacks and obtained considerably more equipment. His word carried weight—lots of it!

◆

It's said that when Patton first came ashore on a Moroccan beach, he found one of his soldiers resting leisurely on the sand. As the story goes, Patton gave the GI a swift kick in the rear. Now, as commander of all U.S. ground troops in Africa, he was kicking a whole *corps'* backside.

This was not received entirely enthusiastically. To his newly assigned troops, Patton had the image of an iron-fisted martinet—a stickler about things that many soldiers didn't think they should be bothered with in a war zone.

Dress code immediately rose high on Patton's list. A new mandate stipulated that all men had to wear helmets with strap fastened, trouser legs tucked into boots or leggings, sleeves never rolled up and—the one that became famously least favorite—neckties had to be worn, under threat of a $25 fine. "It is absurd to believe that soldiers who cannot be made to wear the proper uniform can be induced to move forward in battle," Patton said. Corporal Dillard B. Oakley, 1st Armored Division, comments:

> Patton told all us boys to wear leggings and neckties. On the front and everywhere. I thought it was crazy. If the Germans captured one of the 1st Armored boys, I guess he wanted them to know we were the best-dressed soldiers there was!

New directives were especially unpopular in units such as Darby's Rangers, where it almost caused mutiny. Two Rangers credit the directives for some of the friction that led to ongoing conflicts between their chief, Colonel William Darby, and Patton. Lieutenant Lester Kness, who received a field commission in the 4th Ranger Battalion, speaks bluntly:

> Most Rangers disliked Patton. Patton was extremely excitable. The day he fined me was just stupid—$25 for not wearing a tie! I stood in front of his desk while he screamed at me and hammered on his desk, saying, "Is this true? Is this true?" He turned to a man to his left and said, "Recommend that this man is sent back to the States and separated from service." Well, he might as well just kissed me on both cheeks. I was ready to go home. I saluted, did an about face and headed out the door. I was a brand-new second lieutenant, 13 days old. Of course, I was not sent back home.

Loren Evans of the 1st Ranger Battalion adds:

> General Patton was there after I came in from the patrol. It was just getting daylight and he was already there at our headquarters. I recognized him right away. The pearl-handled revolvers and shiny boots. Spit and polish.
>
> There I was, without a tie. Disheveled. Dirty. Unshaven. Had hit the dirt many times and looked like it. He started to chew me out for not having a tie. It didn't surprise me. I had heard about General Patton. Before I could make some smart answer, Colonel Darby interceded for me.
>
> Darby said, "General, wait a minute. You need to know that this man has been all night long on a patrol." And he told him about the success of the patrol.
>
> The general backed off and I recall him saying something like, "Nice job, soldier." Then it was back to business with Colonel Darby.
>
> No fine was mentioned. It was only a verbal reprimand—or the start of one. Only, *pffft*, we all knew he was capable of giving you a pretty good verbal reprimand!

Dueling in the Desert

Chester B. Hansen, on General Omar Bradley's staff, observed changes that included even a more disciplined eating schedule. It would become a scene depicted in the movie *Patton*, when the increasingly impatient Patton character confronts a cook, glowers at two lax officers, then shuts down the mess hall. Hansen writes in his wartime diary:

> When Fredendall was the corps commander, the II Corps people generally went to breakfast at about nine o'clock in the morning. When Patton came, however, he changed all that, and in Fairlana they stopped serving breakfast at six o'clock in the morning. Therefore it was necessary for us to stumble out of bed at about five, hurry down and grab a breakfast. It was quite cold at that time in the morning. Patton also insisted that the aides stand a watch, which we did all night long.

After being wounded in February, Lieutenant Paul Skogsberg was rejoining the II Corps just as command was passed from Fredendall to Patton in March 1943. Changes were immediately evident to him.

> Also while I was away, the command of II Corps had passed from General Fredendall to General Patton, and with him came a passel of strictly enforced regs designed to spruce the corps up. Helmets had to be worn at all times by everyone, and the chinstraps had to be fastened securely beneath the chin. No one was allowed to roll up his sleeves. Everyone had to have his pants tucked into his boots or leggings. All officers had to wear neckties properly tied. And every vehicle with a radio sported a small red flag attached to the antenna. Since we were all in woolen uniforms and it was now beastly hot during the day, these regulations were not at all popular, but to violate them was to invite punishment under the 104th Article of War on the spot. However begrudgingly, I must admit that the troops did look more professional and maybe this was part of the aura that I had detected on my return.

◆

The disastrous defeat at Kasserine Pass had prompted talk, primarily among the British, that "Americans can't fight." Patton took this personally. He became obsessed to prove the mettle of American fighting men.

A firsthand account of the Kasserine Pass gives an idea why Patton wanted so badly to overcome the humiliation of the defeat (even though Patton himself, then in Morocco, was not in command at any level at Kasserine). Lloyd L. Haas, a tanker and platoon sergeant in the 1st Armored Division, tells about the debacle:

> We were ordered [by Fredendall] to make a road march to Gabes, on the eastern side of Tunisia. Simple enough, right? (laughs) All there was between us and Gabes was Rommel and a whole German Army!
>
> We kind of joked about it: "We're on our road march to Gabes."
>
> At Kasserine Pass, it was a nightmare. But the most memorable incident that kicked the thing off was comical. There was a battery of artillery on a hillside and the Germans were starting to shoot at us. It was all 88s along the right flank. And there was a big valley between us and them.
>
> Here comes an Arab with a herd of camels. So he was between us and them, and he was rushing around like a madman trying to get his camels out of there. Risking life and limb to do it.
>
> I never did see if he succeeded in getting those camels out of there. An 88 hit our tank, but bounced off. A second shell hit us—an armor piercing shell that went right through the armor plate.
>
> When an 88 armor piercing goes in one side it doesn't come out the other. Fragments stay inside, bouncing around and knocking stuff loose. I was hit.
>
> It was white-hot where the shell went through and the shrapnel went in. I got all the hair burned off my face and hands. But I was able to move. Three of us got out and but the other two didn't make it. Our assistant driver and machine gunner didn't get out. The loader got out, but they machine-gunned him down.
>
> I made it out of the tank and didn't realize I was so badly burned until I looked at the other guys and said, "God, you guys got burned." Then they informed me, "You should see yourself."

Dillard Oakley was a member of Haas' tank crew and recounts the rest of the story:

> We could see our tanks just burning all around in every direction. Our own tank had been hit in the rear, and the gas tank started burning. It was probably an 88-millimeter, but I never knew for sure.
>
> We started running to a ditch about 40 yards from where the tank was. It was a small ditch but all of us went for it. I must have sucked in a lot of the smoke, because I was coughing and hacking and could hardly keep up with the rest.
>
> I made it to the ditch and laid there a little while before I looked up. We were all sweaty when we dove into the ditch and got our faces

covered with that fine gritty sand. Against the walls of that ditch, we was all just eyeballs and teeth.

The rest decided to make a run for it, but I stayed with another guy from another tank. It was about 5 p.m. by then and I told him, "It'll get dark in about 40 minutes. That'd give us a better chance to get out of here."

While we were waiting, I could see the German infantry in the distance gathering up our boys as prisoners. And here comes three German tanks followed by troops on foot. So my friend and me played dead. They passed us right up.

We got out [after dark]. Only 14 of us from the company made it back without getting captured or killed. All the tanks were lost.

◆

After Patton was appointed II Corps commander, victories soon followed—much needed after the humiliation of the II Corps at Kasserine Pass.

On March 16, the 1st Infantry Division set out in a downpour through the Tunisian frontier to the village of Gafsa. Approaching en masse, the division scared away its defenders. Gafsa is often cited among the American victories in North Africa, but taking the village itself was certainly not a hard-fought victory that proved the mettle of American forces. Garrison Davidson was there and explains:

Gafsa "fell" practically without a shot. The Italian garrison had withdrawn. The only casualty I saw was an elderly Arab on the main street of the picturesque little Arab desert village. The main obstacle to the advance to the town of the unit we were with was a minefield where I came closest of any time the war of stepping on a mine. They were British Mark Vs. I was the first to discover the field. Treading carefully and gingerly on my toes I had stepped over a mine and was about to settle back on to the spider with my heel when Birdie, who as behind me, saw it and yelled at me not to let my heel down. I didn't, and when I had gotten out of the way, for the practice, I disarmed it.

Others who were at Gafsa said that the gunfire and shell explosions they heard were nearly all fired by American forces, probably after the defenders had fled. Patton himself noted in his diary entry of March 17 that he "could see the troops moving and the shells, mostly ours, bursting." The U.S. troops then marched straightaway down the Gabes road 10 miles to El Guettar.

Chapter Two

Fought in the rugged region south of Gafsa, the Battle of El Guettar was a bona fide victory that *did* show American mettle. As the biggest engagement of the II Corps under Patton's command, the victory would become headline news in the United States, redeeming a lot of the confidence lost at Kasserine. And Patton would be heralded in the press for his decisive leadership. Axis forces included two tank divisions that were forced to retreat, leaving behind 30 burning tanks. Charles Codman writes in his book *Drive* about the intercepted message before the attack and how Patton quickly capitalized on it:

> The key battle was at El Guettar. Victory went to the American forces. A strange incident made this possible. An enlisted man in the Signal Corps picked up a message in German stating that the German attack would be delayed six hours. This enabled General Patton to shift a battalion of tank destroyers and two battalions of artillery, so that when the German attack took place, they were stopped before they got started. Then the 1st Infantry Division, under Major General Terry Allen, completed the rout of the German forces.

Three stories about combat at El Guettar follow, representing viewpoints of the infantryman, Ranger, and tanker.

Infantrymen of the 9th Infantry Division were in the thick of the action in the mountainous region. Italians accounted for most of the enemy forces, as Sergeant Wilbert David Goldsmith relates:

> My baptism of fire was at El Guettar in Algeria [actually, Tunisia]. Our mission was to capture some hills. It was a fixed bayonet attack under darkness about 5 a.m.
>
> It was just getting light. We had lined up in two columns on the road, five feet apart, Colonel Oakes and his people, E Company, and so forth. After we started, fire came immediately from the higher knoll next to the road and we sort of gravitated in that direction. Those of us who were closest got up to the base of the hill where we had a little cover because the enemy was firing over our head. The rest ran out of steam and got pinned down in the flats, even before the mortars and 88s began to fall.
>
> I found myself alone and proceeded around the north side of the hill where I found a path leading up. I started up, only to hear voices coming down. They must have heard me and yelled, "Petri." There being no one in E Company named Petri, I thought to get out, but then I heard somebody coming in.
>
> When he got close I whispered, "Petri, Petri."
>
> "Si, si," came the answer.

Dueling in the Desert

I lunged with the bayonet and ran out over poor Petri. When I reached a sand ridge in about 30 yards, I stopped and took up a firing position. There was no movement so I started to dig in.

After a bit, I was joined by another kid from the company. We could make out that the Italians had four mortars in position up on the hill. Poor Petri had been bringing in ammo, which was stored outside the position. The rest of the bunch tried to get at the ammo but, from our positions, they were sitting ducks. No rounds got out of that position while we were there.

Later, we heard a machine gun firing from the top of the hill to the right, and here came some of our guys running. We fired at the machine gun and covered them. They were from my platoon and had three Italian POWs. We decided to get out of there and found the company in a hold position in the rear.

About three hours later, while I was guarding the three Italian prisoners, an antipersonnel shell burst about 100 feet behind me. I was hit in the rear of my right elbow joint. I did not realize I was hit until the Italians pointed out to me that blood was seeping out of my gas impregnated waterproof jacket around the wrist opening.

This was the first of what would be multiple Purple Hearts for Goldsmith during the war.

Loren Evans had been the sergeant major for the 1st Battalion of Darby's Rangers, but after a lieutenant was killed the day after landing at Arzeu, Evans received the first known battlefield commission in the European Theater during World War II. One of his most memorable experiences in North Africa occurred in the hills and mountains surrounding El Guettar.

As a new second lieutenant, I was leading a patrol. There was a funnel-shaped pass and there were thousands of Axis troops there, both German and Italians, holding up the meeting of Montgomery's Army and Patton's II Corps. It was quite a bottleneck.

We had two patrols. One was headed by another man named Wojcik.

Our mission: Wojcik was to take a patrol through to the backside of the mountain—a torturous route. My job was to take a patrol and engage the enemy there at Djebel El Ank. I was to get close, draw fire, back off; draw fire, back off and so on. This was to keep them busy while Wojcik was on their flank. Plus, it was to probe to see if there were weaknesses in the line.

Just at daylight, we came back to the olive grove where we were bivouacked and reported back what we found to Darby, then a lieutenant colonel.

Based on what we learned on the patrol, the next night our battalion went in from behind and attacked. We took them totally by surprise. Took thousands of prisoners. They thought we were far more than the 500 men we were. Plus, the Italians didn't really have their hearts in the war. They were lovers, not fighters.

A mainstay of Patton's armor: the M4 Sherman medium tank. The Sherman has a cast hull (as opposed to a welded hull like most others) with 62-millimeter-thick armor. Despite weighing in at 36 tons, it could traverse the desert dunes at 25 miles per hour.
National Archives

Dillard Oakley of the 1st Armored Division also fought for the high ground at El Guettar. He tells of his experience as a gunner in an M4 medium tank:

The worst battle was at El Guettar. I was the gunner in a tank. Our officers were told by Patton we *would* take El Guettar, and we'd have to go through a minefield to do it. Our captain passed along to us that we were going to take a mountain [overlooking El Guettar] no matter how many tanks it would cost.

We were getting shelled pretty good before we reached the mine-field. Explosions all around. Our captain, Captain Brush—a good, ol' guy we all called Punjab because he was big—knew we needed to cross that minefield. We liked him. He was a very good officer.

That day, Punjab stopped his tank and got out and walked all the way through [that minefield] and walked back again. The engineers and minesweepers had been through and marked it, and he found the path that we couldn't see from the tanks. Shells continued falling.

Then he drove his tank through first and radioed back to say, "Stay in my tracks and you'll make it through fine."

And we all did.

We started running into resistance. Punjab radioed to tell us to give the Italians a chance to give up. And some were coming forward to surrender. But a lot more were fighting and I saw a tank here and there getting knocked out—about three by this time.

We knew there were Germans in behind the Italians. We were told there were SS troops shooting 88-millimeter guns, mortars, and other things. Our tank commander was a lieutenant, and I told the lieutenant, "These aren't Italians. These are Germans!" They weren't giving up. They wanted to fight!

We came to one place where there was a machine gun dug in. I was fixing to shoot at that gun, but the tank commander told me not to and said we'd just run over it instead. Then I saw another German off to the side, peeking his head out from behind the rock about a dozen times. I said I wanted to lay one into that rock.

While we were occupied, trying to run over that machine gun like the lieutenant wanted to, the German from behind the rock threw a grenade. It hit just below the turret and the concussion of it was enough to take out the lieutenant. I didn't see it happen because I was down in the gunner's seat. But he had been waist-high out the hatch. He slumped down and I thought he'd been shot with a rifle. Both I and the assistant gunner thought he was dead.

I told the driver to stop and I turned my gun around and saw the German by the rock. The German ran and jumped behind where the machine gun was. I blew up the gun, but I'm not sure what happened to the Germans there.

While all this was happening, old Punjab was in the lead tank and kept trying to call our lieutenant. We'd hear "X-ray One to X-ray Two" comin' over the radio. Finally I answered him back that the lieutenant was knocked out but the tank was in good shape. The cap-tain directed us to go up that hill—the one Patton had ordered taken—and we were to follow him. There were two other tanks that followed us up there. When we got up to the top of that hill, I'd never seen so many Germans. There were trucks and vehicles of all kinds. We fired everything we had at them. Fired until we ran out of shells. The lieutenant came to while we were shelling. He rested his arm on the gun just as we fired. And man, he hollered! I saw the recoil and thought, *Omigod, I busted his arm.* We got him out and the medics picked him up.

We had gone in with just a four-man crew. All of us following old Punjab were able to capture the mountain and hold it.

Patton now held the high ground, so critical to armies throughout the ages. In the meantime, he ordered other divisions to advance below, moving against staunch Axis defenses and finally overcoming them.

After the battle of El Guettar, on April 8, 1943, Patton communicated this to his troops: "Soldiers of the Second Corps: After 22 days of relentless combat in mountains whose ruggedness beggars description, you have won the battle of El Guettar. Each of one of you, in his sphere, has done his duty magnificently. Not alone on the front line, where death never ended his gruesome harvest, but everywhere else all of you have demonstrated your valor and constancy."

◆

El Guettar was not the end of the fighting, however. As Patton's II Corps moved toward Montgomery's Eighth Army, attempting to squeeze the life out of Rommel's *Panzerarmee*, there were many other battles. The *Panzerarmee* still had some life left.

Moving past El Guettar, Patton ordered II Corps to continue pursuit. Paul Skogsberg, already wounded once as a platoon leader in the 1st Reconnaissance Troop of the 1st Infantry Division, was given a mission to drive deep into no-man's-land. His memoir tells what happened after the decisive battle, when the biggest threat became landmines laid by the retreating Germans:

> My platoon was sent out on a mission to reconnoiter the northern reaches of the El Guettar corridor to the east and to flush out any enemy troops that might be located there. As we moved forward along a camel trail we encountered a few hastily buried harassing antitank mines. Progress was extremely slow and I was ordered to pick up the pace. I finally got into the lead jeep and moved out at a good speed. I had gone about 3 miles when we heard a vehicle horn

behind us. We stopped and when they caught up with us, I was told that the jeep following me had struck a mine and had blown up.

In a personal interview, he elaborates:

My heart sank when they said the jeep trailing us at some distance had struck a mine and blew up, killing two of my men. We went back and found three other antitank mines in the area. We pulled the bodies from the wreckage. I think they had gone over two mines, one stacked on the other—probably intended for a tank. The vehicle must have flipped, but it was the concussion that killed them. I had been with them for a long time—we trained together in the States. We evacuated the bodies and stripped the vehicle of anything salvageable.

The story didn't end there, though. One of the boys had an uncle over there in our troop. The uncle felt responsible for his nephew. The family had wanted him to watch out for him. The uncle was a very quiet individual, and nobody realized how he was brooding over it. One day, we were eating lunch and we heard what sounded like a rifle shot. We went back over and found him. He was in his tent. He'd put the muzzle of his M-1 in his mouth and pulled the trigger. So with his suicide, really there were four casualties.

A half-track from Patton's II Corps lumbers through a Tunisian village during the advance through North Africa. On April 5, 1943, Patton noted in his diary: "We have fought continuously for 19 days and have never given ground." **National Archives**

Chapter Two

The next day, another scout jeep hit a mine, and this time Skogsberg witnessed it, as is recorded in his memoir:

We moved out again, with my scout jeeps in the lead. Progress was slow as we stopped to probe for mines in suspicious looking places. And we did dig up a few. As we approached the notch, the attention of the lead scouts was focused on a partially concealed half-track located near the notch.

Suddenly I saw a sickening explosion as the lead jeep hit an anti-tank mine and blew up. I rushed forward with my scout car, quickly sent scouts out ahead and tended to the two men who had been in the jeep.

They were both seriously injured, but they were still alive. The sandbags on the floor had undoubtedly saved their lives. We evacuated the two wounded . . . and again stripped the jeep. The scouts who had gone forward reported the half-track to be a German vehicle that had been knocked out some time ago, probably by an air strike.

◆

Axis forces were still taking prisoners, too. Attorney Leonard Bessman had been drafted in June 1941. Noting his "surprise that older men were taken," he entered service at the age of 33. He had joined II Corps headquarters in England and went to North Africa as a counterintelligence officer. He writes about how he was captured and treated decently, in the chivalrous tradition set by Rommel in North Africa:

In North Africa General Patton visited the front contrary to the style of his predecessor. General Bradley and General Robinett impressed me favorably also.

On April 7, 1943, we were surprised by a German tank battalion in Tunisia. Just my driver and I. A round of armor piercing shell hit my jeep. I ordered the driver to get out and warn the column. I gave him covering fire and I was wounded—a bullet in the thigh forcing me to fall—and I was captured. (I did not know he succeeded getting back to friendly lines.)

I was given good care. I respected those capturing me. Gave me medical treatment. No mistreatment. The Afrika Korps was well trained. The Germans competent. Italians had poor morale because of little faith in the war.

Bessman would spend the next 5-1/2 months in a POW camp before escaping and being helped back to British lines by the Italian underground.

◆

Paul Skogsberg writes about one of the final actions in the battle for North Africa:

As the regimental combat teams entered this new area of operations, they took up attack positions along the front of a sector that cut to the northeast. It was a rugged zone, well suited to the defense. Within the bounds of this sector were the towns of Beja and Matuer. Here again the division saw heavy fighting with some hills having to be attacked one or two or three times before the German defenses collapsed.

On the May 13, the last German forces capitulated, and almost immediately the division moved back to the vicinity of Oran to begin preparations for the next phase of the war, the invasion of the island of Sicily.

He adds in a personal interview:

I didn't jump for joy when I heard the fighting had stopped. We knew only part of it was over, and a lot was yet to come in this war.

Near Bizerte, on Tunisia's coast, William Kunz of the 3rd Infantry Division was told the fighting was over, but he relates "a case of youth and inexperience" that nearly cost his life after the surrender:

We were just walking along and there was a pillbox up ahead. In theory, the Afrika Korps had surrendered. Yeah, well, nobody told this pillbox that.

They opened fire on us. But we didn't know it. We heard it, heard *something*, but didn't realize it was the enemy.

We were fairly new to combat. When you first get into this, you haven't learned yet to distinguish friendly fire from "incoming mail," which is theirs. After a while—pretty quickly if you want to stay alive— you learn the sound of the different weapons. At that point, I didn't know the difference. So, you go along, taking your chances, looking up to see what's going on.

Like I said, I saw the pillbox. And then we heard the sounds but didn't realize what was going on until people started to fall. Tough way to know the difference between friendly and not. In this case, we didn't know until we saw people fall.

We quick got into a defilade, a gully, and returned fire. I put my M-1 on the lip of the gully and started firing on the pillboxes. There was a lot of gunfire going back and forth. Our job would have been to call in artillery on them, but we didn't have artillery set up yet, so I couldn't call that in. It was eventually resolved with rifle fire and grenades.

Once the small pockets of resistance were cleared out, all that remained for II Corps in North Africa was rest and refitting—and recovering lots of lost equipment. William Kunz was given the "mundane" task of taking back some of the supplies looted by the local inhabitants—in this case, not so mundane.

After Rommel's Africa Korps had surrendered, I had charge of a small squad assigned to go through an Arab village and reclaim stolen military supplies. [Some of these people] were the world's greatest thieves. They could strip a dead guy in 10 seconds and be gone. Headquarters got word that there was a lot of our equipment hidden in these towns. So they sent us outside Algiers and Oran. I was a corporal then, feeling high and mighty.

In one house in the middle of town, an entire harem, 8 or 10 women, were seated in a circle on a large Arabian carpet. There was something fishy about that already. After much screeching, they were chased off—that was an adventure right there. They were screaming bloody murder. I don't know what they were saying, but I think maybe curses—my future generations have been cursed down to the 19th generation, I'm sure.

Under the carpet, we found the trap door and opened it. In a "basement," we found enough looted supplies—ammunition, food, uniforms, and weapons—to fill a couple two-and-a-half ton trucks. There was even a great big rubber tire and wheel, from a large truck or maybe a downed bomber! I don't know how they got the thing down there. We couldn't get it back out.

In any given town you could get three or four trucks loaded. We found a lot of C rations and uniforms, but what we were really looking for was armament, and we found that, too. M-1s, machine guns—a lot of it in better shape than ours. They really went for shoes, because they didn't have any. They had their survival to worry about, so that we could appreciate that. But there were limits. So if we saw people walking around the towns wearing boots and remnants of uniforms, we let it go. The rest we took back.

◆

Patton was disappointed that he never had the chance for a direct showdown of tactical skill against Rommel. Even before combat was over in North Africa, Patton was called away to plan for the invasion of Sicily, leaving Bradley to finish the job. And well before the German surrender in North Africa, Rommel had been called away to tend to the "Atlantic Wall"—the defenses of coastal Europe.

Soldiers, including Patton, found some much-deserved time for R&R. A member of the G-2 section of Patton's headquarters, First Lieutenant Ralph Luman, recalls Patton's ever-vigilant discipline, even during R&R:

> While we were still at Mostaganem, a group that included General Patton went down to the city's little pocket beach for a swim in the Mediterranean. General Patton was pleased to exercise, which is difficult for anyone in the combat zone, regardless of rank, but especially for the famous. General Patton looked around at his staff officers and paused. One senior officer had gained quite a few pounds and Patton looked him in the eye and quietly said, "Reduce, or be reduced!" The officer complied.

Paul Skogsberg also found R&R—mixed with Patton-style discipline—on the beach. After taking a bullet and being nearly blown up by mines, he thought he was finally in totally safe territory—on a picnic with a pretty nurse.

> It was during this summer that I came as close to being court-marshaled as I could ever hope not to be. I had a day off and permission to use the command car. I went to the 93rd, picked up Vera [Lieutenant Vera Sheaffer of the 93rd Evac Hospital would later become his wife] and we headed for a picnic on the shores of the Mediterranean. As we approached the beach, top down and radio blaring, we spotted an elderly gentleman in the water up to his knees. We gave him a big wave and turned east and headed up the beach. After about three or four miles we turned toward the beach and had a nice afternoon of swimming and K rations. Late in the afternoon, we headed back and there in the water was the same old gentleman. Again we waved and sped away from the beach.
>
> The next day I had to go to division headquarters. As I approached what amounted to the HQ Quadrangle, I saw a group gathered around a figure who was shouting, "These goddamned lieutenants and nurses running wild all over the countryside in government vehicles. . . ." It was General George S. Patton. At the time, I had assumed that the swimmer was General Patton. On reflection since then, I have concluded that it could not have been the general himself, for had it been, he would have nailed us come hell or high water.

Chapter Two

◆

Patton remained in Tunisia through June 1943. During this time, he took part in planning the Allies' next move, the invasion of Sicily.

Roland Farrell was a lieutenant in the 51st Signal Battalion, attached to armored divisions. His responsibilities included carrying secret messages between headquarters. He remembers a key message delivered to Patton:

> After North Africa was completely under Allied control, I was briefed and given secret orders verbally, not written, to travel to [corps headquarters]. The assignment was delivery of a coded message to the commanding general of II Corps, which was Patton.
>
> I arrived and was shown in to General Patton. I decoded the message in his presence, naturally—not before that in case it would have fallen into enemy hands [en route]. These were Patton's marching orders. Patton was to depart from Africa for the invasion of Sicily.
>
> He smiled broadly but said nothing.

◆

Encountering Patton peripherally was something of a brush with celebrity. Seeing Patton on the avenues of war was comparable to seeing a star on Hollywood Boulevard. No matter how fleeting or distant, meeting Patton left an indelible impression—and was something immediately shared with friends and repeated as an anecdote during the decades since the war. True, especially if there were an element of humor. Lewis C. Moorman was a Navy aerographer's mate third class, assigned to an amphibious weather-forecasting unit under Admiral H. K. Hewitt. Moorman's encounter occurred while Patton was aboard ship as he prepared for the invasion of Sicily in July 1943:

> We were aboard the flagship, USS *Monrovia*, part of an armada of American and British warships headed for an amphibious landing on the island of Sicily.
>
> It was late in the afternoon of D-Day (minus one), and we were caught in the throes of a Mediterranean mistral, accompanied by heavy seas and gale force winds.
>
> At the time, another AerM [aerographer's mate] and I were stationed on the signal bridge with instructions to record sustained winds and maximum wind gusts using a hand-held anemometer.

Dueling in the Desert

I remember having my legs wrapped around a stanchion to keep from being blown overboard. It was rough.

Suddenly, General George S. Patton Jr., who was aboard, and his aide appeared on deck and stood close by. (I remember not being too impressed with his presence, for as a young man, new to the service, I knew little of his importance as a military figure.) A glance showed he had his binoculars in hand and was peering at the island of Malta off our starboard side.

All at once, with the pitching and roll of the ship, together with the fierce wind, a huge spray of water washed over the signal bridge. All these elements conspired to knock General Patton and his aide backward on their butts. The two-gallon bucket containing the general's pearl-handled revolvers and his life belt fell from the aide's clasp and the contents slid across the slippery deck, coming to rest at the bulkhead.

In the next five seconds I heard profanity I'm sure no one has ever heard or witnessed before. The general interrupted his expletives with God's name several times during this outburst. Surely had the devil himself been present, he would have shuddered! Nevertheless, both general and aide quickly scrambled to their feet, completely water-soaked and red-faced.

Under the circumstances this could have been a laughing matter but I guarantee, no one laughed!

Chapter 3

Racing Across Sicily

July 1943–January 1944

Some have called it Patton's defining moment. The Sicily campaign was the opportunity to shine—a chance to overcome the stigma of Kasserine Pass and show beyond all doubt that the American fighting man could fight, and as an equal of the British. The amphibious force was the largest ever assembled, even larger than the forces that would land the first day of the Normandy invasion the following year. Combined Anglo-American forces totaling 180,000 soldiers were to storm the southeastern shores of Sicily to overwhelm the German and Italian defenders. By invading the island off the toe of Italy's boot, the Allies could step next onto the European mainland.

At the outset, much seemed uncertain. With pessimism dripping from his pen, Patton complained to his diary: "As usual the Navy and the Air are not lined up. Of course, being connected with the British is bad." (His concerns would prove prophetic.)

Patton commanded the 90,000 troops of the new Seventh U.S. Army, and British General Bernard Law Montgomery led British forces of equal size. The plan called for the two groups to land side by side, then move away from each other, Patton pounding up the western side of Sicily and Montgomery up the eastern side. The ultimate objective of both was Messina, a key port on the northeast tip of the triangular island.

Britain's top commanders doubted American courage and fighting spirit. Their assessment in some ways was understandable, considering II Corps' poor early showing in Tunisia. General Sir Harold Alexander concluded, "They lack the will to fight." And Montgomery added,

"They have no confidence in their generals." With these statements echoing in his head, Patton became obsessed with getting to Messina first. His redeeming victories in North Africa after the embarrassment at Kasserine Pass were not redeeming enough, and Patton saw that the American soldier had a lot to prove. "This is a horse race in which the prestige of the U.S. Army is at stake," Patton said. "We must take Messina before the British." But reaching Messina first wouldn't be easy. The Americans faced obstacles—an interim objective of capturing the capital of Palermo and the tougher route of travel. Political maneuvering had given use of the main north-south highway exclusively to Montgomery.

Despite a ploy to deceive the Axis (purposely washed ashore in Spain was a corpse dressed in an American officer's uniform carrying plans for an invasion of Greece and Sardinia), Germany's Mediterranean commander, Field Marshal Albert Kesselring, reinforced Sicily. About 405,000 Axis troops defended the island by the time the Allies came ashore. Only 90,000 of these were German, however, with the rest Italian, but the best of these defenders—Germany's 15th Panzer Division and the Hermann Goering Division—stood directly in the path of Patton's Seventh Army in the west.

Private Ted Fleser had forsaken the relative safety of the Signal Corps and willingly relinquished his T/5 rank to become a Ranger. (Fleser notes that rules prevented "a noncombatant, say a quartermaster staff sergeant, transferring into the Rangers at that rank.") Having been in a noncombat role in North Africa, Fleser would see his first action in Sicily. He recounts landing with the 1st Ranger Battalion in the Gulf of Gela on the day of invasion, July 10, 1943:

> It was nighttime and we made a wet landing. Our transport was an LCVP—landing craft vehicle personnel—that carried 30 to 35 people. We were all crowded in there waiting for the door in the front to drop down. Great anticipation, waiting for it to drop. After it did, all you were thinking about at that moment was getting to the beach and across it. There was fire coming in on us. We jumped off into waist-high water. I was a BAR [Browning Automatic Rifle] gunner, and wading in with rifle and with ammunition, I ended up with a 40-pound load.
>
> I discovered quickly that my BAR had become a single-shot weapon. Sandy water had gotten into the mechanism and it wasn't operating as it was supposed to. It fired one round at a time—not even like an M-1 that fired each time you pulled the trigger. It had become a single-shot weapon. You'd pull the trigger and then have to manipulate the actuator in order to pull the trigger again, like a bolt-action rifle.

Chapter Three

As Rangers, we were coming in first, ahead of the other invasion troops. The surf was rough, so we weren't able to bring in our heavy equipment. That meant we had to rely on the guns of the Navy, because our artillery wasn't on shore. The Navy was effective.

This was a nice beach that, I'm sure, in normal times was used for recreational purposes. People probably liked to spend leisure time there. But at that moment, I didn't want to spend any more time there than I absolutely needed to! It was a flat sandy beach, and I moved for cover as quickly as I could.

I dispensed with my single-shot BAR when I picked up a Breda rifle—a 6.5-mm Italian auto rifle. It was just laying there, as was the ammunition for it. I used the Breda as I would my BAR as we went forward on the beach. It was much the same, but the mode of loading was different. It didn't use magazines like ours. With the Browning, you load the magazine underneath the receiver. On the Breda, you had a pull-back unit on the right-hand side that you would fold back toward the front. You would inject a strip of 20 rounds, shove that in and pull out the clip and your cartridges remained in that carrier. Our BAR also held 20 rounds in its magazine.

In fire and movement, I normally fired the BAR from the hip. That day was the first time I ever fired at the enemy. I just had seen movement. It was an Italian. To me, I was shooting at a target. Nothing more. I never knew if I hit him. I didn't think twice about it—nothing was on my mind except taking the objective.

Our specific objective was to take out some radio towers. They were defended by Italian troops backed up by German troops. They were physically placed that way—the Germans were behind to see to it that the Italians stayed in the front. We were ordered to take out any opposition that stood in our way.

But our objective was to take the position, not get into a fire fight. You did not fire when you didn't have to. There was no reason to give away your position. If they did not know you were there, so much the better. If, when you did get there, you surprised the heck out of them, all the better. That's what you ultimately want, and that's what we succeeded in doing that night. We managed to get into places with total surprise for the most part and took the objective of the towers. The enemy troops that were left surrendered.

Elsewhere on the Sicilian coast, the 3rd Infantry Division, the 2nd Armored Division, and a Ranger battalion were landing west of Gela at Licata at about 2:45 a.m. Going ashore with the first wave was William J. Kunz, newly promoted to sergeant. As a forward artillery observer for the 3rd Infantry Division, he landed with Rangers. His unpublished memoir titled *Third and Ten* (*third* for 3rd Infantry Division and *ten* for 10 campaigns) describes it:

> There had been heavy German air raids in the harbor. Nightly successive raids. We were showered with spent shrapnel as we stood on the deck and watched. Light from hundreds of antiaircraft searchlights made our area bright as day.

> Very early on the morning of July 10, our LCT [landing craft tank] beached and was disabled by gunfire. The Navy ensign in charge of the disabled LCT went with us and marched 120 miles to Palermo on the northern coast. Untrained for this, he had a very rough time and was heard to remark he would never leave a Navy ship again, if he lived to return to one.

In a personal interview, Kunz elaborates:

> They got the LCT's ramp down. We had one tank aboard with us and the crew drove it off. Small arms fire was coming in, so as the tank rolled forward we walked behind it—kind of a moving protection wall. We kept our heads down low as we heard bullets whistling by. We followed that tank across maybe 200 yards of open beach. We were lucky, because we got our LCT up on the sand and could walk off. Some of the other ones got stuck because it was more shallow than they thought. So the guys had to go through waist-high water to get to shore.

> Once off the beach, the tank went on ahead down a road, and we never saw it again. At the edge of the beach was a hilly area with brush, so we found a place there to set up our radio in a little depression. Then we contacted the shore fire control.

> We were north of Licata about a mile. We could see incoming fire from German 88s in the distance. They were shelling the beach, trying to prevent the landing.

> After we called for naval gunfire, I remember one round came in—a short round probably from the USS *Brooklyn*—that got too close to us. Big explosion less than a football field away. Other than that, they were pretty accurate.

> We used field glasses and looked out to see the German artillery and radioed a position. We'd zero in on them with the usual field artillery language—a hundred yards left, two hundred right.

> We moved some during those four or five hours, so that we could continue to see the target area. As the naval gunfire found its mark, the German artillery moved or they brought others up to fire on the beach.

Despite incoming fire, Patton observes his Seventh Army troops moving into Gela, Sicily, on July 11, 1943. He recounted that day: "Standing on the beach, I noticed two DUKWs [amphibious 2-1/2-ton trucks] destroyed by personnel mines, and about seven small landing craft beached. While I was making these observations, the enemy opened fire with what was probably an 88-mm or a 105-mm gun. The shells hit the water about 30 yards from the beach, but could not get into the beach on account of the defilade afforded by the town." **Patton Museum**

While this was happening on shore, Major General John P. Lucas watched from a ship in the Gulf of Gela. Lucas had been Patton's friend since serving with him in Mexico on the Punitive Expedition. General George Marshall had sent him to Eisenhower "to be of help in any capacity." Eisenhower made him his deputy commander and assigned him to act as liaison with the commanders reporting directly to Eisenhower, such as Patton. Lucas was a man after Patton's own heart in many respects. Seeing inordinate beauty in the carnage, Lucas writes in his journal:

> 7-10-43, D-day: I came on deck at 2:00 a.m. We were off Gela, which had been bombed and was burning merrily. The whole beach seemed to be lighted up. The naval bombardment was majestic. War, with all its terror, and dirt, and destruction, is at times the most beautiful phenomenon in the world. The shells, which could be followed by the tracers, seemed to flock in from the ships until they burst with a flash of light on the target. Every once in a while a

searchlight would turn on only to be smothered with the fire of every automatic weapon within reach.

Later in the day, after Lucas went ashore, he noted:

The battlefield is a mass of wreckage, an astonishing amount when you consider that all worth saving has been salvaged. Trucks, planes armored cars, tanks, all over the place and all burned. Saw several German Mark VI tanks. Unbelievable monsters, over 60 tons, and each mounting an 88 mm gun. The armor plate looked to be well over 3 inches thick. Splashes could be seen where 37 [mm guns] had hit. The crew probably didn't know they were under fire. The 37 is useless against the front armor of any German tank. It must be used against the flanks or, preferably, the rear.

And Lucas heaped particular praise on the Rangers.

We stopped by the Rangers Hq, in Gela, after we got ashore. These people, commanded by an artilleryman named Darby, have done a wonderful piece of work. At the expense of very few casualties they have killed hundreds of enemy and taken other hundreds as prisoners of war.

The Ranger battalions, which landed and took Gela, had over 800 prisoners. More prisoners than Rangers. The prisoner of war situation is becoming serious. More than we can care for. Not enough MPs to do it.

Colonel Wynot Rush Irish, a West Point graduate serving as a civil affairs officer in the 1st Infantry Division, had the perfect vantage point to watch the spectacle of the invasion. He had occupied a building in Gela, knowing he was to serve as the military governor after fighting was over.

Darby's Rangers had brilliantly captured [Gela], but they were having a hard time holding it. From our balcony we could see couriers constantly dashing in and out of military headquarters across the street. A few troops marched below us toward the western outskirts of Gela where the fighting was hottest.

Vague rumors reached us. The Panzers were counterattacking! The Rangers had no tanks! They were being pushed back.

We were joined on the balcony by Lieutenant Colonel [Bob] Kilroe, Judge Advocate of the 1st Division, who reported with a small staff of officers and enlisted men to assist in government. Since Bob and I had no staff, we were delighted with this reinforcement. Kilroe was an able officer who had served all through the North African campaign and took this battle as coolly as he had a dozen others. As long as it raged, however, there was little that either one of us could do for the government of Gela except, on my part, to watch and pray.

And watch I did, from the rooftop of our three-storied quarters, where the entire battle spread out below me. To my rear was the Bay of Gela covered with ships—cruisers, troopships, tankers, destroyers, and landing craft of various types including those motor boats that give me even then a seasick shudder. To the front, the city was ringed with dust and smoke through which at times I could see moving masses, either tanks or artillery. Overhead roared the unopposed German planes that dropped their bombs on the harbor installations 500 yards away or circled over the bay to dive at our ships like angry hornets. Once there was a terrific explosion. A tanker burst into flame! And what a devil's music accompanied this drama—the boom of distant artillery, the crack of exploding shells, the whistlings of released bombs sending chills along any spine, and the staccato of our ack-ack batteries on shore, who at least gave a noisy moral support to this battle, though little else, failing to hit a single German plane.

Meanwhile, the Battle of Gela had reached a crisis. The Rangers were unable to drive ahead and in some places they had been forced back. Ugly rumors still floated about. The Panzers were attacking west of town. We had no tanks. Our troops were falling back all along the line. And sure enough, as we stood there on the balcony, we could see troops retreating from the north into the Square. Bob and I debated what we should do in case the town fell to the enemy. Since there was nothing in the thick AMBOT PLAN about it, we were left to our own devices. Should we fall gallantly at the head of the stairs ringed with 42 enemy dead (we each had 21 rounds for our pistols), or should we remain with true dignity at our post of duty surrounded by our proud and unyielding proclamations, shaming the enemy by "bowed but unbeaten" air, or, to me unthinkable, should we return to the ships in one of those damnable motor boats.

An armored car drove up in front of military headquarters. Out of this car stepped a heavyset man who was wearing two pistols at his belt like an old-time Western bad man. It was General Patton, Old Blood and Guts in person, whose two "shootin' irons" gave a lift to our spirits. Here was a rip roarin', rootin' tootin' to-hell-with-'em son of a gun, a Salt River Roarer, a bad man from out California who would shoot his ——- ———— ——— way out of this ——- ———— —— —— mess!

It was not long before American tanks (the first we had seen) rumbled into the square and headed for the west of town. The cruisers in the bay began to open up with broadsides, which shook the panes of our apartment. Dame Rumor now spoke cheerily: "We've got 'em on the run! We're driving ahead!"

Up to now, only a thin trickle of prisoners had passed beneath our balcony, but within an hour long files began to slouch by. We were standing there looking down at them when General Patton stepped out on the balcony opposite to us and roared down, "Kick those sons of bitches in the ass, if they don't step out faster."

Bob prudently withdrew from our balcony lest the general, seeing two such idle gapers in uniform, might explode again. Nevertheless, I felt like taking off my steel helmet to this man who had turned the tide of battle with his two pistols—a great leader and a magnificent soldier.

Colonel Wynot Rush Irish was a West Point graduate serving as a civil affairs officer in the 1st Infantry Division. Irish observed Patton on the first day he came ashore: "An armored car drove up in front of military headquarters. Out of this car stepped a heavyset man who was wearing two pistols at his belt like an old-time Western bad man. It was General Patton, Old Blood and Guts in person, whose two 'shootin' irons' gave a lift to our spirits. Here was a rip roarin', rootin' tootin' to-hell-with-'em son of a gun, a Salt River Roarer, a bad man from out California who would shoot his ——— way out of this ——— ——— mess!"

When an Axis counterattack threatened to delay the invasion, Patton had come ashore. Axis tanks and troops were poised to reenter Gela.

Patton had penned a do-or-die message in his diary just before the landings: "I am leading 90,000 men in a desperate attack. . . . If I win, I can't be stopped. If I lose, I shall be dead."

He went within sight of the advancing enemy and actually took part in launching 4.2-inch mortars. He later commented, "I personally helped lay some 4.2's at a range of about 900 yards on enemy infantry. The white phosphorus was remarkable in its effect and seemed to make them quite crazy as they rushed out of the ravine, shrilling like dervishes with their hands over their heads."

Ted Fleser did not see Patton that day, but he witnessed an attack with white phosphorus, likely in the same vicinity.

The 4.2 mortars were approximately the same size as a 105. Believe it was a 32-pound projectile. The mortar was not a smooth bore, but a rifled barrel. At the base of the projectile you had an expansion disk that, on detonation of the charge, would be compressed . . . and with the force of the detonation would be forced flat and out into the rifling. That would spin stabilize it. It was originally designed for chemical warfare. Its primary function was laying a smoke screen.

Its primary type of projectile was white phosphorus that would generate the smoke. But that white phosphorus would also burn like hell. And continue penetrating. Phosphorus reacts with water. So if a particle of white phosphorus lands on you, it would keep burning in because of the moisture content. And so it was a very effective weapon. But each component weighed about 100 to 150 pounds for your base plate, your tube and bipod. These were hauled along on a cart. We had the 83rd Chemical Mortar Battalion supporting us. They'd come trotting up the road with their carts, with the mortar and their ammunition. They were a joy to see and they could be relied on, so we referred to them as the "83rd Chemical *Ranger* Battalion." They supported us at Gela and other places.

Seeing the white phosphorus explode was like seeing a field of blossoming chrysanthemums—white flowers, multipetaled. I was at outposts where I could see the "blossoms."

Paul Skogsberg was among those in the 1st Infantry Division who encountered panzers. Actually a member of the 1st Division's 1st Reconnaissance Troop, Skogsberg was assigned as a liaison to a Ranger battalion at the time. He writes about the encounter:

On the morning of the 11th it was reported that an enemy tank column was moving south astride the Ponte Olivo-Gela road. There was a gap between the 1st Division and the Rangers, and this column was headed right for this opening. I was dispatched to see if I could establish visual contact with this unit and to report its location and to keep tabs on it. I set out toward Gela on a route that paralleled the beach. When I reached a point due south of where the road to Gela swung almost due west, I saw an American jeep literally flying down the road toward Gela and it was under heavy fire from the north. I learned later that Captain Ray Regan [commander of the 1st MP

Company] was in this jeep. Fortunately, the jeep was not hit and no one was hurt. . . .

With all the attention given Captain Regan's jeep, I had apparently not been seen and was able to locate myself at a dinky little railroad overpass, which afforded me excellent cover. I could see the tanks clearly from under the bridge, but I realized that I was in a precarious position as there was at that moment nothing to stop the tanks from driving directly to the beach, and my position afforded me no means of escape without exposing myself to direct fire.

Again the tanks opened fire. I thought at first they were firing at me as the rounds zoomed directly above my position, but I soon realized they were firing at a cargo vehicle that had just crossed the dune behind me. I reported my observations to Blake at the Rangers and to the 1st Recon liaison at division.

At the moment, there was nothing to stop these tanks from reaching the beach, and had they continued on they could have raised havoc. But for some reason, they halted. Perhaps they felt they were being sucked into a trap. What ever the reason for this halt, it was costly for the enemy. An infantry cannon company soon moved into position to the east of my position and took the tanks under fire. This unit was soon joined by an artillery battery, which I could not see.

In short order, most of the German tanks were put out of action and the few remaining withdrew. With a total of 16 wrecked panzers burning in their wake, the Hermann Goering Division pulled out that afternoon, bound for Messina and escape to Italy. Lucas elaborates in his journal for July 11:

Parts of the 15th Panzer and the Hermann Goering Division hit our 1st Division. The blow came where I had predicted, but was a day early. The 1st was somewhat disorganized and its left, including the Rangers, was thrown back in confusion at Gela. General Patton was ashore and his presence, more than any other single factor, restored order. At this time (2:30 p.m..) the situation is better. . . Am glad Patton wasn't shot.

I feel sorry for George. The strain is terrific. I think he does pretty well. I would be more irritable than he is. He has trained his staff to accept their responsibilities and take action, which is a big relief to him.

Patton, aware of Lucas's doting concern, groused in a letter to his wife, Beatrice: "John Lucas and Beedle all lecture me so much against taking risks that it is making a woman of me."

Chapter Three

In his journal, Hap Gay adds his view of the value of Patton's presence:

It appears to me that Gela was in imminent danger of falling, particularly during the hours before noon, and I personally believe that the commanding general's presence in the front lines had a great deal to do with the enemy attacks failing.

Major General John P. Lucas, long-time Patton friend, watched the situation deteriorate on Sicilian shores. In his journal, he privately credited the turnaround to Patton: "General Patton was ashore, and his presence, more than any other single factor, restored order."
U.S. Army

◆

On the night of July 11, elements of the 82nd Airborne Division went in to reinforce the Seventh Army's holdings. Parts of the 82nd Airborne had parachuted in early the first day, but encountered many problems on the ground. Airborne landings would become even worse the second day, for different reasons. During planning talks, the Navy had been very nervous about the approach of aircraft, knowing how vulnerable the ships were. Navy brass initially disagreed with a plan that sent low-flying formations of transport aircraft roaring over their flotilla in the dark, but finally agreed *if* the aircraft approached through a narrow corridor at a prescribed time.

The C-47 troop transport aircraft did fly when and where planned, but something went terribly wrong. A single machine gun, it was rumored, opened up on the defenseless formation, then another and another, until finally the sky filled with tracers. Antiaircraft gunners on ships and shore joined in, and flak bursts dotted the sky.

For the airborne troops, conditions became catastrophic before they even confronted the enemy, as friendly fire raked them from the ground and sea. Edward Sims was a second lieutenant in the 82nd Airborne Division. His 504th Parachute Infantry Regiment (less the 3rd Battalion, which had landed in Sicily the first day with the 505th Parachute Infantry Regiment) was the unit caught in the debacle. Sims tells about a peaceful flight that turned into pandemonium:

We took off in C-47s from Karouan, North Africa, on the night of July 11, 1943. Half of my platoon was in one plane—14 troops plus me. The other half was in another plane. It was our first combat parachute jump—our initiation to combat.

As we approached Sicily, I stood at the open door of the aircraft. The night was calm and the light from the quarter moon reflected off the white caps of the Mediterranean Sea below. I could see land as it appeared under the port side wing.

It was a pretty tranquil scene until I started seeing red tracers coming up from below. My initial thought was, *What the hell is going on here?* We knew right away it had to be friendly fire. Couldn't be anything else. There weren't any German ships in the area. All hell broke loose and you couldn't get it to stop.

I felt our plane shimmy as it passed through the first flak burst, and then the antiaircraft guns of our own forces at sea and on the beaches opened up with all they had. I didn't get shook. I had too much to do to think about. I had to be calm—for the troops. They were putting their lives in my hands, just as I was putting my life in theirs.

We could hear the hits as the flak penetrated. From the door, I scanned the sky for other planes, but the only planes I could see were going down in flames. Our starboard engine must have been hit, because it was no longer running smoothly and the whole plane had developed a distinct shudder. Our pilot was banking away from the fire.

I had my men stand up and hook up and then, as I walked forward to talk with the pilot, I instructed my platoon sergeant to get the men out fast if the plane started to go down before I got back.

Chapter Three

The pilot said, "We're lost." He had known where he was until he started to bank away from the fire. I looked out the windshield and said, "You can see land down there." With the moonlight you could distinguish land from sea. And I could see flak coming up. Flak all around. Fiery red, bluish bursts. You couldn't see the smoke because of the darkness, just the little explosions.

I told the pilot he'd never get back to North Africa with this load on. I said, "Give me a few seconds to get back to rear and give me a green [go light]. Then I'll take this crew out."

I didn't know where we're going to land, but I knew I'd much prefer that risk to going back toward Africa and ditching at sea.

When I was making my way back, the red light had come on. Just as I got to the door and hooked up, the green light came on. So I tripped the equipment bundles—our ammo, automatic weapons, and [other supplies] fell from underneath the plane. I stood at the door and yelled for everyone to get ready to jump. Then I jumped into the darkness with everyone following.

The formation around them was being annihilated. Sims would learn later that out of 144 airplanes carrying airborne troops that night, 23 were shot down—6 of them crashing before the troops could jump. Another 37 were badly damaged and 8 aborted the mission, returning with paratroops still aboard to the base near Karouan, Tunisia.

Sims and half his platoon were plunging toward earth destined for "who knows where," but certainly not in the drop zone near Gela. Sims continues:

Landing was quick and rough. My parachute opened just seconds before I hit the ground. The plane had been only a few hundred feet off the ground. We all landed right together, so we were able to assemble quickly. I learned then that one man had hit a stone fence and injured his leg.

I had to find out where the hell we were. At a nearby road, I sent a two-man patrol each way down the road. One of them came across a sign that said "Augusta 40 KM." Knowing that, I was able to figure out our general position on the map. We were southwest of Augusta, which put us about 25 miles from Gela. That meant we were on the other side, the *wrong* side of German forces who were opposing the beach landing of the 45th Infantry Division.

No other airborne troops had dropped near us. Soon, I saw what appeared to be small enemy patrol. We fired on them, and never knew if they were Italian or German. They were too far away and left quickly, not interested in fighting. We saw a larger group, probably three or four times our number [15], but we didn't want to open up on them. Didn't want to expend our ammunition until we got closer to our troops. I knew this group was German, because we could hear them speaking German.

The next forces we met were advance elements of the 45th Division, and we had trouble convincing them we were friendly. There was a one-sided fight there. We could identify who they were, but they didn't identify us. We started talking to them, but they still thought we were Germans. We had to use just about every swear word we knew to convince them that we were paratroopers. [Possibly confusing them was our uniforms.] Our intelligence people in the regiment had had us "paint" our jump suits with oil-based paint to make a camouflage effect. We hadn't had camouflage uniforms at that time. Plus the jump suit was something most hadn't seen before, with its old baggy pants and sporty jacket. And the troops in the front line had not been briefed that there would be paratroops. Once they finally realized who we were, we went on. From there it was easy to get to Gela walking on foot. The 45th Division had already moved forward, so we were walking through secured territory and joined the rest of our company at Gela.

◆

After going ashore on July 11, John Erbes and others from the 2nd Armored Division experienced many air attacks from Messerschmitt Bf 109s, whose "black crosses . . . seemed as large as the sky itself and were coal black."

We finished unloading . . . and were on the beach, digging slit trenches . . . and diving for cover at least once every half hour. We learned an important thing about slit trench protection when one of the men dived into a slit trench to avoid the strafing. When he dove into the slit trench his feet were pointed into the direction of the oncoming plane, and of course, his head was pointed in the other direction. There was just enough angle to the path of the machine-gun bullets so that when the bullets passed over the front edge of the slit trench they struck him in the head, killing him instantly. The lesson to be learned from this experience was to position yourself in the slit trench so that your head is pointed toward the on-coming plane. You may get a bullet in the foot, but that is better than the alternative. One other important point was to position the slit trench crosswise to the usual path approach of the plane, if there was a usual pathway.

Chapter Three

James Burt also experienced air attack against elements of the 2nd Armored Division that landed at Licata. Instead of Messerschmitt fighters such as the ones Erbes saw, these were Stuka dive-bombers with their dive sirens wailing.

The Stuka was supposed to be a terror-maker with its sound. It was something of a laugh. We saw them some in Sicily hopping over the dunes. Our ground crew shot down several. But one day a gas truck driver lost his vehicle to strafing from a Stuka. He went back to the beach and got another truck. Later in the same day ground people shot down a Stuka that exploded in the air and the engine landed on the gas truck and destroyed it. That poor boy had two in the same day.

◆

The Rangers who had landed at Gela were given new objectives for their second night on the island. Ted Fleser would see the use of a new and effective weapon—the bazooka—used in combat for the first time.

The second night, our company was assigned a detail of taking a pass. It was guarded by a battery of 88s and pillboxes on the side and machine gun pits.

There was about a five-mile plain between Gela and this pass. So we had to cross this plain by stealth. As we moved, the Germans shot up flares and we'd freeze so that we wouldn't be seen. I don't recall that this disturbed us that much. We almost got into a rhythm with it, expecting the next one after a certain number of steps. Each time, we just did as we were trained—we froze. We crossed the plain, took out some outposts, and got through the barbed wire entanglements.

As we approached the pass's defenses, I remember getting to a place where we hadn't been able to dig in yet before we started getting mortared. I remember *my stomach* trying to dig into the ground. And I was thinking, *Mama, take care of your little boy*. But we were able to go on and take out the machine gun pits and move in on the pillboxes.

We were using bazookas in combat for the first time. Bazookas had been issued to us in North Africa, just before we left for Sicily. They were the battery-operated type. You had to make sure the contacts were clean and that the batteries were in good shape.

Visualize the effect of a shoulder-fired artillery piece firing in on the slits of the pillboxes. That's how we used them for the first time. The Italian troops came streaming out. The psychological effect was devastating. They had not seen anything like this before. And we were just issued these, so it was new to us, too. The bazooka had been designed for use against the lighter armored vehicles, like the German Mark IV tank, not the Mark VI—they'd be useless against the Mark VI. But we used them on pillboxes very effectively in this case.

For the battery of 88s covering the pass, we directed the Navy guns on them. That let our forces advance. We had taken the pass, which let them go on through.

As Rangers, we had come ashore with very little. Weapon and ammo, and a canteen of water. That was about it. No rations. No blankets or anything of that sort. We were getting pretty hungry by then.

There were two brothers, Joe and Bill Cain. Before becoming Rangers they had joined the Canadian forces in 1939 in France. They had escaped from France through Brest back to England. So I had the benefit of their combat experience. I remember walking along with them and seeing there were bursacks on the forward slope of the hill. There were no longer any Italians to be seen. They had just fled moments before, chased away by the approach of the whole company. The three of us went down the forward slope. Each of us picked up two packs and crept back up. That gave us some rations and blankets.

But the Italians would have their revenge: The blankets contained lice.

Fleser would suffer something more longstanding than lice from the biotope of Sicily. He, like many GIs, took away a case of malaria that caused fever and chills for years.

◆

The work of the Rangers and others, which relied on coordination of naval and air support, was aided by the intelligence sections of the various commands. First Lieutenant Ralph Luman served in the G-2 section of Seventh Army headquarters.

We controlled all photo reconnaissance flights over Sicily in our zone assigned by the tactical plan. From British and U.S. troops in North Africa, we set up a photo interpretation center. Daily at least, Colonel Koch would come in with General Patton, who would ask: "What's new?" Or "What's important?"

With the perfect weather of the central Med and the new U.S. cameras and aircraft, we soon were amassing thousands of important facts. All data was posted on 1/25,000 maps, the largest scale maps used at that time. We also had topographic map makers update the maps of Sicily to replace the 1848 Italian map used as base data. The shore lines were corrected. Road, railroad and airfields data were drawn in, using drawing on acetate made by the photo interpreters. We located every enemy fixed position, including underwater obstacles, beach defenses of land mines, barbed wire, and machine guns and artillery pillboxes. Even troop reserve areas, written with an accuracy of one meter in X, Y, Z (three dimensional) coordinates. Each was given a target designation number, so that could be radioed to supporting naval gunfire control, who would assign it to the appropriate ship to fire upon.

◆

Patton's men moved away from their landing areas and up the west coast as quickly as they could. Edward Sims of the 82nd Airborne moved out from Gela along the shore to seize the coastal town of Sciacca and then moved on to Salaparuta. In an unpublished memoir, he writes:

At one point during this move, enemy planes strafed our column. We did take up dispersed positions and opened fire, but all of the planes continued to fly south. It was obvious there were no serious hits. As we approached Sciacca, I was leading with my platoon when I noticed smoke rising from the road ahead, so I dispersed my platoon into firing positions and went forward to check out the smoke. The road had been mined with antitank mines and a two-wheeled cart, driven by an old man with a young child, had set off one mine killing both of them and the mule that was pulling the cart. To our left on the crest of a small rise were a number of pillboxes with white flags being waved from the gun ports. We advanced cautiously and flushed out a large group of Italian soldiers who wanted to surrender. After disarming them, they were sent under guard to our rear. I will never understand why they allowed the old man to drive his cart into the minefield.

We cleared Sciacca, then headed for Marsala. In an area called "Tuminello Pass," we were forced to make a frontal assault when a strong German force caught us by surprise and opened fire on our column. This turned into a long, hard fire fight.

Sims elaborates on the ambush in a personal interview:

The first thing I did personally was to curse at the people from the rear who were telling us to speed up the damn thing all the time. All that did was close up on the people ahead of us. Bunched us all together. I kept thinking how stupid that was.

Racing Across Sicily

I took what cover I could alongside the road. But I realized quickly it was no place to stay, so I got up and said, "Let's go."

The Germans were up on a small hill to our right. We weren't close enough to see an individual and fire at him.

We had encountered mostly Italians to this point. But these Germans fought us hard. They had the element of surprise on us, but they took on too many people—our whole battalion was on the road. They pinned us down until we figured out what was happening, then we made a frontal assault on them. We turned to the right and attacked them head on.

Eventually, they fled. There I lost one more man. By then my platoon had united—about 30 of us together. The other half hadn't had too much problem landing. They landed right in the Gela area. They were shot at coming in, but no serious damage.

British General Bernard Law Montgomery joins Patton at the midpoint of the Sicily campaign, on July 28, 1943. If the relationship was uneasy in North Africa, it turned decidedly competitive in Sicily. On the day this photo was taken, Patton wrote: "This is a horse race, in which the prestige of the U.S. Army is at stake. We must take Messina before the British." **U.S. Army**

Sims concludes the movement up the coast to Salaparuta in his memoir.

Marsala was soon taken and then Trapani was seized and secured. Near Marsala a friend, Lieutenant Lutcavage, was accidentally shot in the left elbow by one of his own men, who was shooting at wine barrels. His elbow was shattered and he was evacuated through medical channels to the U.S. for treatment.

After seizing Trapani, the fighting in our area subsided and we were placed on occupational duty. My platoon was assigned to police an area near the small town of Salaparuta, which was the milling center for a larger area. I established my command post in a house vacated by a Nazi collaborator and selected a local citizen, who had been deported from the U.S. in the late 1920s, as an interpreter. He was a great help to me and served the community well. We immediately set out to search the surrounding area for holdouts and soon found a large building that had been used by the Germans for food storage. The large amount of food supply remaining was confiscated. I then arranged with the local clergy to distribute the food to the most needy in Salaparuta.

◆

The 2nd Armored Division began the push toward Palermo. John Erbes writes about venturing out to find the wounded, but finding only dead as they moved to an inland crossroads:

On July 13 we received a message that there were wounded at a crossroad in the direction of Mazzarino. I took my jeep and an ambulance half-track and started in that direction. Chaplain Ernie Northen came up and asked if he could come along, so we put him into the ambulance and took off. We drove about 8 or 10 miles to the crossroads. When we got there the roads, were littered with dead Americans and Germans. The 1st Infantry medics had already evacuated the wounded. I told my medics to pick up the dead Americans and that we would leave the dead Germans to be picked up by our graves registration unit. Chaplain Northen would have no part of that. He insisted that we at least bury the Germans and mark their graves. I didn't like the idea because there was still plenty of gunfire around us and artillery was still shelling the crossroads. My men were beginning to grumble but the good chaplain was insistent, took a shovel from the ambulance and started to dig a grave, so I told the men to pitch in to bury the 6 or 8 dead Germans. Suddenly an artillery shell dropped about 100 yards away, followed by another about 50 yards away. I looked at Ernie and he looked at me and I yelled at the men to mount up and get out of there. The Germans shelled that crossroad for about 10 minutes. When I related the experience to Colonel Hillyard, he said that the enemy must have had an observation post nearby looking right at us and directing the artillery fire at the crossroads.

Patton's men moved away from their landing areas and toward their interim objective of Palermo. Patton turned to a trusted subordinate general, Geoffrey Keyes, whom he appointed his deputy Seventh Army commander. He assigned Keyes to lead both 2nd Infantry and 2nd Armored divisions on a very fast ride of 100 miles in only a few days. The result was 300 American casualties and enemy casualties numbering 6,000. More than 44,000 Axis prisoners were taken. Capping the drive was the foray into Palermo itself on July 22. William Kunz remembers:

> There wasn't organized resistance in the town. Once we got within 5 or 10 miles, it opened up for us. There were Italian battalions up in the hills, but when we'd encounter them, they'd come down and surrender right away. The Germans fought to the end, but they didn't take a stand against us at Palermo. Not like there was on the way into Messina, when we had to fight our way from town to town along the coastline.

Once Palermo was secured, the rear-echelon units commandeered some parts of the city. Roland Farrell, a second lieutenant who had served also in Africa with the 51st Signal Battalion, was assigned to the message center. He says:

> We took over the large post office building in Palermo as Seventh Army headquarters. We started a message center in the building. In those days, a message center was a lot like a post office, because everything literally was "mail." So being in a post office building was very appropriate.

> There was a back stairway that went from the general staff office up above to our message center. With urgent message traffic, I was able to take it right up to them. It happened a lot.

> General Patton came down the back stairway once and found us walking knee-deep in envelopes and packages. Most of the stuff was for units that hadn't even gotten over there yet. Patton really tore into the signal officer for the mess. We were all scared to death. He was a very stern man.

"The best damn ass-kicker in the U.S. Army" was a title Patton himself boasted—particularly appropriate after the turnaround of II Corps—and he continued to live up to it on Sicily. His troops found their leader wasn't finished with monetary fines for minor violations. Farrell witnessed one such fine while he fulfilled a collateral duty:

> As a payroll officer I went to a construction company that was bivouacked to pay them. They were all eating at the time. They had C ration cans open and were sitting on their jeeps, trucks, or on the ground. Up drives General Patton and his aide, a bird colonel. I'm the closest one to him, so I high-tailed it down there and gave him a highball.
>
> He asked, "Who is in command here?"
>
> I answered, "Captain Torcia."
>
> By then Torcia had seen what was happening and was coming quickly. When he got there, General Patton asked him, "Is this any way to run a bivouac site?"
>
> What are you going to say? All the captain could answer was, "No, sir."
>
> General Patton said, "I don't ever want to see anything like this again. Captain, do you want a court-martial or Article 104?"
>
> Again, what are you going to say? He said, "An Article 104, sir." [An Article 104 is a unit commander's prerogative to discipline personnel for minor infractions and doesn't require a court hearing.]
>
> Patton said, "That's going to be a hundred dollar fine. Now square your unit away."
>
> The bird colonel aide stayed behind to ask, "Captain, what's your full name, serial number and the name of your unit?" Sure enough, the next week, it was out of his pay.

◆

North Africa had been sweltering and dusty for Patton's unacclimated troops (the Desert Training Center came too late for them) and Sicily had similar conditions, as Garrison Davidson describes:

> The campaign was the first time I had been so physically active in a semitropical climate dressed so heavily. Operating over dirt Sicilian country roads during a military campaign in the middle of a hot, dry summer must be experienced to be appreciated. The talcum-powdery dust clung to every bead of perspiration and hung like snowflakes from sweaty eyebrows and eyelashes. It worked its way up under helmet liners to turn the hair of the others as gray as mine. At day's end we looked more like fugitives from a blizzard than people who had just come from a sunny Mediterranean day.
>
> The white dust billowed up in dense clouds from under the wheels of our jeeps and the tracks of our tanks, to settle on the red

pasta sauce spread to dry in the sun on large boards next to the doors of the village homes. It was questionable whether the dust contributed more to the ultimate flavor than the hoards of flies that blackened the spread. I am glad I never had to make the test.

At any rate, it was a hot, dirty campaign even without the fighting. Our engineer troops played a key role in the operations over the beaches and in the pursuit across and around the island of Sicily.

As Davidson had described the characteristics of Sicily's environment, John Lucas summarizes the characteristics of fighting there:

This is the roughest country in the world, and everything favors the defensive. Patton's answer is the correct one—a continuous and unrelenting attack. Prepare during the day, get artillery and mortars in position and registered, then advance your infantry at night under an overwhelming bombardment, light the fire and close with the bayonet. German prisoners say we never sleep and they must be getting rather hopeless. They still fight with remarkable stubbornness, however, and still put mines and booby traps everywhere. Two dead children were found a day or so ago who had played around a haystack that had been mined. The roadsides are mined in many places that we haven't found yet and hand grenades are all over the place. The country will be dangerous for a long time.

◆

Lieutenant Loren Evans had been reassigned to the 3rd Ranger Battalion, which landed at Licata, 20 miles to the west of Gela. After leading a platoon in Africa, he now was a company commander. A key assignment for his battalion was to serve as flank guard for Patton's forces moving up the western coast.

When they reached Palermo and were going across the north coast of Sicily, Patton wanted one of the Ranger battalions to guard the flank from the inland. Colonel Darby was going to send the 4th Battalion, because they were the most rested. But the 3rd had had the most action, so Patton asked specifically for the 3rd Battalion. I was there, so I heard it myself.

"I like what they've done," Patton said. "I want the 3rd Battalion."

As we got closer to Messina, the opposition got tougher. We went up against more and more crack troops. And face it, these *were* crack troops on Sicily.

Chapter Three

Often I led the point company for the 3rd Battalion. If I wasn't at the point, another "old-time" officer was at the point. The other old-timer was Joe Larkin [another company commander]. Either he or I was at the point or bringing up the rear.

I have a selective memory. I can remember little of the blood and guts. You know that I had six campaigns, four invasions. Fought every battle of every campaign. I saw a lot of it. But somehow I've just closed it out of my mind. It's not that I don't want to. I've just spent so much time forgetting it.

We lost some men, about the usual, on Sicily. We worked hard to rebuild to full strength. But you know, every time we had to rebuild, we weren't quite the unit we were before. If we had time to work with them and build up an *esprit de corps*, we could get there. But if they were just a replacement thrown in, you couldn't count on them. That wasn't their fault. That was just the fact that they hadn't been there.

As the Rangers repelled flank attacks, the infantry divisions continued a steady advance toward Messina. But even in the absence of attacks, there were other dangers. William Kunz of the 3rd Infantry Division says his most vivid memories of Sicily were the murderous minefields on the way to Messina.

After Palermo—now *there* we started losing a lot of people. We set out for Messina on the coast road and found hundreds of land mines per mile. That place was really loaded with mines. It was mountainous. Rugged to travel through. And we faced some enemy infantry, artillery, and air raids. But what I remember most were these land mines.

On one particular day, we were going along a road. A dusty one. It was hot, and the guy up ahead of me was lugging a BAR. He was walking along and noticed a spring, a flowing fountain, where he could get a drink just off the road. He stepped out of line and took a couple steps to the spring, and he got it. There were mines around that spring. Seeing that, you learn to be careful.

Something else we learned was . . . when you see somebody dead, yours or theirs, and there's a hole next to them, you *don't* throw them into it. It'll probably blow—they were booby-trapped just waiting for someone to do that. On that stretch of road, we probably lost 20 or 30 people to mines.

You learned to follow very carefully in the footsteps of the guy in front of you. You watch very closely. But it was difficult, because you had people digging the mines out with bayonets, you had people stepping on them, you had artillery fire from our batteries and their batteries firing back. And medics trying to get in and out for the mine casualties.

I had a close call myself. We were on foot most of the time, but I had a command car one time and I backed it off the track and flipped up a couple of Teller mines—one under *each rear wheel*. A Teller mine looks like a round disc, or a discus like you throw. In the center of it is a spring-loaded plate that's set for the weight of a vehicle, like a jeep or a half-track or a tank. You might be able to stand on one without it going off. There were littler mines for people. Any way, the tires had run across the sides, not the detonators. The rubber was within an inch of the edge, which caused them to just tip up out of the ground. They were real shallow in this case and it was real sandy. I got out and looked. It would be hard to duplicate that!

At that point, I thought to myself, *I made it this time*. Once you get to the point where you've lost 20, 30 people, then 100 people, and you come upon a scene where artillery fire laced into a platoon and you see people lying dead all over the place, you can get pretty insulated from it. It's either that or you get killed. If you panic in that sort of situation, you're in big trouble.

The heavy mining of the route was part of a well-executed delaying action. The Germans were no longer fighting to hold the island, but to delay its conquest long enough so most of them, such as the Hermann Goering Division, could escape across the Strait of Messina to Italy. Lucas notes in his journal:

8-1-43: The destruction of the bridges and mountain roads by the Germans in their retreat is the most expert and successful demolition operation I have ever dreamed of. They must have an unlimited supply of high explosive.

William Kunz had his first and only encounter with Patton somewhere en route to Messina:

I had gotten a couple nicks from shrapnel. Nothing major, just enough to draw a little blood. I was sitting by the side of the road putting on a little sulfa and a bandage on my shoulder. Patton came roaring by, and then stopped.

He asked, "You hit, sergeant?"

I said, "Yes, sir."

"Going to the hospital?"

"No, sir."

He said, "Good! Get back up there and kill some more Krauts!"

Chapter Three

◆

In mid-August 1943, the Allies were considering more seaborne landings on Sicily's northeastern tip, but they became unnecessary when the 3rd Infantry Division moved into Messina at 8 p.m. on August 16. Lucas writes in his journal:

> 8-17-43: Gay woke me at 2:40 to say that Messina had fallen to the 3rd Division at 8 p.m. last night.
>
> Patton, Keyes, and I joined Truscott on the top of the mountain this side of Messina. I didn't like the place, as it was an important crossroads and I hate crossroads that are within range of the enemy's guns. Our artillery in the valley was firing at Italy.
>
> The Italian commanders, left behind by the Germans to be the goats, were there and were very military, polite, and seemed relieved.

When the British arrived in Messina at daybreak the next day, they were greeted by GIs and astonished to find the city in American hands. A few hours later, a senior British officer was shaking Patton's hand and congratulating him on "a jolly good race." Montgomery later begrudged that Americans had "proved themselves to be first-class troops [who got to Messina] more quickly than we did." This has been played up dramatically in movies and big-picture histories, but William Kunz comments about it from the GI's point of view:

> I missed out on all that stuff about Patton beating Montgomery in there. Often, we [in the infantry divisions] would get there first. You'd take a town, but don't wait around for the photographers. You go right through to the other side, chasing the enemy out, and then set up a perimeter on the other side. By the time the hoopla gets there, you're long gone—at the other end. Same thing happened in Rome. By the time Clark [Fifth Army commander] got to Rome, we were 15 miles on the other side of it.
>
> One thing I do remember about Messina. We got into the town itself and it was night. But the place was burning up. Alongside of the wall were a bunch of Italian civilians who had been shot by firing squad. They had been looters, shot just before we got there.

◆

During the closing days of the Sicily campaign, Patton's stock stood sky-high. During the week of July 26, 1943, he made the cover of both *Newsweek* and *Time* magazines. The Germans now took notice of Patton for the first time. A captured document from the German high command stated Patton was "the most dangerous general on all fronts" with tactics that "are daring and unpredictable. He fights not only the troops opposing him, but the Reich." High praise by any standard.

Patton made a regular practice of visiting wounded troops, like these awaiting evacuation to field hospitals in Sicily, even though, as he wrote to his wife, "it always makes me choke up." Losing his temper twice over suspect patients during such visits in Sicily nearly ended his military career. **National Archives**

Triumphant, Patton carried out his duties of an Army commander by visiting many field hospitals to see the GIs wounded in the great victory. Lieutenant Colonel Charles R. Codman recounts it in diary form in *Drive*:

August 2, 1943. Went with the boss [General Patton] to the hospital this morning, where he distributed 40 Purple Hearts, and, God, he did it well.

"Where did you get it, boy?"

"In the chest, sir."

"Well, it may interest you to know that the last German I saw had no chest and no head either. To date you have captured or killed over 80,000 S.O.B.s—that's the official figure, but as I travel round, my nose tells me that the figures are much bigger and before the end they will be double that. Get well quickly—you want to be in on that final kill . . ."

A rousing collective speech to each ward, to the nurses, to the interns. The last guy he decorated was unconscious, oxygen mask, probably won't live. The boss pulled one of those quick switches of his—took off his helmet, knelt down, pinned the medal on the pillow, whispered in the guy's ear—stood up at attention. Elementary if you like, but I swear there wasn't a dry eye in the house.

The next day, Patton made another hospital visit—one that nearly ruined his career.

While walking through the 15th Evacuation Hospital on August 3, 1943, Patton happened upon a soldier, Private Charles H. Kuhl, sitting on supplies. When Patton asked what was the matter, Kuhl answered, "I guess I just can't take it." Patton was instantaneously livid. He verbally lashed out, then physically lashed out—slapping him with his gloves. The man was later diagnosed with malaria and chronic dysentery.

On August 10, a second incident occurred. As Patton walked down long rows of cots at the 93rd Evacuation Hospital, he had words of praise for the wounded. Then he came across Private Paul G. Bennet, who appeared fine. Patton again asked what was the matter. Bennet said, "It's my nerves." Patton's voice pierced the ward: "What did you say?" Bennet replied, through sobs, "It's my nerves. I can't stand the shelling anymore." In the words of the medical officer who witnessed and reported the incident:

He was still sobbing. The general then yelled at him, "Your nerves, hell; you are just a God-damned coward, you yellow son of a bitch." He then slapped the man and said, "Shut up that damn crying. I won't have these brave men here who have been shot at seeing a yellow bastard sitting here crying." He then struck the man again, knocking his helmet liner off and into the next tent. He then turned to the admitting officer and yelled, "Don't admit this yellow bastard; there's nothing the matter with him. I won't have the hospitals cluttered up with these cowardly bastards who haven't got the guts to fight." He then turned to the man again, who was managing to sit at attention though shaking all over and said, "You're going back to the front lines and you may get shot and killed, but you're going to fight. If you don't I'll stand you up against a wall and have a firing squad kill you on purpose. In fact," he said, reaching for his pistol, "I ought to shoot you myself, you God-damned whimpering coward." As he left the tent, the general was still yelling back at the receiving officer.

Lieutenant Vera Sheaffer was a nurse in the 93rd Evacuation Hospital. Although not in the same ward, she was in the hospital as all this happened. She recounts the aftermath:

> Word of it spread quickly in the hospital. I did not actually see him slap the soldier. But immediately there was a lot of talk among the nurses. Everyone was very upset. Our commanding officer let us know he was not going to stand for this and not just let it pass. He wrote a letter to Corps.
>
> Of course, for us it was right back to caring for the patients. Back to duties. There were many patients and much to be done. All these really young people who had such wounds they would carry with them their whole lives, like amputations—so traumatic for them. You tried not to think about it. But it affected you. Our doctors saw things they'd never seen before in civilian life. Not in a whole lifetime of practice.
>
> Other than the [slapping incident], it was a day like any other day. People were dying and they'd be talking about their wives and family back home. It was a hard time. I just listened and responded to what they said. My concern was with them and not the actions of a general.

The "slapping incidents" made news around the globe. A news reporter named Drew Pearson broke the story after Eisenhower himself asked reporters not to. It completely overshadowed Patton's dazzling victory on Sicily. As Charles Codman would later say, "This campaign by the Seventh Army was one of the most successful campaigns ever made by an army in history. It was thought that great credit would be given to General Patton for this magnificent campaign. Such was not to be the case."

As his superior, Eisenhower faced a dilemma. He didn't want to lose his best fighting general. But the public outcry was too strong to ignore. In his book *At Ease: Stories I Tell My Friends*, Eisenhower writes:

> All kinds of protests arose, and General Marshall cabled to say I would have to decide this one on my own and he would support my action, as usual. . . .
>
> I made up my mind to hang on to him. . . . I decided to let him suffer for a week or so to impress upon him that he could not continue to sound off this way and still be a worthwhile commander in a great Allied organization. I sent word that I would make a final decision in a few days and would let him know his fate.
>
> George would sweat, I knew, because if there was one thing he wanted to do it was continue in the war. So, after an interval, I sent for

him, told him that I had decided to keep him on, and said at the same time that he had to learn to keep his mouth shut on political matters.

Patton always lived at one extreme or another of the emotional spectrum. He was either at the top of his form, laughing and full of enthusiasm, or filled with remorse and despondency. When I gave him the verdict, tears streamed down his face and he tried to assure me of his gratitude. He gave me his promise that thereafter he would be a model of discretion.

It wasn't quite so simple as that. Eisenhower also ordered Patton to apologize to the two men slapped, the hospital staff, and his troops. Many Patton veterans today praise the movie *Patton*, but the apology scene—showing a penitent George C. Scott choking out his regrets before troops who relish the humiliation—is not accurate, they say. The real-life scene is described by Major Ted Conway of the 9th Division:

[W]e were assembled in a large . . . olive orchard. . . . General Patton arrived in that famous command car of his with the two metal flags on either side . . . a long trailing cloud of dust, and MPs and so on. We all stood at attention and put on our helmets as the bugler sounded attention and General Patton mounted this sort of PT platform in front of these 3,000 troops. General Patton had a rather high, squeaky voice, and as he started to address the regiment, he said, "Take seats," so we sat down on our helmets—it was a practice of those days to keep us out of the mud or the dust—and General Patton started to give what we knew was to be his apology. But he never got past his first word, which was "Men!" At that point, the whole regiment erupted. It sounded like a football game in which a touchdown had been scored, because the helmets (steel pots) started flying through the air, coming down all over, raining steel helmets and the men just shouted "Georgie, Georgie"—a name he detested. He was saying, we think he was saying, "at ease, take seats," and so on. Then he had the bugler sound "attention" again, but nothing happened. Just all these cheers. So, finally General Patton was standing there and he was shaking his head and you could see big tears streaming down his face and he said, or words to this effect, "The hell with it," and he walked off the platform. At this point the bugler sound "attention" and again everybody grabbed the nearest available steel helmet, put it on, being sure to button the chin strap (which was a favorite Patton quirk) and as he stepped into his command car and again went down the side of the regiment, dust swirling, everybody stood at attention and saluted to the right and General Patton stood up in his command car and saluted, crying. . . . He was our hero. We were on his side. We knew the problem. We knew what he had done and why he had done it.

Speaking from the point of view of patients in that hospital, Leon Luttrell of the 2nd Armored Division leaves no doubt about his sentiments:

> I was in the hospital recovering from my wounds, for which I received the Purple Heart, when he slapped the soldier and branded him a coward. I can only say none of us felt sorry for the soldier. After recovering from my wounds, I was placed in limited service and assigned to the 600th Medical Ambulance Company and later to the 2670th Ambulance Company. I picked up the wounded and the dead in Italy, France, and the Battle of the Bulge, where only Patton was able to advance. I never heard anyone say that he was not the great leader, and best general in the Army, and certainly not the "prima donna" that George C. Scott portrayed him as being in the *Patton* movie. I am proud to have served General George S. Patton.

Luttrell would have offered a decisive vote for the "popularity poll" that Charles Codman cites in *Drive*:

> In regard to the soldier-slapping incident, it now seems to be closed except for the continuous fan mail, which it is one of my jobs to handle and which is running rather better than the Gallup poll on the same subject—about 89 percent pro and 11 percent con. Taken as a whole, it forms quite an illuminating human document. [There is] importance in backing a leader, 'specially one who has the rare quality of making people *want* to fight.

Garrison Davidson received a letter from Paul Harkins, Patton's deputy chief of staff, that shares some insights into the slapping incident:

> After the Troina fight, which was pretty rugged as you remember, the ol' man visited a hospital. There must have been two to three hundred very badly wounded men there as the result of the fight. He went along talking to most of them, and at the end of a line of such vets he came to a man whimpering, sitting on a box. He asked him what the matter was and the "guy" without standing said, "I can't take it. I can't stand the sound of shells anymore." Whereon the general became upset—you know how he felt about malingerers—and took a swing at the man with the fingers of a pair of gloves he was carrying. The man ducked, his helmet fell off and the "old man," giving out some of his best language told the C.O. to get the malingerer back to the front and out of sight of the men he called heroes. In a letter he said, "I think I saved a soul."

As it later turned out, the man was AWOL from the front at the time. He went back to his unit and stayed with it for the remainder of the war. I heard he became a pretty fair soldier. In the U.S., his father said if he was doing what the general said he was doing, he would have beat him himself.

The members of our headquarters were incensed that a reporter like Drew Pearson would cast the incident in such an exaggerated light to make public news, and at Ike for not giving an able field commander the understanding and support he deserved.

The reports of the incident and the action against General Patton by General Eisenhower angered our headquarters. We felt General Patton did nothing more than one would do to a drunk to bring him to his senses. The whole thing was magnified out of all proportion to the true nature of the incident and the punishment out of all proportion to the "crime." A contributing factor was the fact that the incident wasn't made public news right away. The efforts to keep it hidden just magnified a minor incident out of all proportion to its true significance.

John Lucas saw Patton often during the time, and notes Patton's state of mind in his journal:

Patton feels very depressed, as he believes he is being shelved and doesn't know the reason why. He thinks it goes deeper than anything that has happened to him over here . . . Patton was suffering from repercussions of the "slapping incident," though neither of us knew it at the time. He was certainly wrong in his violent method of handling this affair, and yet his reaction was not entirely an unnatural one for a man who had seen many brave men die for their country's safety and who realized the unnecessary casualties that can be caused in battle by one weakling who fails to do his duty.

A diversion from his woes from the incident came in the form of visiting celebrities. Patton hosted comedian Bob Hope and singer Frances Langford at his headquarters in the Royal Palace at Palermo. The general felt at ease around this pair, who had come to do a USO show for troops of the Seventh Army. Codman recounts the memorable dinner:

August 22, 1943. Last evening our guests at the palace were none other than Bob Hope and Frances Langford.

It couldn't have been better. Supper with lots of Asti Spumante. The boss [General Patton] was nothing short of terrific. With Hope was a guitar player, a tenor, Langford of course, and his scriptwriter, a Mr. Block. He was fascinated by the boss—they all were, but he especially.

After about the second of the boss's sallies—in his best vein, Mr. Block just put down his knife and fork and gave out.

"But, General, that's *beautiful*—Bob, did you hear that reading?—and what *timing*—say, General, can we use that one in the next Thursday's show?"

A little later, "You might as well bow out, Bob—he's topped your every line so far."

Hope: "He's right; from now on I'll just play it straight—and tomorrow I'll get a new script writer."

And so on for hours.

Langford sang some old songs and also some of Cole Porter's new ones—then we got her on Gershwin. . . .

The boss gets eloquent again—then sentimental—has them in tears. Hope brings them back to normal with: "Not the old blood and guts *I've* heard about."

The boss goes over his campaigns—is very modest about it—says he just prays he's done his job as well as he could.

Hope leans over—conspirator stuff. "Look, General, if you should ever be out of a job, I *believe*—" his timing is perfect—"I believe I can get you a solid week at Loew's State."

Good-byes—pictures (I saw to that).

The boss tells Hope that entertaining the soldiers is a fine thing. "It is wonderful," he says. "You can see how they enjoy *anything* in the way of entertainment."

Hope: "How do y'mean, *anything*?!?"

The boss thinks for a moment. "Well, let's say *everything*."

Mr. Block is practically cataleptic with joy. "It's beautiful—see what I mean, Bob? Now he's *double*-topping you."

Another diversion was a visit to the nearby island of Corsica. Perhaps in an attempt to draw strength from a historical figure he revered, Patton flew to the capital city of Ajaccio, birthplace of Napoleon. Patton believed he had served in Napoleon's Army in a previous life. Several of Patton's staff accompanied him, as Colonel Garrison Davidson remembers:

Ajaccio was the birthplace of Napoleon. Soon after we arrived, General Patton asked to be taken to Napoleon's birthplace. We all went along and he took a picture of us and General [Alphonse] Juin at the door.

Napoleon was born on a Sunday. His mother was at church when she got labor pains. They hurried her home but she did not make the bedroom. He was born in the living room on a sofa. When the sofa was shown to General Patton he walked over to it, closed his hand loosely and rubbed his fingernails over the covering and then blew on them, saying with a twinkle in his eye, "Just for good luck."

But nothing could make the trouble from the slapping incidents go away. Severe judgment for the transgression had been handed down in several forms. Patton was relieved of command of the Seventh Army and left to await a new, unknown assignment. On January 22, 1944, Patton received orders to go to Great Britain without delay. Even in the dark days of uncertainty, Patton carried on with the formalities that go along with a changeover of command and, unnerving as it must have been, he maintained professionalism and his soldierly bearing. Roland Farrell attended a send-off banquet.

Before Patton left Palermo to go to England, we had a banquet. It included all his staff and others in headquarters. It was a luncheon, served on a long, long table with him at the head of it. I was way down at the end of the table with the signal officers and even a Red Cross girl. When General Patton is at the head of the table, you better be facing him. Especially when he's talking. I learned by watching him with his staff that when anyone would turn their head away from him as he was talking, he *demanded* their attention. If they were distracted or looked away, he'd holler out their name. In his presence, I was scared stiff. He was like a god.

[At the time of the banquet] he had just been relieved of Seventh Army command and was on the way to England. Right up that road was the hospital in Sicily where he slapped that soldier. I had visited that field hospital at least once, but I heard about that later. Nothing came through the message center about it. I heard it through the newspapers. I'm sure he was glad to be leaving all that behind on Sicily.

He gave a little speech to us. He thanked his staff for their support and for doing a good job. He said to carry on their assignments, as well as they had done for him, for the rest of the war. He already knew that they, as a part of the Seventh Army, would be part of the invasion forces. Perhaps a few of the upper ranks like the G-2 and G-3 knew, too, but the rest had no knowledge.

Many in that room would be part of the invasion forces, but Patton himself would not. After the slapping incident, Omar Bradley, formerly his subordinate, became his superior.

The most self-destructive acts of Patton's life—the two slapping incidents in Sicily—changed the course of his career and probably the course of history. He was no longer considered for command of the cross-Channel invasion—an honor that went instead to the new Army group commander, Bradley. Dwight Eisenhower describes Patton's reaction in *At Ease: Stories I Tell My Friends:*

> General Bradley was to be commander of the American Army group when we had one established in France. There was a potentially delicate shift. I had communicated with General Patton and invited him to join us. But I told him that if he did so, the positions of him and Bradley would be reversed, with Bradley commanding a group of armies, and Patton a single one. He did not hesitate a second and I was happy to have him. After all, we had been friends for twenty-five years. There came a time when we needed all the friendship we could muster.

Chapter 4

Preparing in Britain

January 1944–June 1944

One of Patton's favorite maxims was "A pint of sweat is worth a gallon of blood." In Great Britain during the first half of 1944, he would sweat many pints preparing for battle on the Continent.

Patton had to start from zero. Since entering the Army, he'd been through the drill many times before—transforming a fledgling unit into a spirited fighting force, by his count, 27 times. "Each time," he writes in his diary for January 26, 1944, "I have made a success of it, and this one must be the biggest."

He would be in charge of the Third Army—an untried union of commands being drawn together even as Patton waited in Great Britain. Still in the States, troops of this embryonic legion realized they were being organized to go overseas, but they knew little more. Many did not know they would become part of the Third Army. And none knew Patton would be their new commander until, well, *Mrs.* Patton told them. Fred Hose, a warrant officer in the headquarters intelligence section, explains:

> General Hodges had already left at that time to take command of the First Army. So when we left Fort Sam Houston, we didn't have any idea who our commanding general [CG] might be. We were at Camp Shanks, New York, when we found out that General Patton would be our CG.
>
> Somebody at the post office, the APO, noticed a letter from Mrs. Patton. It was addressed to General Patton at APO 403, New York, New York. Well, APO 403 was the Third Army post office. The guy

looked closer and saw written on the envelope: "Lt. General George S. Patton, CG Headquarters Third Army." *That's* how we learned that we'd be getting "Old Blood and Guts."

We really wouldn't have thought it would be Patton, who was down in the dumps after the outing in Sicily.

The "somebody" who noticed the letter was Coy Eklund of Third Army headquarters' personnel section. In a personal interview, he says:

I was sorting the mail one morning when I came to a letter addressed to Lt. General George S. Patton Jr. I wondered, *How can this be?* And then I looked at the return address and saw it was from Mrs. George S. Patton.

I was the first one to know we had a new Army commander. His wife would not be writing to him at APO 403 unless she knew that was his proper address.

I gave this letter to my boss and he ran over to our chief of staff, Brigadier General [George] Davis. Davis turned white, as you can imagine, because he knew his days were numbered.

The Third Army's advance party had shipped out for Scotland before the word spread. So, the men aboard ship did not know they had a new commanding general. And that particular general's appointment had consequences for the most senior of them. Citing Patton's "reputation of handpicking his own senior staff officers," Colonel Robert S. Allen tells how Patton met the stunned advance party at the port:

When their ship docked at Glasgow, the advance party was assembled in a mess hall to hear a welcoming speech, as was the practice. Even when Patton entered, aglitter in gleaming brass and boots, they still suspected nothing. They thought he would do the spieling.

He did. But not what they expected.

"I am your new commander," he said. "I'm glad to see you. I hope it's mutual. There's a lot of work to be done and there's little time to do it. There's a special train waiting on the dock to take you to our CP [command post]. We leave in an hour." ·

That was it. On the train, the advance echelon was ordered not to say or write anything about the new CG.

Patton did not meet the main body. But several orders did. They relieved the C/S [chief of staff] and, with one exception, all the senior general staff officers, who were rolled before they got off the transport.

They were replaced by Patton men who had served under him in the African and Sicilian campaigns. Later a number of the special staff chiefs also gave way to Patton veterans. The purge did not affect subordinate officers. Subsequent combat operations wrought many changes in their ranks, but Patton confined head-lopping to the upper brackets.

Practically all of Patton's section chiefs were cavalrymen. A number also were veterans of the 2nd Armored Division, his first divisional command. With the exception of Macdonald [previous commanding general], Hodges' senior officers had been doughboys. Under Patton, Hq Third Army became predominantly cavalry, the only one in the ETO. It was the only headquarters where riding breeches and boots were common articles of attire. It was the only headquarters where every officer always wore a necktie.

Patton had been forced to leave behind his battle-hardened troops in the Mediterranean, but he received permission to transfer key staff officers from the Seventh Army to join him in England. Among them were Hugh Gaffey and Hap Gay, who would continue as Patton's chief and assistant chief of staff, respectively (Gaffey was chief of staff until December 1944, and Gay became chief of staff from then until the end of the war), Oscar Koch was in charge of intelligence, Walter J. Muller marched on ever efficiently as quartermaster, and his chief medical officer remained Charles B. Odom. Accompanying Patton directly from Sicily were his aides Charles Codman and Alexander Stiller.

Army headquarters usually were given a code name, such as "Eagle," "Liberty," "Danger," and so on. For the Third Army, Patton chose the code name "Lucky." Lucky Forward was a small group of key officers within the G-1 (personnel), G-2 (intelligence), G-3 (plans and training), and G-4 (supply), along with sections for miscellaneous subcomponents. Lucky Rear was a larger administrative group located in the rear area. Each section had its own set of dynamics and responsibilities critical to the Third Army's success.

Fred Hose offers insights about Lucky Forward, and particularly the G-2 section:

We learned that the two parts of our headquarters detachment would be called Lucky Forward and Lucky Rear. Lucky Rear had the noncombatants in a large administrative group. I was part of Lucky Forward, [which was a smaller group who advised him and] consisted of the chief of staff, G-1, G-2, G-3, and G-4. Then there was the artillery section, the engineer section, and the signal section—all part of the forward section.

When we got to England, the G-2 section had only two officers who had their jobs retained. Lieutenant Colonel [Robert Sharon] Allen retained his job in intelligence and I retained my job as the administrative officer. Our colonel in G-2 was gone. Patton's G-2 from the Seventh Army, Colonel Koch, took over.

There were several teams within G-2: counterintelligence, CIC, military intelligence teams, prisoner of war team, and more. At the time when we went operational, G-2 section had 1,500 men running around in teams. It was a huge task keeping track of all these men.

I saw General Patton a lot through all this time and worked closely with Colonel Robert S. Allen, who had been coauthor with Drew Pearson on the newspaper column called "The Washington Merry-Go-Round." Colonel Allen had lived in Germany for five years and spoke good German. Drew Pearson had been the one who had written about the slapping incident. I asked Colonel Allen what he thought about that, and he said, "Pearson is a horse's ass who doesn't know when to break a story."

Everyone wondered what Patton's reaction would be when he realized that Colonel Allen had been coauthor with Drew Pearson. But at the time the story broke, Colonel Allen was already in service and couldn't have had a role in it. So there was no hard feelings toward Allen. Allen fit right into Patton's mold. Very aggressive type, like Patton.

The vague wartime caption reads: "Lieutenant General George S. Patton, who commanded the American Seventh Army in Sicily, inspects troops of his new command somewhere in the British Isles. April 21, 1944." Censors have whited out shoulder insignia to keep the Germans guessing. It's not known if the white conceals the Third Army's circle-A or a divisional insignia. Also whited out is the inspecting officer following Patton. **U.S. Army**

Chapter Four

◆

Vast American forces were assembling in the British Isles for the cross-Channel invasion. As they arrived, boatload by boatload, the Third Army became part of the olive drab masses overrunning Great Britain during the first half of 1944. But the Third Army would not be part of the invasion forces of Operation Overlord. It would remain behind in England and arrive in time for the breakout from Normandy. Patton's mere presence, however, gave his Army and himself a role in D-Day. Advised by the *Abwehr* (German military intelligence), Hitler felt that the invasion wouldn't happen when or where it did, largely because the *Abwehr* concluded Patton was not committed to battle.

Patton was initially quartered in London, but soon decided to move his headquarters five hours' drive away to Knutsford, near Chester in Cheshire. Before Patton took up residence at a mansion named Peover Hall, a contingent of Third Army troops, among them MPs, was sent to Knutsford to prepare the area for use as headquarters. Peter P. Joseph had been among the first assigned to the 503rd Military Police Battalion (activated in San Antonio in February 1943) and among the first nonheadquarters Third Army troops to arrive in England in January 1944. He also was among the first at Peover Hall. In a letter to the author, he writes about duties quite unconventional for MPs that put him often in Patton's presence:

Prior to the general's arrival, our unit was asked to volunteer as waiters and orderlies for the staff stationed at Peover Hall, a short distance from our quarters [at Toft Hall]. Many of us did and I, along with two of my close buddies, were chosen to table-wait Patton's staff in his private dining room.

After a week of training, teaching us the formal way of serving the general and his staff (around 10 or 12 officers), we began our new assignment. Shortly thereafter, we were informed that the general had arrived and would be joining his staff for dinner that evening. After we had prepared for the serving, we stood outside the dining room in the hallway awaiting the general's appearance.

I first heard the footsteps and turned to see this tall, straight, perfectly groomed officer walking down the hall. I immediately recognized him as General Patton, stood at attention, saluted him as he entered the dining room and proceeded to follow him to his chair. All his officers in the room were greeting him with great enthusiasm. I pulled out his chair and he sat down, and then the three of us proceeded to serve the food, meat platter, followed by potato platter, and then the vegetable platter. We served according to rank, the food from the left, the beverages from the right. In short, we were there around two months and did orderly work between meals.

A humorous incident occurred during my tenure of cleaning the general's private rooms and office. I walked in on him while he was in his bathroom, seated on the "throne." I immediately apologized for walking in on him (he had not closed the door) and he courteously informed me, "No problem. I will be out in a moment." I relayed this to his valet, Sergeant George Meeks, who calmed me down and assured me there was nothing to fear.

I'd thought, *This is it! I'll be sent to the front lines!*

———————————◆———————————

Meanwhile, the bulk of the Third Army's original troops were en route from America. In the beginning, Patton's Army was composed of these four corps: Troy Middleton's VIII, Gilbert Cook's XII, Wade Haislip's XV, and Walton Walker's XX. Within the corps were a total of 12 armored divisions and infantry divisions. (During the course of fighting on the Continent, many divisions and even entire corps would be exchanged with the First Army, Ninth Army, and others, including the polyglot Allied forces under Montgomery, which caused Patton's command to fluctuate between 100,000 and 400,000 troops at any one time.) Most of the original troops traveled on the ocean liners *Queen Mary*, *Queen Elizabeth*, and *Ile de France*, disembarking at Glasgow, Scotland. Among them was Fred Hose, who set out on March 12 and finally arrived on March 21. The voyage began much later than expected.

We should have been to England in January 1944, but the *Queen Mary* got caught in a big storm on a return voyage and that delayed things. We got to Camp Shanks at the first of the year and they told us we would ship out in five days, but it became two months. We traveled instead on the *Ile de France*, and embarked on March 12. As we left we saw the *Queen Mary* at port, lit up from stem to stern because she had been hit by a wave so big that it had even damaged the superstructure. They had men crawling all over it to get it back into shape. That set us way back.

On the *Ile de France*, we were up in a little companion way on the boat deck—38 of us crowded in there. We ran into some major storms and I remember one in particular, when I was assigned as duty officer. Men were getting sick all over. I was starting to get seasick and went to the promenade deck to ask if we had any empty buckets. Everybody there was sick, too. No spare buckets.

We had to zigzag all the way over. Standing on the fantail of the ship, you could see how we were moving across the ocean.

Hose speculated along with others "in the know" what it would mean for Patton to be in command of the Third Army:

At the time, we didn't know what that would bring for us. Number one, the Third Army had been the Army of Occupation in World War I. They hadn't participated in the actual fighting. The First Army took care of that and the Third Army was the Army of Occupation, so we didn't know if we would be involved in combat. It was possible that the Third Army would be the Army of Occupation again.

We found out that with General Patton it would be different than our previous commanders. In the United States, the only time I ever saw our first CG, General Krueger, was when he blurred past in his staff car. And I never saw General Hodges, because he was always down with the troops on maneuvers in Louisiana. I would see Patton countless times over the next two years.

Chief Warrant Officer Fred Hose of Lucky Forward saw Patton for the first time in Great Britain. He comments: "We found out that with General Patton it would be different. In the United States, the only time I ever saw our first commanding general, General Krueger, was when he blurred past in his staff car. And I never saw General Hodges, because he was always down with the troops on maneuvers in Louisiana. I would see Patton countless times over the next two years."

The first time Hose heard Patton speak, any conjecture about being in the Army of Occupation was put to rest. Hose says:

The day after we arrived in England, the officers were to meet at Peover Hall and assemble at 1300 hours. So all the officers were there, promptly at 1300 hours, to hear General Patton. He came out in his tailor-made cavalry uniform with Willie [his dog] marching alongside him. He passed by many of the officers and when he stopped, Willie immediately sat down on his haunches like a good dog. Patton had a crop under his arm, shining cavalry boots, and a new shiny helmet liner with the Third Army insignia on it. He proceeded to talk to us and the first thing I noticed was, well, you'd think that a man of his stature would have a booming deep voice. But he had a high voice, and we had a hard time to keep from laughing.

What he said immediately settled the idea that the Third Army might be the Army of Occupation, as it had been in the last war. The first thing we were going to do was get to France and kick the shit out of the *Boches*. He proceeded with his speech, and the most memorable thing was when he reminded his officers: "From the standpoint of distance, there's not much of a difference between a pat on the back and kick in the ass." And that we should be just as liberal with one as with the other to the troops. In the ensuing months, that was the credo that he always adhered to.

Frank Pajerski, a major in the G-2 section, was at the same assembly:

All of headquarters assembled in front of his headquarters building. He came out and gave us a welcome. He always appealed to me—liked his idea of spit and polish. If you're going to soldier, you get up and *soldier*. None of this sloppy business.

I knew I was with a winner. The way he dressed, the way he talked—the minute he started talking, you knew who was going to be boss. There was no question about who was running the show. He might have a chief of staff, and a staff with 17 subsections and five generals with him, but you knew who was in charge. And you knew that he was a winner. He had the reputation of being a winner from Africa and Sicily.

He gave us a little pep talk. One thing I remember: "If you don't do your job, I'll find you out and kick your ass out of here." About those words, but maybe a little stronger.

Coy Eklund also remembers the first time he heard Patton speak:

He lined us up in formation at Peover Hall in Knutsford . . . He said, as we stood stiff and straight: "Take a look at the individuals standing next to you, on your left and your right. Of the three of you, only two of you will get home alive." He paused before saying, "What the hell? Do you want to live forever?"

It was ironic that Lieutenant Colonel Joe Pelton was standing next to me. He [originally] had the job of reporting casualties, which I later did. But we hadn't started yet—weren't on the Continent yet. Just as soon as we got over to France, here's what happened to him: He got killed while driving across a railroad crossing by the only train that was running in the whole nation of France that day—and he was one of three of us standing there when Patton said that.

MP Peter Joseph listened while on duty at Peover as well:

One of the things [General Patton] told us in England after he came from Sicily was that "Being afraid is normal. Being a coward is another thing." This was after the slapping incident, and it was clear he wouldn't tolerate a coward. He gave this speech by Peover Hall, standing by a microphone on the steps, talking to a huge formation of us. In his speech he said, "If you come across a coward, you shoot the coward. Otherwise he'll go back to the States and breed more cowards like him." He gave this stern speech with all the terrible language he was known for. But I had to admire the man, because he was what the people said about him—a real warrior.

Patton was later quoted in more diplomatic phrasing: "Cowardice is a disease and must be checked immediately, before it becomes epidemic."

◆

Major Frank Pajerski served first in the engineer section and ultimately as the air liaison officer in the G-2 section of Lucky Forward. He had numerous encounters with Patton at Peover, but none so literally face-to-face and memorable as the first meeting.

When I first arrived in Great Britain, I was responsible for intelligence mapping. I made many a trip to London to get our feet on the ground and get the maps we needed. We met with the corps commanders and division commanders to figure out what maps they would need once across the Channel. We worked out of offices that were located in these mess hall type buildings.

I was just opening the screen door to go out and there was Patton standing on a step below, just reaching for the knob to come in. I'm 5'10", but Patton was so much taller that we were eyeball to eyeball. I mean, *six inches* between eyeballs. When you come face to face with stars looking at you—and attach to them the Patton reputation—you get a real wake-up call.

Hell, I knew my military courtesy. I jumped back and hollered *"Attenshun!"* I had two officers and nine men there working with the maps. They popped to attention and I said, "Come in, sir."

First table he came to, I had some maps spread out and he started looking at them. Then he said, "Do you have any Michelin maps?" Those are very good French maps.

I said, "I'm familiar with them. But we have no use for those as yet."

"We used those in World War I. Those were great maps," he said. "Our artillery could hit a brick shithouse at 20 miles." Those were his exact words.

We talked some more and finally he said, "Where's Colonel Conklin?" John F. Conklin was Third Army engineer—my boss. Patton had come to the wrong building.

We were behind a barbed wire enclosure, so I said, "He's in the next building. I'll take you there." And I led him through. I stayed ahead—I wasn't going to have him opening a door for me.

I opened the door of the Army engineer and executive officer, S-3, and I shouted, "Attenshun!" so loud I rattled those windows. Conklin popped out like a gopher out of the ground. The minute he began to say, "How are you, general—?" I got the hell out of there!

Later on that day, Conklin—great engineer but one with a peculiar way—never sent for you, never picked up a phone. He always *shouted* for you. You could hear it five blocks away. He hollered, "Pajerski!" and I galloped over there and he said, "Pajerski, it's all right to shout 'Attention,' but goddammit, you don't have to scare the hell out of us, even when it's General Patton."

I smiled and said, "Yessir."

We all lived at Knutsford, 3 miles away from Peover. Peover was a mansion, a country house with a huge surrounding estate with "Upper" and "Lower Peover." And we'd attend church that was actually a part of Peover. The Third Army left a plaque on the wall there saying that Patton had the pleasure of worshipping in this church.

At Peover, you'd see him taking a walk every morning near the compound, Willie at his heels all the time. He'd come down through the meadows about midmorning, after morning briefing and after he got everything rolling. And we had briefings every night, so you could see Patton every night—if you wanted to miss sleep all the time.

Otherwise you attended briefing on a rotation basis, and took turns going when assigned.

◆

Not everyone was privy to speeches at Peover Hall or had reason to be in the headquarters compound. After they arrived in England, many troops in the rank and file were not even informed that their ultimate commander was Patton. In fact, in keeping with the military's "need to know" policy, some would not know until they were on the Continent.

For a private in a foxhole, the chain of command above the platoon meant little or nothing. Battalion, regiment, division, and corps levels were at best obscure and their commanders largely nameless to the rifleman. But Patton wanted his name known among the frontline troops for the aggressiveness and pride he wanted to instill.

Apart from that, Patton was a well-known personality—a celebrity who had been featured on *Life* magazine's cover on July 7, 1941, precisely five months before America entered the war (and *Time* and *Newsweek* in July 1943)—and in the absence of facts, "Dame Rumor" stepped in to claim Patton as her own. Walter Unrath writes:

> In England . . . rumors were strong that our battalion would be part of a newly formed Army, which would serve under the legendary General George S. Patton Jr., the one of Africa and Sicily fame. "Old Blood and Guts" certainly did have an amazing reputation, and the GIs loved him.

Frank Thomas, 4th Armored Division, enjoys a cup of hot coffee with a Red Cross girl. He sensed what it meant for his armored division to be placed in Patton's command: "We'd all heard a lot about Patton—his reputation of being a real gung ho general. To an 18-year-old like I was, *that* was exciting."

In the 4th Armored Division, Frank Thomas was also in the dark, but caught the glint of a star:

I saw Patton drive by in Chippingham one Sunday afternoon. He was in a big black Cadillac. We knew he was there for some reason. But at that time, I knew nothing about the Third Army, knew nothing about Patton being its commander. I knew something big was cooking. And I knew he was an armor man, so I figured we might have a part in whatever would take place. We'd all heard a lot about Patton—his reputation of being a real gung ho general. To an 18-year-old like I was, *that* was exciting.

Even when Patton gave motivational speeches, he sometimes couldn't divulge that he would command the very men he was speaking to. Vince Gish, a T/5 in the 6th Armored Division, remembers:

The only time we heard a Patton speech was in England. Even then we didn't know he was going to be our commander for the Third Army. He just gave a speech to the 6th Armored—to the whole division of about 15,000 men . . . [at] Spring Hill Lodge.

Essentially, he said, "You've trained good. . . . You've trained for this in the desert. You've trained as a division and I will see you over there."

He wasn't able to divulge that he would be our commander, even though he probably already knew. . . . They didn't announce that we were part of the Third Army under General Patton until we were up on the Continent.

◆

Patton wasted no time launching a training regimen. He was known to get into the act himself on occasion, critiquing the exercises and maneuvers on the small-unit level. Phillip W. Robbins, a sergeant and later an officer serving as a field artillery observer, remembers such an occasion.

My first encounter with Patton was in about late March 1944 at the town of Armaugh, Northern Ireland. He had just come from Africa and Sicily. He had a little problem over there and they relieved him. He came to inspect the troops for three or four days. We pulled a field problem and he was just an observer. But after the field problem, he made a speech to tell us what we did right and what we did wrong.

I remember it very well. We all got a big bang out of it. He was a pretty rough talker and did his "act" (and it was that) to inspire the officers and we senior sergeants of how to kill Germans by socks full of shit.

He got up on the hood of a jeep to talk to us. But it wasn't just us. There were a bunch of Army nurses and Red Cross people who came out to hear him speak. They were curious to hear. This was in the town square and all [the townsfolk's] windows had been opened to hear the words of this famous American. Most memorable was the rapid closing of those windows as he "revved up."

He said, "Now we whipped them sons of bitches in Africa and we have them on the run in Italy. But if you ever get one down, don't take pity on him. Use your bayonet on him, twist it, then kick him in the balls."

All the GIs looked back to see the reaction of those women, and we saw they were laughing, too.

Training in England included all the challenges Patton expected his troops would face on the Continent. For instance, since a wet landing was anticipated, all drivers were expected to be experienced in disembarking vehicles from a ship while still away from shore. Frank Thomas was a jeep driver (or "peep" driver in Patton's own parlance) in the 24th Armored Engineers of the 4th Armored Division. In a personal interview, he tells about his training. For the Britons who swear they witnessed disembodied heads fleeting around a pond in 1944, here's an explanation:

When we got close to D-day, they sent us down to Land's End, to help get people ready to go over on barges and other ships. In preparation for that, we set up our equipment for disembarking into water. We had to put Cosmoline all over—this black grease a lot like Vaseline but very black, turned your hands black, and sealed all the water out. It was terrible to get off. Didn't have gloves. And we had an exhaust pipe running up the side. . . .

We practiced in a pond. Each driver had to do that. We had to drive right off the edge of a barge into the water. You had to drive off pretty fast so that you didn't get hung up, so you'd put it into low-low, four-wheel-drive, wind the engine up, foot to the floorboard. You didn't just ease off, you *zoomed* off, to stay level as much as you could, so not to let just the nose drop down. When you landed you'd hit the bottom of the pond and it was a pretty good jolt. You really had to hang on to that steering wheel.

All you'd see is the driver from the neck up. You'd watch them driving around with just their heads visible above the water (laughs) in the pond. Waves right under their chins.

It came easy the first time. I drove all the way at least a football field long, feeling the current pressing up against me, until I drove up onto dry land. You didn't shift. You just moved along in the same gear. They had us doing that until the unit stalled out. I turned around and went back to go again, like we were supposed to. On the second trip, my peep died and they had to pull me out.

Thomas offers this footnote: "From Southhampton, we went over to the Continent at about D + 35 or so. We went to Omaha Beach and unloaded. We drove right off onto dry land."

◆

They rehearsed everything they could. The moment they hit France's coast, they knew no excuse would be good enough for a delay. Patton was famous for his freewheeling operations, yet his unyielding discipline demanded strictly a do-it-by-the-numbers approach so that a job is "mechanical and automatic." Consider a small field manual titled "Operations Sub-section, G-3, Plan for Operations in the Field," dated May 29, 1944, prepared to exacting standards for Lucky Forward's G-3 section "to ensure its rapid advance on the Continent"— and imagine the men practicing with precision while still in England (because it's doubtful if it happened on the Continent!):

There must be no lost motion. Each officer and enlisted man must know his job so well that is mechanical and automatic . . . assignments have been made and are covered, in detail. . . .

The Operations Sub-section is the nerve center. . . . It must . . . be mobile . . . and have a workable standard procedure for breaking camp, loading and moving which will enable it to be read to displace on a moment's notice.

And, in no uncertain terms, the "Pitching of Tents and Unloading" chapter did just that:

a. Upon arrival at CP area Sgt. Whitehall will spot truck with equipment near area where tent will be pitched.

b. Men will remain in truck until ordered by Sgt. Whitehall to detruck.

c. After detrucking, men will ground personal equipment, and proceed with the following plan for pitching the storage tent:

(1) Sgt. Callan and Pvt. McRae will "lay out" rectangle rope and drive corner tent pins and guide rope pins. At the same time, the remainder of the men will bring storage tent, poles and pins.

(2) Tent will be unrolled and placed in desired spot by all men under supervision of Sgt. Whitehall.

(3) Ridge and center poles will be assembled and placed in tent by Sgt. Lydon, Sgt. Riportella and Cpl. Clark, who will also place guide ropes on end poles. At the same time Sgt. Callan and Pvt. McRae as a team, and Cpl. Wisehaupt and Cpl. Whitmer as a team will lace up center flaps.

(4) Sgt. Callan, Pvt. McRae, Sgt. Lydon and Cpl. Clark will each take a guide rope and pull the tent up, with Cpl. Whitmer and Cpl. Wisehaupt assisting at the center poles. When tent is in upright position Sgt. Riportella will place corner tent ropes on pins, which have previously been driven. Each man with a guide rope will then tie them to the guide rope pins, which have previously been driven.

(5) Sgt. Callan and Pvt. McRae will drive in remaining pins while the remaining men under direction of Sgt. Whitehall unload equipment for this tent, and carry it to the proper place in the tent. (See Charts B and C).

(6) Other tent or tents will be erected in the same manner.

Sergeants Whitehall and Callan, Private McRae and the rest were blessed with similar enlightenment for "Tearing Down Tents and Loading." In Patton's own words: "There is only one type of discipline, perfect discipline."

◆

Being a pioneer in armor, Patton had many ideas for innovations to improve his units' performance. Walter Unrath attributes one such innovation for his half-track battalion that would later be attached to XX Corps:

As a self-propelled armor unit, our battalion was excited with the thought of serving under General Patton, whom we later learned the Germans called the American Rommel, after their famous field marshal.

It was midmorning one day in June that written orders were received from higher headquarters, allegedly from General Patton himself. The orders directed that all 80-plus half-tracks of the battalion were to be modified in a most strange manner. Brackets were to be welded on each side of the half-track, of sufficient length and depth to hold five-gallon cans (Jerry cans) on each side of the half-track. It appeared that General Patton, an advocate of mobility and rapid movement of armor, wanted to ensure that each half-track carried sufficient gasoline above and beyond tank capacity to travel fast and without refueling. Each half-track had two 30-gallon tanks and now was to be given an extra capacity of carrying 50 additional gallons of gasoline—in short, almost doubling its fuel capacity from a 300-miles range to a 550-mile range. The work commenced with top priority and was completed in record time. Commanders were deeply concerned as the placement of the five-gallon gasoline cans along the entire both sides of a half-track made that track vulnerable to an explosion and fire if any shrapnel or tracer bullet hit one of the gasoline cans. The GIs, normally apt at creating terminology to suit any occasion, began to refer to the tracks as "Flaming Coffins." Knowing General Patton only by reputation at that time, many began to wonder whether Old Blood and Guts was for real and what else we could expect from him. Also, we had no knowledge of whether any other units were given identical orders (although later in our drive through France we observed other units with similar welded appurtenances on their tracks).

While in Great Britain, First Lieutenant Walter Unrath of the 456th Antiaircraft Automatic Weapons Battalion (attached to the XX Corps) heard rumors that Patton would be the commanding general: "As a self-propelled armor unit, our battalion was excited with the thought of serving under General Patton. We later learned the Germans called him the American Rommel, after their famous field marshal."

Unrath and the others wouldn't realize until several months later what foresight this was:

> At about 2:00 p.m. [on September 4, 1944], my half-track unit was rushing along the road to Metz. The 4th Armored Division was ahead of my element. I had to pull my unit into a deserted airfield at Etain, France, as we had run out of gasoline and could not proceed farther. Matter of fact, the entire Third U.S. Army was halted for lack of fuel to proceed farther.
>
> We now recognized the military genius of that Great Captain, General Patton, when he ordered our battalion to carry the extra gasoline on the sides of our tracks. The extra fuel we carried was sufficient to carry us across France, while other Third Army fuel could be used to feed the bottomless tanks of the armored divisions.

◆

Part of a general officer's lot was attendance at formal functions in a hosting country. One such function was a luncheon with the King and Queen of England. Even in their royal presence, Patton wore his famous ivory-handled revolvers. When asked about them, he made reference to the outlaw Pancho Villa of Mexico and pursuit by the expeditionary force commanded by General John J. Pershing in 1916. A shootout during a foraging mission had resulted in the deaths of three outlaws, including renegade General Julio Cardenas, head of Pancho Villa's bodyguard. A crack shot, Patton himself had felled two of the outlaws on their horses, using the single-action Colt he had purchased in March 1915. He carved two notches in the grip of the revolver. Dwight Eisenhower recounts the conversation in his book *At Ease*:

> At [an] outdoor luncheon, senior officers of both British and American Armies were present. Seated directly across from the King was George Patton. During the conversation, the King asked General Patton if he had ever shot anyone with the pistols he was wearing.
>
> George said promptly, "Oh yes." But he added, "Really, not these pistols. These are the ones I carry socially. I carry my fighting pistols when I'm out on campaign."
>
> "How many men have you killed in war?" asked the King.
>
> Without batting an eye, George said, "Seven, Sir."
>
> This was too much for me. "How many did you say, General Patton?"
>
> Instantly he replied, "Three, Sir."
>
> "Well, George," I said, "I'll let you get away with that." George had

often told me that during the Pershing expedition into Mexico in 1916, he and a small cavalry patrol ran into a handful of Villa's brigands and in the melee he shot one [actually, two] of the enemy. I think this was about the limits of his personal lethal accomplishments.

In another social activity, Patton wasted no time getting into trouble again. After the slapping incidents, he had written to his wife that the adversity had made him a better general. But something he still needed to learn was discipline in speech, especially when the press was in earshot. A few words to a "Welcome Club" in Knutsford led to another censure by Eisenhower, who writes:

Not long after his arrival in England, he attended a meeting which he thought was private and off the record. Called upon for a comment, he made a statement to the effect that after the war was over, Britain and America would have to rule the world and other nations would have to conform. Georgie should have done three things: thought about what he wanted to say, watched his tongue, and checked the roster. There was a newspaperman present and the story made vivid headlines the next day. Again, George Patton was on the hot seat.

◆

On June 5, 1944, the day before D-Day, Patton delivered a famous speech to the Third Army. He exhorted his men to fight, because "Americans love to fight, traditionally. All real Americans love the sting and clash of battle." Later that same day, Fred Hose was present for a smaller, more intimate elaboration of the pre-D-Day speech.

General Patton spoke again to us as a group at a briefing just before D-Day. I'll never forget his concluding remark. It was one of Patton's hallmark statements. He told us: "It won't be long before we'll be going to France where we'll either make history, or we won't be back to alibi why we didn't." Prophetic? Prescient?

At the end of June 1944, the Third Army stood poised for challenges awaiting on the Continent.

Chapter 5

Rampaging Through France

July 1944–August 1944

Once on the Continent, Patton turned the Third Army loose on a drive that would become legendary. The speed of the advance—as fast as 60 miles a day—would make even the vaunted German blitzkrieg look like a Sunday drive.

As Third Army units assembled in France, Patton welcomed many of them with a pep talk to rev them up for the drive. This was not common practice among Army commands, as Phillip Foraker of the 13th Armored Division notes: "We were assigned to four different Armies. General Patton was the only Army commander who personally met with all the officers and noncoms of our division." Carl Ulsaker, a junior officer in the 95th Infantry Division, records one such talk:

> Orders came down the line that all officers except one duty officer per battalion and a representative number of noncommissioned officers were to assemble in a field behind a large chateau. At the appointed hour General Patton appeared on a terrace overlooking the field. Accompanying him on the terrace were Major General Walton Walker, the XX Corps commander, and Major General Twaddle, our division commander. Because it was a chilly, overcast fall day, "Old Blood and Guts" wore an overcoat which concealed his normally resplendent uniform and his ivory-handled pistols. He was taller than the other two generals and wore a helmet with three silver stars prominently displayed thereon. Erect in bearing and wearing his famous scowl, he made an impressive enough figure for us despite the absence of his normal accoutrements. Among the early

arrivals, our battalion group found itself standing in the front row of the audience, only a few feet from the speaker's stand . . . we were called to attention and the generals walked out on the terrace. When Patton began to talk, I was surprised at his high-pitched, squeaky voice. From such a big, aggressive person one expected to hear the words roll of his tongue in deep, resonant tones. Once the general swung into action, however, what he had to say captured our undivided attention and the timbre of his voice became inconsequential.

After an opening statement of welcome, he launched into a litany of how he wished us to fight and behave in the Third Army. Much of what he told us seemed very practical and, to our surprise, often ran contrary to what we had been taught as Army doctrine. He spiced his talk with considerable profanity and colorful figures of speech. I understand he did this on purpose because such was the general practice of soldiers and the general wanted to communicate clearly with them. He must have been right because I can remember to this day most of what he told us. I'll repeat some of it much in the same language he used:

"Now you men were all taught to assault the enemy using fire and maneuver; that is, some of you take cover and fire while others advance in short rushes. Well, in practice that doesn't work. First of all, when you get close enough to the enemy to get shot at, you'll find that half your men won't get up and rush when they're supposed to. They feel too secure hugging the ground. Secondly, you won't see the German son of a bitch until you're right on top of him. Therefore, I want you to use marching fire to attack from the last point of cover to close with the Hun. Get as many rifles, BARs and machine guns as possible in a line of skirmishers, and put a hail of fire in front of you. Shoot at every bush, tree, house—anywhere an enemy might be. Hell, we may be short on artillery rounds but we've got plenty of small arms ammunition. The old Bunker Hill crap of 'don't shoot till you see the whites of their eyes' doesn't work here. Besides, the Germans don't have any whites to their eyes; the bastards have goddammed little yellow pig eyes!

"On maneuvers in the States you were all taught to dig in whenever you halted for any appreciable time. I believe the slogan was 'dig or die.' Well, my motto is 'dig *and* die.' Troops who spend all their time digging are too exhausted to fight when they finally close with the enemy. I want my troops to save their energy for our principal purpose, to kill as many of the bastards as we can. Anyhow, where we're going the Germans have already been; and they've dug enough foxholes for all of us. Along the same lines I don't want you to walk if there's any way you can ride. Overload the vehicles. If you squeeze hard, you can get a dozen men on a jeep and trailer in addition to its normal load. The ordnance people would have you think that the truck would break down if you put more than a quarter ton on it. Don't you believe it; those sons of bitches have been putting overload safety factors in the vehicle specs ever since we relied on escort wagons for supply. Why wear yourself out walking when you can ride? Anyhow, if the damn thing breaks down, we can get another one. It's a damned sight easier to replace a truck than a combat-trained soldier.

"When you were children I'll bet your mother would make you go inside when it rained. You know the expression, 'He doesn't have sense enough to come in out of the rain.' Well, I don't want that said of anyone in the Third Army. It so happens that in Europe everywhere you look the people have built houses. I want you to take advantage of this shelter to the maximum. Now, in France we are allies and liberators, so just say politely, 'Move over.' But soon we'll be in Germany; there you tell the Nazi bastards, 'Get out!'

"I am concerned about the health of the command. A sick soldier cannot fight. Don't drink water from any source other than our engineer Water Supply Points. If you can't get water there, purify your own with Halizone tablets. Hell, all water in Europe is piss; you wouldn't willingly drink piss, would you?

"If you believe what you read in the papers, you'd think that generals win wars. Hell, generals don't win wars; you are the people who do that. You junior leaders—sergeants, lieutenants, captains—do the things that win wars. An army in combat is nothing more than a whole bunch of small unit actions where the issue is decided by how those small unit leaders behave. Jesus Christ, any old fart can be a general. Look at Walker here."

With that, Patton slapped the shorter General Walker across his rather expansive stomach and let out a loud guffaw. Walker looked slightly pained but endured his leader's little game in stoic silence. I noticed also that our general, Twaddle, who we knew to abhor the use of profanity, also looked somewhat pained. But Patton was in the saddle; he talked the language of the troops. Furthermore, he talked common sense. I made a mental note of the fact that much of the guidance he gave us wiped out a lot of the Mickey Mouse stuff that we had been forced to digest on maneuvers in the U.S. Here was a leader of men worth following into battle.

Waverly Green, another junior officer in the 95th Infantry Division, heard a different welcome speech with some overlap in content.

I was in one group that was assembled on a racetrack, in a steady rain and on slippery ground. We were carrying on much small talk when suddenly five jeeps, each with a .50-caliber machine gun with a gunner in the back roared around the track and stopped. We all saluted General Patton as he got out and stepped upon a stand with a loudspeaker arranged for him.

He was not as handsome as [George C.] Scott who played his part in the movie. Somewhat ruddy faced, barrel-chested, and he spoke in a high voice.

"A hundred and sixty-nine years ago, some goddamned son of a bitch was writing about the Battle of Bunker Hill. To show you how dumb the bastard was, it wasn't Bunker Hill, but *Breed's* Hill. Anyway, it was said, 'Don't shoot until you see the whites of their eyes.' And ever since then, the American soldier has had it in his head not to shoot until you see the whites of their eyes.

"Hell, you are going to get killed that way and a lot of American soldiers have been killed because they didn't shoot. In North Africa and Sicily, we found that only about 18 percent of the men fired their weapons when they attacked. The Germans would sight their automatic weapons and small arms fire when troops would be crossing open ground and places with good fields of fire. The American soldiers would not fire back but hit the ground as he was trained in the States. The enemy artillery had already zeroed in on the site and would then deliver a heavy bombardment causing many casualties. Now when you attack, shoot. *Fire, fire, fire.*

"Once you get ground, hold it.

"Now this idea that the German soldier is some superman is a lot of bullshit. The reporters have made people think this. But you are stronger, tougher, better trained and better equipped than he is. Hell, the American soldier can beat the daylights out of a German soldier any time. So don't be afraid of them.

"Civilians who behave themselves properly will be treated properly. Those who do not behave properly will be buried properly.

"Don't drink their water unless you use your Halizone tablets.

"Now if we attack all out and vigorously . . . the war should be over by Christmas. Then I will meet you in the South Pacific. Do like I have told you so that you can go home and vote against the damned politicians who are responsible for your being here."

This is the way I remembered General Patton's speech. The wording is most likely not exact, but I have tried to get over what he stressed to us. As we were leaving one of our sergeants said, "That old son of a bitch makes you feel like you can do anything and nothing can stop you."

Chapter Five

And nothing would stop them. From the moment of disembarka-
tion, they barreled out of the landing area. Patton was there to make
sure of it. Fred Hose of Lucky Forward's G-2 section tells about his
arrival on July 6, D + 30, and Patton's personal "welcome":

We disembarked about two or three o'clock in the afternoon. It
was ironic that every vehicle had to be waterproofed as we went over,
including my jeep, because when we got there they ran that LST up
on the beach as far as it could go and then waited on the tide. They
opened the huge front doors on the ship right over dry sand and all
the vehicles drove out in a column on to land. The first thing everyone had to do was get rid of all the waterproofing so the vehicles
could function efficiently on land.

All the unloading went smoothly. We fell into another column
for the Third Army headquarters convoy to get us the hell out of the
beachhead and into the area we were assigned to. We got into an
apple orchard and set up. Unfortunately it rained, so I slept the first
night in a bedroll under a six-by-six truck to get out of the rain.

General Patton was nowhere to be seen in Normandy, until we
started the advance. He was always gone up to the front. When we
moved out, we were sitting in a jeep and I heard the blaring of a
horn—like an 18-wheeler coming down the road hell bent for leather.
What came through was not some big rig, but a little jeep with stars
on the front.

I turned to my driver and asked, "What the hell is this?"

He said, "It's the Old Man."

Here he comes with the flags waving and horn blasting for everybody to get out of the way. That was his way of letting the troops
know that the Old Man was going up to the front. It was funny.
Humorous. Really was, going hell bent for leather like that.

Right behind was a jeep with his aides trying to keep up. I didn't
realize at first that it was all theatrical—his way of putting on a show.

We would move in such a way that half of our section moved forward and set up, and once that was set up, then the one that was left
behind would fold up tents and move forward. Each time you moved,
everything had to be done all over again. You had to line up your convoy, get on the road at 7 a.m.., then scout out a new location forward,
then you had to camouflage, you had to dig latrines—we really had
our work cut for us.

He insisted on being as far forward as possible, and having Lucky
Forward with him. So we were moving constantly. The Old Man could
come in at any moment wanting an intelligence briefing. We were really
working on a 24-hour a day basis. We slept right there with our maps.

Men learned quickly about Patton's expectations. From the outset, "ASAP" took on a whole new meaning. Colonel D. Kenneth Reimers, commander of 343rd Field Artillery Battalion of the 90th Infantry Division, realized immediately that life would be different under his new boss, as he records in a wartime diary:

2 August 1944, Montgothier: I guess we are now in the Third Army under the command of General Patton. Last night our easy life ended with a speedy conclusion. Ever since we arrived in Montcuit we have been on a four-hour alert. This was later reduced to two hours. I didn't pay much attention to it because we have had short alerts before that dragged into 8 and 12 hours. This time we were called and given less than two hours.

The 357th Regiment had invited our battalion to see a USO show. I had given the battery commanders permission to load their men in trucks and go to the show. At 2030 I received a rush order, by messenger from division, to report to division for further orders and to have the battalion ready to roll at 2300. The USO show had just begun and the first act was about half through. I collected the battery commanders, told them what I knew and advised them to get back to their batteries in time to leave at the prescribed time. I then rushed to division expecting a false alarm or a postponement, but found the 344th F.A. Battalion. Ready to move out and the 358th Regiment entrucking. The 1st Battalion of the 357th was scheduled to follow the 344th. This didn't give us much time to get ready. . . .

By 2300 the battalion was ready enough to leave but we didn't actually get moving until 2330. The battery commanders and I followed K Company of the 3rd Battalion of our regiment. The ride to our new positions turned out to be an all-night march. We had only 60 miles to go but the roads were so crowded it took us until 1400 today to reach the positions. It looked as if the entire Third Army was moving south [toward Avranches].

Patton was "hell bent for leather" from the very beginning of the drive, perhaps motivated by what Bradley writes in *A Soldier's Story* was Patton's "greatest fear"—missing out on the glory and victory:

When news of the attempted assassination of Hitler reached Patton in the Cotentin, he bounded down to our CP at Colombieres.

"For God's sake, Brad," George pleaded, "you've got to get me into this fight before the war is over. I'm in the doghouse now and I'm apt to die there unless I pull something spectacular to get me out."

I've often wondered how much this nothing-to-lose attitude prodded Patton in his spectacular race across the face of France. For certainly no other commander could have matched him in reckless haste and boldness. Someday a definitive biography of Patton will go into the issue more exhaustively than I. Until then I shall go on believing that the private whose face he slapped in a Sicilian hospital ward did more to win the war in Europe than any other private in the Army.

Patton talks with his two superiors, Gen. Dwight D. Eisenhower and Lieutenant General Omar Bradley, about progress in Europe. Desperate to join the fight and get out of the "doghouse" after the slapping incidents in Sicily, Patton lobbied Bradley to let him advance. Bradley writes in a *Soldier's Story:* "I've often wondered how much this nothing-to-lose attitude prodded Patton in his spectacular race across the face of France. For certainly no other commander could have matched him in reckless haste and boldness. Someday a definitive biography of Patton will go into the issue more exhaustively than I. Until then, I shall go on believing that the private whose face he slapped in a Sicilian hospital ward did more to win the war in Europe than any other private in the Army."
U.S. Army

For the first 60 miles, Patton's Army moved easily through an area cleared by the First Army. But ahead in the French interior was a gauntlet of German defenses. To open the way, the U.S. Army Air Force sent a great air armada to blast a hole in the German lines at St. Lô. Private W. King Pound of the 4th Armored Division remembers the armada and its destruction:

We were all straining at the bit to get into action. My first vivid memory of Europe is the bombing that blew open the hole for our breakout. We were told that up to that time, it was the heaviest bombing anywhere in World War II: 3,000 planes involved—B-17s, B-24s, P-47s, the whole nine yards. We were about 5 or 7 miles back from all that bombing. A good thing we were back like that. We could see the smoke from the smoke bombs dropped for guidance to mark the target, and the wind came up and blew the smoke our direction. No problems for us, but that's when friendly fire killed General [Lesley] McNair.

Bombing went on into the morning, *all* morning. We didn't see how the Germans could survive it. And they didn't. We had a big hole that we could go through. We hadn't seen action yet; we had been only a reserve force only till then. Didn't even have patches on or identification on our tanks, because we were a "secret army" still.

The doggies would yell at us, "Who are you?"

And we'd just say, "Georgie's Boys."

Then we got our identification back—tank insignia and shoulder patches.

A shoulder patch on a uniform could communicate a lot. It told which outfit a GI belonged to and, for the knowledgeable observer, where the unit had been and what action it had seen. To one man, it meant his brother was in his midst. After spotting the "arrow-8" patch signifying the 8th Infantry Division, George Davis realized his brother Mike also must be at St. Lô. The brothers were from a farm family in Tennessee. Sergeant Mike Davis was a member of the 17th Photo Tech Squadron (component of the Ninth Air Force) attached to Third Army, while Tech Sergeant George Davis was an infantryman in the 8th Division. Mike Davis also recalls the bombing of St. Lô intermingled with the quick and fruitless search for his brother.

Near St. Lô, we woke up one morning and the sky was just full of our bombers and fighters. I originally had been an aviation cadet, but found I got so airsick I couldn't continue training. I ended up in photo tech. As those hundreds of B-17s and B-24s filled the skies, I remember thinking that some of those guys overhead must be men I knew in training.

They were coming and going all day long, and simply annihilated St. Lô. We could hear the explosions, but because it was such a forested area and we were about 6 miles back, we couldn't see any of it.

It was them who blasted open the hole for our breakout. That sent the troops streaming through. I saw units going past—armored divisions and infantry divisions, one after another.

Chapter Five

Unlikely things happened sometimes. Of the divisions I saw going through, I noticed the 8th Infantry Division—my brother's outfit. I knew it was his unit because of the 8th Division insignia on their sleeves. But I never was able to catch up with him. That happened just south of St. Lô on the way to Avranches, and his outfit turned toward Brest after that. I really felt for him, thought a lot about him and his buddies on the front, and hoped they'd make it.

His brother George *did* make it—winning a Silver Star in the process for his actions at Brest (but more on that later). As a platoon sergeant in the 8th Infantry Division, he had already seen heavy fighting as part of the First Army. During June, his division had fought its way inland to relieve the 82nd Airborne Division, which had been dropped inland and stranded. Afterward, his unit became part of Patton's VIII Corps, pointed toward Brest.

I never did link up with my brother that day at St. Lô. I had an idea he was in the area, but we were moving quickly and there was no time to find him.

I was a platoon sergeant. And a platoon leader practically all the way through because we were short on lieutenants. They offered me a battlefield commission, but I refused it. I didn't fancy the job that much and knew I didn't want to make a career of the military. We had some good officers above us. So I stayed a tech sergeant all the way through.

When we got inland enough so they could start bringing in the armor, that's when Patton's Army came. When we finally made the breakout, they attached us to the Third Army.

Not too many tanks had passed by before here comes Patton in his Dodge command car. He blazed right through as we walked on foot. We would see him every day driving up and down those roads. . . . He was right there with the troops. Patton was a good general. Always in the middle of the action.

Once we had the breakthrough, Patton just opened up and sent those tanks right on through France. Nothing was going to stop them.

◆

Patton's first real combat action on the Continent began at Avranches, a town in southwestern Normandy that became the launching pad from which Patton's troops would thrust southward toward the Loire. Military policeman Peter Joseph was among the first from the Third Army to reach Avranches. He says:

> Supposedly, no one was left in the town—not even French civilians. Our job was to go through the town and make sure there were no German snipers left. We did do a lot of sniper-clearing duty. We went to Avranches' city hall, which became our headquarters [for our assignments to search sectors of the town]. From there we went in groups of four or five from building to building, searching closets, looking under beds, and so on.
>
> We had been told all the French civilians had left, but we went into one building and were surprised to find food on the table! We knew somebody must be here and just then we heard footsteps coming down the stairs, so we drew our guns.
>
> A woman appeared and we yelled "*Boches, Boches?*"
>
> She said, "No Boches, no Boches"—no Germans here.
>
> We rushed upstairs and looked all around. Nothing. She had told the truth. That same day, after four or five hours of searching for snipers, it was getting to be dusk and we were ready to stop for the day. We came out of the last building we were to search that day, and just then a sniper took a shot at us from the church steeple of Avranches. I jumped behind a stairway. Our jeep pulled up and we all jumped in and took off to headquarters. We reported what had happened, so that they could send in some troops to take care of him.

Then the Germans tried to take back Avranches—with a vengeance. Elements of the 4th Armored Division went in, among them W. King Pound, part of an M5 light tank's four-man crew.

> Avranches was a circus. It was at night, in the middle of the town. Hell, our tanks in the dark, in the middle of town. Germans were every place. It was a wild night, racing around town like kids in a Plymouth trying to find Germans!
>
> We had been told to hold the town after it was counterattacked, and not much more. There were pockets of resistance throughout the town. In buildings, every place. They really wanted to win Avranches back and we didn't want to give it back.
>
> There could be fire from any direction. So you got your bow gunner buttoned up. The tank driver, too. But we always kept an open turret. We didn't close that down because that would have meant no vision. I was the [37-millimeter] gunner down below. That required looking through the sight and aiming the gun. The tank commander standing in the open hatch would call targets down to me: "Traverse right. Building on the corner." Constantly telling me where the

enemy was. Then we'd give it everything we had—spray it with .30-caliber machine gun fire and then hit the thing with the 37-millimeter.

If there were any civilians left, we supposed they were in the cellars. If anybody was out there, he was suspect and we held nothing back. If there was fire coming from a house, we didn't hesitate to shoot. No quarter given, no quarter asked. We were paired with one other tank from our platoon and given a certain sector of the town to cover. In the end, we managed to survive and keep the town.

Many prisoners of war were taken in the vicinity. Prisoners were turned over to combat MPs, when they were available, for dispatching to the rear. MP Peter Joseph says:

Not long after [retaking Avranches], our forces took a lot of prisoners. Probably between 500 and 1,000. All were standing in big circle in an open field, surrounded by U.S. tanks. Our soldiers were standing on the outside of the tanks behind machine guns.

Our MP company was brought in to search these prisoners who had just put down their weapons. We pulled anything we found out of the pockets of their coats, jackets and shirts, looking especially for knives, small pistols and any other weapons. We found medals and things and threw it all into a pile. I took a sword from an officer and threw that in the pile, too.

There was fear in their faces. They were at our mercy and they knew it.

After the search, they were loaded on our open six-by-six trucks, all of them standing in the backs of the trucks. We MPs each got on a front fender of the trucks to guard the truck immediately in front of us. So there were many trucks in succession, each with two MPs riding on the front fenders guarding the prisoners riding in the truck just ahead of them. We took them all to a POW camp nearby. That was one role of a combat MP, as opposed to the MPs back in the towns on patrol.

◆

The preliminaries in Avranches were over. The Third Army charged out of the Cotentin Peninsula like a racehorse out of the starting gate, and the headlong dash through France began. Simultaneously, elements of the Army would roll west for objectives on Brittany's coast, while others would sweep east on a relentless drive toward the German border.

The 4th Armored Division spearheaded much of the drive toward the Rhine. W. King Pound talks about being among the lead tanks in the spearhead:

We were driving every day across France, right out front. We were always up on the point, because the idea was for us to feel out the Germans. If we [in M5 light tanks] couldn't handle what we came up against—say the Tiger, the Panther—we'd call up the "persuaders," which is what we called the Shermans. We'd peel off and go to the flanks while they took care of them. We had many engagements with small German infantry patrols that we could handle.

Gas was never a problem, until Metz. We could go 90 miles in a day without refueling. There were two gas tanks on the back. They would fill us up that night when we stopped, and we'd be ready to head right out in the morning.

George Davis tells about the drive from the infantryman's point of view:

The tanks would go into these towns up ahead and knock out the big stuff. But the German foot soldier was still there. So our infantry on foot would follow them up and clean out those pockets of resistance.

We found that the tanks were moving ahead faster than the infantry could keep up. They finally got enough trucks to move us. They'd move us 8 or 10 miles, we'd detruck. Then the trucks went back to get more of us. We just leapfrogged all the way through like that behind the armor. And we'd ride the tanks into those little villages.

You went in blindly as an infantryman, you know, expecting most anything. But through it all, I had the feeling I was coming back home. I would tell people my biggest worry was being captured. I think I would have died before letting them capture me. It nearly happened once when our regiment was behind the lines. We broke through their lines, or maybe they opened up and let us go through and closed behind. But we ended up there three or four days, surrounded. It was a farm area with some farmhouses around. There were hedgerows where we dug in. This particular hedgerow was L-shaped and two pairs of us dug in at the corner of it so we could look down both ways. Two of us had one foxhole and the other two had a foxhole. During one of the days when it seemed quiet, we got out and sat talking. Suddenly an 88 shell came in. It hit the top of the hedgerow, exploded, and these other two boys were sitting directly in line with it. I was four feet away from that pair of men when the shell fragments just tore through them—mangled them and killed both instantly right in front of my eyes. We had several

Chapter Five

things like that happen. I can't explain my reaction at that moment. You were scared all the time, but trusting that a higher power was taking care of you.

One time, another fella and I went forward alone to get a sniper. He was about 200 yards away in an old building made of rock and mortar. They happened to start throwing shells in on this little village, so we laid down by this road. This boy was behind me after a shell hit the building.

There was mud flying, debris and dust went everywhere. Both of us were laying there just scared to death, and once the debris settled down to earth, this boy behind me yells, "I'm hit! They tore my rear-end off! I'm bleeding bad—the blood is running down my leg!"

I turned around and crawled back there to him. I looked at him and saw there was a piece of shrapnel as big as your hand laying on the cheek of his butt. The shrapnel was hot. He was laying there, afraid to move. I said, "You're not bleeding. You're just burned." I flicked the piece of shrapnel off. I laughed at him about that the whole time we moved through Europe. He had been so sure he was hurt that he could actually *feel* the blood running down his leg. We needed something like that to laugh at.

◆

For Patton's very mobile type of warfare, there was no greater natural obstacle than France's rivers. Because of this, bridges were as important to rapid movement as anything in the arsenal. Lieutenant William Baker had been an infantry officer when he landed on D + 5, but an unexpected number of engineer casualties resulted in his reassignment to the 989th Engineer Treadway Bridge Company. He served with Patton throughout the drive across France and here he explains how assault bridges were put in place:

There were only about a half-dozen treadway bridge companies in the whole ETO. Originally, the idea was for each armored division to have one, but they decided that was too much of a luxury. So we remained a separate unit—assigned to the Third Army and attached down the line to whatever division was on the offensive.

We were already on the Continent supporting the First Army and very glad when we were assigned to the Third Army. We knew what kind of general Patton was. His reputation preceded him. He was an aggressive general—and this was going to be his kind of warfare. It was fast moving and it required bridges.

It was like we hit the open road when we had Patton. As a company, we were on the move constantly during those four weeks across France.

A treadway bridge was an assault bridge. It goes up fast. It's a bridge that is on pneumatic floats—pontoons that had to be inflated. We were immediately put in the advance elements of the Third Army, right after the breakout. We were in support of the 5th Infantry Division and 7th Armored Division. We traveled with them through much of France.

The first river of any size we needed to cross was the Seine River at Fontainebleau. We got some small arms fire there. It's a very vulnerable bridge to fire of any kind. So we never wanted to put them up under small arms fire. The floats, made of a rubberized fabric, could be punctured easily by any bullet.

The idea was for the infantry to go across the river and establish a bridgehead first, then we'd come immediately to put in the assault bridge. That would carry the armor, trucks, anything—our bridge could carry anything the Army had.

On the Seine, our infantry crossed first, as was the usual practice. The 5th Infantry was good! After a short time, they cleared out the enemy infantry. But until then, they were firing us from the woods, scattered through there. They were firing at anything and everything. We had to stop and pulled back and waited a few hours for the infantry to clear them out.

The bridge did go up fast. The first thing was to get the bridge truck to the site. There were two bridge platoons in our company—each platoon with 18 trucks. Each eight-ton truck carried 24 feet—two sections of bridge. With 36 trucks in all, each carrying 24 feet, we could cross even the widest rivers. (We later crossed the Rhine, which was 1,080 feet wide.)

The first step putting it in was to draw a strong cable across the river, because the whole bridge would be attached to this single, very strong cable. Then roll the pontoons—rolled up like old inner tubes—off the trucks and inflate them with our own air compressor. They would put on each pontoon a "saddle." The saddle held the treads. The treads were lifted off the truck by this little crane, made for that—the only thing it would have been good for. So we'd put together two pontoon and two treads, and that was a section. It was about 12 feet long. Each truck carried two sections, so about 24 feet per truck.

A large crane, which was also part of our equipment, would then lift each section, one section at a time, and simply place it into the water. Then we had a powerboat that would take it and maneuver it around to attach it to the existing section of bridge. So the bridge was built one section at a time. The first section of bridge would have a trestle and be attached to the friendly side.

The amount of time depended on how much fire we were taking. We always got artillery fire, because the Germans were retreating and knew we had to cross the river and where we would do it. We could put in a 250-foot bridge in about four hours. It was a like a big erector set. Everything fit, everything had a place. And when everything was in place, it all worked.

The drive across France required many river crossings. In the words of Lieutenant William Baker of the 989th Engineer Treadway Bridge Company: "We were very glad when we were assigned to the Third Army. We knew what kind of general Patton was. He was an aggressive general—and this was going to be his kind of warfare. It was fast moving and it required bridges."
U.S. Army

The Third Army moved quickly, but some of the gains were hard won and setbacks were inevitable. Not far past Avranches, the 17th Recon Squadron, attached to the VIII Corps, ran into heavy resistance. Arthur Schladerman was a radio operator and machine gunner on a half-track in the squadron. He describes his personal Armageddon:

We had stopped because of mines in the road . . . when all hell broke loose as artillery was landing everywhere. Lieutenant Woods, the platoon leader, was wounded trying to get back in the vehicle.

Then a jeep drove up and Lieutenant Colonel Lindquist jumped out and ordered me to pursue the Krauts on foot. I grabbed a rifle and ran in the direction he pointed. I never saw any Krauts, just retreating GIs. After running about a half-mile, I saw several disabled vehicles. They were from Troop C that had been ambushed. They had encountered superior forces and were in full retreat. I recognized one of our tanks that was assigned to Troop C from our 3rd Platoon and was running toward it, when machine guns and mortars opened up. Crawling on my belly toward the tank, I had a closer view and noticed a man in the 50-caliber turret. I thought I would be safer with a tank than alone in the open. When about 10 feet away, I could see the man was dead.

There was no sign of damage to the tank, so I presumed the crew was still aboard. Every tank had an escape hatch in the floor of the tank, so I crawled under the tank and the hatch was open. I heard some movement and moaning inside and found a wounded crewman—Johnson. He had been hit in the lower legs and was bleeding. I found a strap and made a tourniquet for one leg and used my belt for the other leg. He told me a sniper had hit the turret gunner and the crew exited through the floor hatch. He was the last one to leave, and as he stood up to run, he was hit. He then crawled back to the tank through the escape hatch where I found him.

The tank was still operable and I thought I could drive it back to safety, but did not have any idea where that was. I decided to get him out of the tank through the escape hatch. The hatch is large enough for the average man to squirm through, but Johnson was short and bulky. Getting him out posed a problem as every movement of his legs was agonizing and he resisted my every effort. I then went up the open turret to see if there was anyone who could help me. There were many retreating GIs fleeing from an unseen enemy, and I called out for help. Finally, two men stopped and I explained what we had to do to bring this wounded man up through the open turret. One man went though the open floor hatch and fastened his rifle belt onto Johnson's belt.

I was pulling Johnson up the open turret when a cannon shell hit the dead machine gunner next to me through his midsection. His upper torso dropped on the man outside [and he] left screaming in horror. The lower torso dropped on the man inside the tank [and he] exited through the escape hatch, also terrified, leaving me holding Johnson halfway out of the tank. I don't remember how I got the strength to pull him up and out, but I did. Johnson was still conscious but did not give me any resistance, and I carried him on my back like a sack of potatoes. . . . I was trying to reach a farmhouse when more mortars started up, so I dropped to the ground with Johnson's heavy body on top of me. One of the mortars landed close so I remained on the ground till they stopped. I needed the rest, as he was about 150 pounds and I was only 130 pounds; I was completely exhausted and had a migraine headache.

I was just ready to get up when two Germans pulled up in their vehicle. This was the first time I felt fear because I was in a helpless situation and expected I would die. One Kraut kicked me and then left, assuming we were both dead. Finally, I got up and put Johnson on my back and carried him to the farmhouse where three French women and one old man helped me lay him on a table. The women were jabbering in French and I understood not a word. They released the tourniquets and bathed his legs when I noticed his back was punctured with shrapnel. It was then that I realized the last mortar had landed too close and he was again wounded. His body had absorbed the shrapnel, but I was not wounded. Now panic hit me as I did not know how severe these wounds were and fearing he might die if medical help did not reach him in time. I ran out of the farm-house in the direction that I assumed our troops were. I cannot remember how long or far I ran until reached our lines. Chaos and confusion was rampant. Burning vehicles and dead GIs everywhere. No one had any idea where the medics were, so I continued on till I met some tankers who directed me to a group of vehicles.

Approaching the group, I recognized Brigadier General Herbert L. Ernest and saluted him—a mistake I will always remember, as he read me the riot act.

"Never salute an officer in a combat area!" Snipers pick off offi-cers and he did not want to be a casualty.

I was embarrassed, but was able to explain about Johnson. The general commandeered a jeep and some medics and I led them back to the farmhouse where Johnson was given plasma (he had lost a great deal of blood). Even though the general had given me a tongue lashing, I take my hat off to him for personally responding to the needs of a wounded soldier in a still highly hostile area. Later I learned that Johnson was safely evacuated and was recovering.

———————————◆———————————

Patton's VIII Corps rolled on through Brittany to take Lorient, St. Nazaire, and, in particular, the port of Brest, home to German U-boats. Three GI's accounts about the Brittany drive follow.

The 8th Infantry Division faced heavy fortifications at Brest. George Davis describes the action there that would result in a Silver Star for him:

They had fortified Brest. Part of Brest's defense was a big old moat. My platoon was spearheading an attack that morning that required us to cross this moat. In our area at least, the moat was dry. It was maybe 50 yards across, and the Germans or maybe the French had built stairs of wood and stone down 15 or 20 feet to get to the moat's bottom. I took two boys with me and went down into the moat using those stair steps. As soon as we got down into the moat, Germans dug in on the other side started throwing hand grenades at us. We had not known they were there.

I had left the platoon on the bank to protect us while we were trying to see what was going on. But the Germans were on higher ground, so every time our boys stuck their heads up, the Germans could see them and would fire. Three of us were killed, one or two wounded—just like that. Our boys started firing back.

We hurried back to them and knew we had to get out of there. But there was wide-open spaces for 200 or 300 yards to get out of there. We had no choice. Nothing we could do but withdraw through this wide-open area. I knew we were in trouble.

The lieutenant had been wounded, so I had charge of the platoon. I set up two squads firing. One would fire while the other dropped back. One set covered the other set, then they'd drop back and cover the [first] set in retreat. That's how we made it out. Finally, we got to a point where the rest had to go on and I stayed behind to cover.

By staying behind, Davis bought the time and opportunity for his platoon's escape. For the disciplined way he handled his platoon in getting them out safely, he was awarded the Silver Star for gallantry in action. His citation for the Silver Star reads:

For Technical Sergeant George H. Davis, 34147451, Infantry Company I, 121st Infantry Regiment, for gallantry in action on September 10, 1944, in the vicinity of Lambazellec, France, when a platoon was pinned down by heavy enemy artillery, mortar fire, and small arms fire, the platoon leader was wounded. Sergeant Davis moved to the position and assumed command. Although his action exposed him to enemy fire, he moved among the men, encouraging them and directed their fire. When he directed the platoon to occupy a new position, he remained behind, delivering covering fire until each man had reached the new position. His quick thinking and inspiring courage were responsible for the safe movement of his men and the continuance of their part in the attack.

Technical Sergeant Milo Flaten's 29th Infantry Division had landed with the First Army, but now was attached to VIII Corps on the way to Brest.

In August 1944, the *Stars and Stripes* newspaper said General Patton had taken Brest, which was a large French seaport. The news story also said we'd now be able to supply the troops because we'd captured that seaport—and that we'd be "home in a couple of weeks."

We soon found out that the armor might go through a territory but they wouldn't go into a town and hold it. They'd just bypass the town, maybe at 20 miles per hour, but they wouldn't actually take control of the land. The infantry would be required to fight from house to house in towns we heard were already liberated. But the tankers would get credit in the newsreels for taking the town. Going up the coast of the Brittany Peninsula, I remember capturing St. Malo, Morlais—towns like that [bypassed by armor]. Our leaders said we would spend about a week flushing the Germans out of the submarine pens so the Allies could use that city [Brest] as a seaport. It was France's second largest seaport.

The hedgerows weren't as numerous in Brittany as in Normandy. But they still had plenty of them for the Krauts to hide behind.

In St. Renan there were not only Germans remaining but tough aggressive ones. Those Germans would counterattack viciously. They came back over the hedgerow with bayonets, the whole bit. They had these funny little hats. That's because they were the paratroopers. We found out it was the 2nd SS paratroopers which had been in Italy at the bloody battle of Casino.

When we ran into an SS unit, they were tougher than shit . . . it was like 15,000 rattlesnakes. These guys were vicious and well trained. Soon we started getting terrible casualties again. This time there were more small arms casualties not so much from artillery. The ground fighting was more like cowboys and Indians up there. Hand-to-hand combat. Oh, there was plenty of mortars, tanks, and machine guns but it wasn't self-propelled 88s. In addition, the Germans had coastal artillery guns that they turned away from the sea and pointed inland. They also had built big forts to defend. I think they also were old reinforced French forts or something. We were in a town on the outskirts of Brest called, I think it was called Recouverance, a suburb of Brest. The boundary line between Brest itself and Recouverance was a river. In the harbor they had a narrow peninsula that stuck out into the harbor of Brest like a finger. Ships landed and unloaded. They had a tunnel going through the base of the finger of land which contained rails and little railroad cars hauled by donkeys which would go back and forth. That way they could unload a ship and transfer cargo without having to take it all the way up to the top even though they were separated by this peninsula of land.

As our unit pushed up near the harbor, they sent me out on a patrol, me and one of my squads. By then I was promoted to platoon sergeant, and held a rank of tech sergeant. Earlier that week we moved across some hills to a huge structure called the Great Wall of Brest. It actually looked like the Great Wall of China. It had trees and roads on it. It was about a quarter of a block wide and 100 feet high. You could see tunnels every once in a while on the side of the wall. It had roads going up the side of the wall at a gentle angle to get up to the top of it. I guess that had been some old Roman or French fortification.

By then I was sort of well known. I had survived. Colonel Purnell, the regimental commander asked me whether I thought we could take that wall which was actually a combination of a wall and a hill. I said I'd go up there and look around. I took two guys from my first squad and started up the ramp running like a stairway on the wall. The colonel was watching our progress through glasses. All of a sudden from one of these holes a white flag stuck out and Christ, out came more goddamn Germans that I ever saw in my life, all wanting to surrender. The regimental commander had apparently heard that I was a reliable patrol leader, which is why I was selected. That made me very proud. He gave me the right to do exactly what I was supposed to do. He said he could count on me. And within a half an hour I came back with at least 300 prisoners. There were so many Germans that if they wanted to throw rocks at us they could have overwhelmed the three of us on that recon patrol. But they just wanted to give up. I got another Bronze Star for that because the regimental commander was up on the opposite hill watching us.

Actually, I did lots of things more deserving in 12 months of combat. But he happened to be watching me on that day. Getting decorated is always a matter of luck in the infantry. I got another Bronze Star one time because our company commander got hit. We were in our initial attack when we got to Holland after we left the hedgerow country. This new captain was walking around when he should have been on the deck and took a bullet in his leg. He was right next to me so I dragged his ass back to the battalion aid station. Because it was the C.O. being rescued I got the Bronze Star. I had done it a million times for other guys and never even got a thank you.

But to get back to the battle for Brest, after all those Krauts surrendered, we thought: *This is it—they're ready to collapse.* We literally had captured hundreds of Germans that day. Later on I read that they were mostly cooks and quartermaster soldiers. There were even some Navy guys. In the German forces up near Brest, the Navy and the Army and everybody all wore the same uniform. I didn't know who these guys were but they weren't the tough infantry soldiers we have encountered up to then.

We thought, *God, if those were only SS soldiers and paratroopers that were giving up.* Those were the ones driving us crazy with their counterattacks and aggressive patrolling and had caused all these terrible casualties. But Colonel Purnell saw me bring in all those prisoners and he was excited about that.

After capturing so many prisoners, Flaten tempted a fateful turn of the tables in his next assignment. He and two other "volunteers" were sent to reconnoiter a small suburb of Brest.

When we got into Recouverance we could hear a machine gun, and we thought, "They've got one of our heavy machine guns shooting down this boulevard. It was a main street. On that patrol was a . . . cook. He wasn't a rifleman. It was a dumb thing to allow him on that patrol but he wanted to go. He wanted to get some French brandy. He was a boozer . . . so he volunteered to go on the patrol. The other guy, named Ritter, was either a squad leader or platoon sergeant from the 3rd Platoon. So there were two sergeants and this cook on this recon patrol.

As ordered, we went into this town to see how far we could go. For about eight or ten blocks we didn't encounter a thing. Then we came upon this boulevard and there was a great big 500-pound bomb crater right in the intersection. It was a huge crater that had sides over your head when we stood on the bottom.

Up in Brest we had a lot of air cover. It was odd, because we not only had the usual P-47s but we also had Australian Typhoons for close air support. We even had big bombers. We found out later it was because we were sticking out right into the ocean in Brittany, all by ourselves, without organized air support. The pilots were volunteers. After they'd come back from their regular missions, they asked these pilots if they'd want to help out the guys at Brest.

Then, to our surprise, we ran into these SS paratroops. . . . When we came to this boulevard there was this heavy machine gun up the street, so we jumped into this huge bomb crater. Ordinarily on any patrol, when you get into a bomb crater or any hole, each guy looks out a different direction. You do that instinctively. Each guy establishes security. You protect your buddy's ass that way and he protects yours.

But this cook wasn't watching down the street the way he was supposed to. All of a sudden I heard this voice say, "Hands up," and it was a Kraut down in the crater with a burp gun, a Schmeiser, pointed at us. We had to put our hands up and drop our rifles and he marched us down the street to a big stairway and we climbed down about ten flights of stairs, down into this subway tunnel. It was the tunnel running through this hill connecting the two harbors in the city of Brest.

Once in the tunnel, they fed us some meat and sauerkraut and questioned us. They knew what unit we were in from our shoulder patches. But those Germans didn't want information. They wanted manual labor. There was a bunch of other American prisoners there, about 20 of them. So the next day they got us out of that tunnel up to the street with a shovel to fill in bomb craters so they could move their tanks and trucks around. The streets were narrow and they had lots of bomb holes in them. I figured we were still near the outskirts of town kind of because there were only scattered houses with woodsy empty lots.

As we worked with our picks and shovels, we got strafed by our airplanes. One P-47 came down to strafe and the other was to protect the first one's ass. Of course from the air they couldn't tell we were Americans. To them we were just "Krauts" filling the bomb craters. To guard us prisoners they had a Kraut on our side of the road with a gun and two other guards on the other. When those P-47s strafed, 20 guys went in the ditch on one side with the two Kraut guards. Ritter and I and the one Kraut guard dove into the other ditch.

The planes were on their second pass when Ritter took his shovel and hit the Kraut in the head. The edge of the shovel split his head right in two like a pineapple. He wasn't wearing a helmet, just a little gray cap. So that German died instantly. Then we had to run while the planes were still diving. We wanted to get away before they found the guard that Ritter had killed.

We ran into this big copse of bushes, trees and stuff. It was like an overgrown park. We hid there in the bushes until dark. Fortunately the planes kept coming down and coming down and coming down, so the Germans couldn't look for Ritter and me. We hid there until after it was dark and then we decided we were going to try and go back to our unit, if we could find it.

I knew the way because I had been guiding on that church steeple in our approach from St. Renan. So we went back out of town retracing our steps right through St. Renan which was a tiny little place. Finally we got to about three fields beyond that church, three hedgerows toward where they'd started us on that patrol. It was dark and we didn't want the Germans to see or hear us and we didn't know where they were. Then we started to approach this place where we had left our company that day. We knew our unit would be sending out patrols because they usually did that.

For background I must explain that each morning headquarters would declare a password and a countersign for the day. However, that password changed every 24 hours. Each morning they'd tell you what the new password and countersign was. Ritter and I had been gone from our unit either two or three days up with those Germans before we had escaped. As we crept through this field I said, "I think we're getting close."

All of a sudden you could hear this guy say, "Halt, who goes there?" from our hedgerow. He then pulled back on the bolt of the machine gun. In order to fire that gun you have to pull the bolt back twice to get the first round out of the belt into the receiver. The second time the bolt is pulled back to put the first bullet in the chamber so it's ready to fire automatically and continuously. Anyway, then he gave the password to us again just before he pulled back to bolt for the second time. The way it works is the challenger gives the password and the other gives the countersign. So you'd have to know both words each day in order to pass.

So when Ritter and I got near our front hedgerow, the machine gunner on the outpost hollered out the password and mumbled, "This is the last time I'm going to tell you."

We could hear the bolt go back a second time and we knew machine gun bullets were coming any second. So I cried, "I don't know what it is today but I knew what it was two days ago."

And the voice said, "Ah shit, it's Flaten."

What a relief. The guy on the outpost recognized my voice. Later on I talked to him and he said he was expecting an F Company patrol, which was due back at the time.

Here I had spent two days captivity filling in holes in the roads. Ritter killed a guard and then we had escaped. All that time our unit was still sitting there in the same spot.

Converging on Brest at this time was the 6th Armored Division. Vince Gish was an engineer and demolitions expert in the unit. And after being wounded almost immediately in the approach to Brest, Gish found that at least some rules of the Geneva Convention were followed.

Rampaging Through France

The 6th Armored went 250 miles in 10 days. A whole armored division—*that* fast. I traveled in a half-track. We took mines out as we went. The Germans would leave snipers behind in the villages to harass us and slow us down. All that delayed us but we got up to Brest quick, although the Germans still had enough time to mob thousands and thousands of troops into Brest.

When we got to the outskirts, somebody got sent in under a white flag to ask for surrender. It was a lot like Bastogne in reverse: The Germans essentially told *us* "nuts."

It was about one o'clock in the morning when we pulled into fields up there and dug in. By daybreak the Germans, who were on higher ground, had us zeroed in. And they really poured it on us—artillery and mortars. The darn 88s you could hear; the mortars you couldn't hear. I lost three men right away in my squad.

I tried to dive into a hole, but they got me in the arm. I didn't even know how bad I was hurt. It just felt like someone had thrown a brick at my arm. When the shelling subsided temporarily and I could run for the hedgerows, I finally had the chance to look down. We wore those long-sleeve olive drab shirts and my sleeve was just saturated with blood, and dripping off my fingers. I thought I would lose my right arm.

I ended up traveling 250 miles back toward Avranches through the night to get to a field hospital. That same night, I traveled the same 250 miles we had just fought through over 10 days!

We had been sent back without an escort, but no one was supposed to attack something with red crosses. There were two or three ambulances traveling together. And no one on the ambulances carried a gun.

Somewhere in those 250 miles, German soldiers stopped our ambulance. These were Germans who hadn't been cleared out. Or the French had hid them as we went through. They stopped the ambulance to make sure it was carrying only wounded.

I was seated in the rear with the rest. I didn't have to be in a gurney in the ambulance, like some guys with neck injuries, or legs or arms off, or chest torn open and taped up.

I couldn't see anything out of the ambulance, because there are only those two little windows in the back. All we knew in the back was that we came to a stop. We thought we had arrived at the field hospital.

Then suddenly the doors were flung open and Germans stood there—three or four of them. They raised the muzzles of their rifles to the ready. They made the driver get out, and he was standing there, too. They shined their flashlight all around. They wanted to see what was in the back, to make sure there was no ammunition or mines.

I never thought they would pull the trigger. Honestly wasn't really thinking about it. I was still too concerned with losing my arm at that point—I'm right-handed. No one moved. Some with us were so heavily sedated they didn't know what was happening. The Germans didn't make us get out, even though some of us could have. They just wanted to make sure there was wounded in the ambulance and nothing else.

I was in the field hospital for a month. By the time I got out, the 6th Armored—half of it—had gone east in the pursuit of the Germans across France, toward Paris, the rest stayed back and contained Lorient. I rejoined at Lorient. We sat there until the 94th Infantry Division came fresh from the States. Then the rest of us packed up and caught up with the outfit as it was moving east.

Fortunately, rather than going back to another outfit—infantry unit or whatever—Patton himself made sure we could get back to our own units. He knew what camaraderie meant for morale. Patton did this, I know. He arranged that any man wounded who could return to combat could return to his own original unit. Everybody appreciated that. I know I did.

◆

The battlefield was a harrowing place for anyone. But there was a hierarchy of risk faced by GIs, depending on role—tanker, rifleman, combat engineer, and so on. Clearly topping the list for harrowing ordeals was the medic's role. When a sudden burst of machine-gun fire or explosion of shrapnel sent soldiers grappling for cover, the cry of "Medic!" was almost sure to follow. And a man with a satchel and red crosses painted on his helmet would emerge low, then bolt for a writhing, blood-covered comrade. Oftentimes, the result would be the medic lying in his own blood.

John Gill was a medic and private in the 2nd Infantry Division. In an unpublished memoir written fresh in 1948, he recounts a long day sometime in August 1944 that ended with a Purple Heart—not for those he delivered to safety but for himself:

> Some infantrymen from the main line said they had seen their buddy fall a little ways down the hill and asked us to have a look at him on our way to the outpost. They didn't believe he was seriously wounded and said he had just been hit.

Buntello [medic squad leader], myself, and two others proceeded over the hedgerow we had been waiting behind, walked a little ways down the hill where we came upon the soldier. He was dead; his wrist had already become stiff, as I felt for his pulse. We found no visible wounds on his face or body. We signaled back to the main line of defense that he was dead and caught the surprised faces of the men, who believed he had been just slightly wounded.

We felt as though the Germans could see us as we moved further down the hill, although trees were everywhere and gave good concealment. It was a strange feeling being between our lines and the Germans, but I wasn't quite as scared as I had been a few hours before during a light shelling.

We found the outpost, which consisted of two wounded men lying near a little stream of water. One had been hit in the back and neck by bullets that had caused flesh wounds up his back and a light wound in his neck. It didn't seem to be too serious, but he couldn't walk. The other soldier had a sprained ankle and could only hobble. These men had come as close as possible to the Germans, which was their mission. I took my scissors out to cut some bandage and tape and then lost them in the excitement. We now had to rip the tape and bandages with our hands, because I had had the only scissors left.

We were talking over what should be our next move when our infantry started opening up with their rifles and machine guns from the hill above us. This quickened our decision to start back up the hill. Going uphill carrying one casualty on our litter was slow, and we had to wait for the fellow with a sprained ankle. It was steep and tiring. We figured we were safe near the bottom of the hill, because the Germans were busy firing at the top. We wondered how it would be when we got up there.

We could see one of our tanks coming down the hill from up above and then heard the roar of a German antitank gun. Two shells burst almost upon it, when the fellows driving decided it was an unwise move. They drove quickly behind a farmhouse on the hill and stayed there, not daring to move until the gun could be silenced. We were halfway up the hill and saw it was impossible to go any further. We all would have been killed by our own or the German small arms fire, had we attempted to get back to where we had started, for our attack with all its fury had begun and the Germans with great tenacity were resisting fiercely.

There was a shack of some sort nearby and we took cover in it, although I don't know why because the walls were as thin as paper. The noise outside was deafening, louder than I had ever heard before, gunfire from both sides was pouring across the valley over our heads and we could hear shells from our artillery over our heads as they arched into the German lines. We felt that at any moment a burst of machine gun fire might come crashing through the walls of the shack, as we hugged the floor for as much protection as possible.

We waited, listening to this noise outside—more noise than we had ever heard before. Noise that meant the Germans would have begun to withdraw in the face of our heavy firepower, or that our troops would have to seek some other way of pushing them back.

The noise gradually lessened after what seemed like an hour in the shack and came to almost a complete halt. We went outside to see what had happened and found that our troops had moved down through us and the valley and were now up on the hill where the Germans had been dug in so firmly.

Now there were left the wounded in the wake of this battle. Not as many as you'd think, if you had heard all the commotion, but enough. Enough that it would take us trip after trip the rest of the afternoon to get them back to the aid station and there were many who would crawl or get back under their own power. It wasn't humanly possible to take care of everyone at once, so we had to take care of those we came to first. The Germans were increasing their shell fire now, in an attempt to cut our infantry's supply lines and we had to dodge these as best we could. Quite a few shells were falling in the general area and made evacuation hazardous.

We started back for the aid station with our original casualty from the outpost and passed a squad of infantry with fairly clean uniforms. They were sitting dazed near some trees doing nothing. We knew by their looks and actions they were replacements who had just come up form the rear and had been hastily thrown into this battle. They were all badly frightened and a few of them had leg wounds that looked suspiciously like they had been self-inflicted but we couldn't be sure.

I felt sorry for them. Combat isn't always as bad as it was today. If they had been more slowly indoctrinated into it by the veterans around them it would have been easier. They had been too fresh, their minds too clear and rational.

To go into a battle like the one today or any other one, it is easier to take if you are completely exhausted in mind and body as most veterans . . . as we usually felt. You are literally drunk from lack of sleep, from fear and from all that has happened to you. So that your body and mind are numb. You actually reach a point where you don't care what happens to you. Sometimes you're so exhausted that your body refused to do what your mind tells it. So that you would rather risk getting killed than summon the physical effort necessary to move out of danger.

We got back to the aid station and went into the house near the aid station for water and talked about how easy it would be to hide here for the rest of the day, if we wanted.

We left the aid station and went back for more casualties. On the return route we could see shells land in front of us about 200 yards. They made small willowy puffs of smoke as they landed on the previous route we had come. In a road we passed a tank and armored car of ours that had been hit and were burning. Some of the crew lay dead on the ground, while medics from a medical half-track were getting some of the wounded out of the tank.

We continued bringing casualties to the aid station and the doctor there was finding it impossible to take care of them all. The ground was covered with litters and there must have been at least 50 of them, with more coming in all the time. Soldiers suffering from combat exhaustion were standing around in a daze, with no one paying attention to them, a few were helping load the ambulances from the collecting station. The doctor was just filling out medical tags, because it was impossible for him to even begin to take care of any wounds.

It was around 6:30 now and the infantry had pushed through the town and were now just outside it. We left the aid station and went back to locate the company of infantry we had started with. We had evacuated all the wounded we could find and had orders to report to this company.

We found the company just outside the town, and there weren't many of them left. They hadn't dug any foxholes as yet and were just waiting behind some hedgerows.

Speaking to an infantry sergeant in one of the platoons, we asked him if they had sent us down to some of their casualties in the valley, knowing they would start their attack on the Germans while we were in between. We told him we couldn't get back to where they were, but had to wait until the attack passed over us. He replied, it was just one of those things and went on to say that one of our own platoons had been shelled that day by our own artillery, because they were too close to the Germans. So he continued, "Why should we worry about the lives of a few medics?" We figured he had something there, so we kept our mouths shut. So many of his men had been shot up in the attack . . . that he didn't care what he said anyway.

Howitzers pummel German forces retreating swiftly through France. By mid-August, Patton could write triumphantly in his diary: "In exactly two weeks, the Third Army has advanced farther and faster than any army in the history of war." **U.S. Army**

When it seemed like it couldn't get worse, the Germans began shelling again. And Gill had to face horrors that anyone else would turn from reflexively.

A soldier came running toward us from the town. His jaw was gone and tattered bits of flesh showed where his chin had been ripped apart. He had no mouth and not much remained of his nose. It was a wonder that he was able to walk, but I suppose he was in such a state of shock that he didn't realize what had happened. Everyone who saw him shuddered at the terrible sight. Infantry walking by turned their heads because they couldn't look at him. The only thing we could do was put a large compress over his face, to hide it from the infantry walking by and send him back to the aid station.

The jeep made trip after trip and on one of these I rode along and stood between the two top litters with a medical compress in each hand, in an attempt to stop the bleeding of two soldiers, one of whom had his foot blown off and serious body wounds. The other had his stomach ripped open and was bleeding profusely. Their skin was ripped off in places and you could look right inside their bodies. One of them died in the few blocks to the aid station and I doubt if the other lived. At the aid station, men lay all over the ground on litters, waiting for the ambulance to take them to the rear.

The aid station was only about four blocks from the town where the shelling was so heavy and I thought if the Germans should raise their fire just a little all these wounded would get it.

I rode back to the collecting point and helped load four men on the jeep again. This time I didn't ride back to the aid station. As soon as the jeep left, the artillery fire reached its height in our area. We were all lying on the ground while the shells were coming in so close that it was suicide to try to get up. We huddled near a house, which was right in front of us and to our left was a high bank. Scotty and Gregory and one casualty that we hadn't had room for in the jeep. We were caught in the heaviest shelling we had so far witnessed. Usually we'd receive maybe one real close shell burst and then the others would land further away from us, or we'd have the protection of a foxhole.

This time our luck ran out. One of those shells hit us. It knocked me out instantly and I came to in a few moments. I could feel a trickle of blood running down my leg, and felt my breathing to be somewhat difficult. My ears rung from the concussion, but I felt very much alive. Gregory had been hit in the head but not seriously, and we kidded one another about finally getting wounded after all this time.

Buntello and a couple of other medics had been under a culvert and hadn't been hit. They now came as the shelling let up and they loaded us up on the jeep for our ride back to the aid station.

Back at the aid station there were now over 100 casualties and the doctor was busy filling out medical tags. Kitty Buntello put some sulfa powder on my wounds and I felt extremely sorry for him, because I was getting out of the war and he was getting ready to go back into the tow for more casualties. He was Mexican and the bravest man that I ever knew. Sergeant Sam Hill, my squad leader, was wounded twice that day, the second time by the shell that hit me. Scotty, Gregory and several others of the old gang got it but fortunately none of us were killed and were all happy to be getting out of there.

One of our ambulances came up to the aid station and we were transported back to our collecting station. As we were unloaded from the ambulance Captain Fiedl C. Leonard and some of our other officers came up and greeted us. I supposed they were wondering what they were going to use for litter bearers now that there were so few left. We stayed here only a short time and then were loaded on another ambulance and driven back to the clearing station. Here to my surprise were many of the men from my company who had been removed, suffering from combat exhaustion. They were working back here and felt rather sheepish about greeting us. It was around 10 in the evening and we were in a tent where our clothing was cut off, being an easier way than trying to get it off us. It was only then that I found out that I had been wounded in the back as well as the fanny. I was taken into the X-ray room and then into the operating room. They didn't waste any time. They put me under and the next morning I awoke in a ward tent with the sides up and the sun streaming into my face.

Once medics had done their job of retrieving the wounded and dying from the battlefield, medical doctors such as H. G. Tousignant had to make immediate decisions about treatment. They also had to accept the fact that some soldiers were hopeless cases for whom nothing could be done, and their priority must go to those they thought they could save. Tousignant, battalion surgeon in the 5th Infantry Division, which replaced the 1st Infantry Division at Normandy, learned a lesson of discernment when a certain soldier was carried into the midst of chaos in a crowded field hospital.

When our stretcher bearers brought in a soldier at 6 p.m., I examined him and saw that his entire brain was on the litter and his type of breathing indicated to me that he would be dead in a few minutes. I called over the chaplain and told him the soldier was dying and did he want to say a prayer or something. He leaned over the litter and picked up the man's ID chain and called the soldier by name. Imagine my feelings—I had just said the soldier would be dead in a few minutes. He answered the chaplain as clearly as if his brain were intact! I have never forgotten that experience, and have been very careful of what I said around badly wounded soldiers after that.

The soldier did indeed die within minutes, as Tousignant predicted.

———————◆———————

Several years before, in the pleasant rolling hills of Georgia, Patton had said to the officers of the 2nd Armored Division at Fort Benning: "There is an old Chinese saying . . . 'A look is worth a thousand words.' This means that the commanders . . . must be close up to attain full knowledge of what has transpired." He demanded this of his commanders, and he demanded it of himself. Sergeant Phillip Robbins of the 80th Infantry Division remembers a surprise visit from the brass turned out to include Patton himself.

My forward observer team was held up on the forward side of a hill facing the Germans by Manincourt-sur-Seille. It was about September 15, when suddenly up scampers our battalion commander to quickly make friends with the three of us there. This was his first time: He didn't know us from Adam. Anyway, after that two-minute reconnaissance he bugged out. To return in another minute with Generals Patton, McBride (commanding general, 80th Infantry Division) and Serby (assistant division command—soon to be killed), treating us with the familiarity of well-known members of his battalion. Jeez! How lucky.

Patton joined us at the observation post as the others closed in by him and they discussed the plan for the attack on Delme Ridge, some 20 K to our front. I don't recall his ever asking our names, but he was solicitous, rather friendly and ate the C rations we offered him and his companions. We had no neckties and were poorly shaven. But, no comment from him. That episode led me to accept he was an actor and would play the role of the moment. Yet, he was a lethal one.

Incidentally, that was both the first and last time we saw our battalion commander.

A *photo* is also worth a thousand words. While Patton would not have approved of a photo as a substitute for firsthand visits, another way for battlefield commanders to view the battlefield was through the use of reconnaissance photos. Special units attached to various Third Army commands had the mission of providing photos taken by aircraft. Mike Davis tells about his specialized role in the 17th Photo Tech Squadron:

Our P-38s were rigged with cameras, and we developed their film for commanders on the front lines to use [in planning]. So we followed the front right behind the Third Army across Europe. I worked in the "laboratory."

At first when we over to the Continent, we had a semitractor and trailer. The trailer was all outfitted as a developing lab. But we abandoned that in short order. We found with the rapid movement that we could do better in a smaller truck and set up makeshift darkrooms wherever we stopped.

We used anything that could serve as a darkroom. We'd go into buildings still standing and set up our developing equipment. If we didn't have a building, we'd set up a tent and seal out all the light in order to do our work with black and white prints. We'd be busy every day the aircraft were flying.

Chapter Five

The Germans used airpower effectively, too. Aircraft on the Luftwaffe's forward airfields had to drop back along with the ground troops, as German-controlled territory shrunk. As the bulk of the Third Army continued east, building tremendous momentum as it went, German ground forces were knocked off balance and began reeling backward. Even when the Germans seemed powerless to resist on the ground, the Messerschmitts and Focke-Wulfs could still materialize instantly overhead to strafe and bomb. In his journal, Colonel D. Kenneth Reimers of the 343rd Field Artillery Battalion describes an air attack:

13 August 1944, Alencon: What a night last night turned out to be. It was just after dark when we pulled into position and it may have been a good thing because the darkness may have saved our necks. If the German plane that came over had obtained a better location on us I might have written a different story. Fortunately the plane came over when it was getting quite dark [and] barely possible to distinguish objects for more than a couple of hundred yards away. Also when the pilot flew over everyone was quiet and they were careful not to flash lights or light cigarettes. For a long time after the plane passed over nothing happened. We relaxed and were so tired we didn't bother to dig slit trenches. Those that did didn't dig deeper than about six inches. The ground wasn't any help. Six inches down it became so rocky we couldn't penetrate it. The FDC personnel started digging a hole for themselves but got only a foot down before deciding it wasn't worthwhile. I also said to hell with it and spread my bedroll on top of the ground under a tree. I hadn't been in my sack longer than about 10 minutes when large planes began coming over us. At first we thought they might be our own planes but soon awaked to the fact that these were enemy planes when they began dropping flares.

They first dropped red and green flares which we noticed formed squares. Then in the center of each square appeared a white illuminating flare. I was still feeling pretty brave until one white flare looked as though it would drop right on top of me. Shortly after the white illuminating flares started dropping, the bombs began to fall. That's when I lost my bravery. I'll never forget my telling everyone to lie still and he would be perfectly safe. That was before this attack. I scrambled out of my bedroll and headed for a shelter I had noticed when we first arrived in this location. Down the stairs of the shelter and at its door I found I wasn't the only one present. The entire personnel section had beat me there. Sgt. Sergeant was the nearest to the door and apologetically said,

"Colonel, I'm afraid there isn't any room for you." I yelled back, through the noise of the bombing, "The hell there isn't, move down." I managed to squeeze in behind the door. The bombing lasted about 20 minutes. From then on everything was quiet except for the clanking of picks and shovels. I can't get over how badly my legs shake whenever we get heavy bombing or shelling. I guess it's a nervous reaction. When the bombs stopped dropping, I got out of the shelter and settled down in my bedroll. I didn't try digging, but near me I heard *clank, clank, shovel, shovel.* Suddenly it stopped and I heard, "To hell with it." I looked over and there was Captain Ford, in his bedroll, with only his butt in a very shallow hole about two feet in a diameter. I said, "Ford, that isn't giving you much protection." He replied, "The most important part is protected."

As the Germans reeled in retreat, stragglers surrendering became more common. Reimers continues:

13 August, Cuissai: After selecting battery positions I paid a visit to the 3rd Battalion. The route is up a ridge and through a forest to a forward slope of a hill. I would have enjoyed what could have been a beautiful ride except for the burned-out German vehicles lining the way. From the base of the hill and all the way to the top the road was littered with German vehicles. . . .

While on reconnaissance for our present positions I had an experience I won't soon forget. The battery commanders and I had turned off the highway and into a field of grain about chest high. Off the highway I called back to the BCs to hold up a minute to give me a chance to look around. As I turned back to the front, immediately to my front was a German soldier. He jumped up from the grain field and ran toward me waving his hands in the air. I reached down to grab my carbine lying on the camouflage net over the windshield of my jeep. The carbine was stuck in the net and I couldn't get it out. Fortunately the German wanted to surrender. If he'd had a weapon and wanted to fight, I could have been killed. As soon as I returned to the battalion I called Captain Hott at Service Battery and asked him to get me a .45-caliber handheld machine gun we call a grease gun. From now on I'll carry it around my neck where it will be easy to get at.

We ended our reconnaissance, which ran through several grain fields, and ended up near a French farm. From there I sent the BCs to make a more thorough reconnaissance for their battery positions. Later, when the BCs brought their batteries forward, they captured some more prisoners plus a machine gun that could have been used against us. These prisoners were picked up in a ditch not more than 100 yards from where we had been. The Germans had enough machine gun ammunition to have made a good fight. They could have wiped out all of us. When Captain Hott looked around the same area for his battery his men picked up four more prisoners. One was almost dead from shock and loss of blood. Both of his hands had been blown off. Hott brought him and his comrades to our CP tent where Doc gave first aid to the injured man. He also gave him some plasma before sending him to the regimental aid station.

◆

Daniel Kennedy is a veteran of *both* world wars and the oldest person, at age 101, interviewed for this book. He had served in the 35th Division, in the First Army, and was wounded in combat. "I was in the first [war] and shouldn't have been in the second," he says, "but I volunteered. And Patton didn't gave a damn who you were, as long as you could do the job he threw at you." Kennedy was a lieutenant colonel in Lucky Forward's engineering section. He remembers the relentless drive:

We [in Lucky Forward] were right up front with Patton as we moved across France. We traveled in jeeps followed by trucks with our equipment. We were in pup tents all the way across France. We never got settled anywhere along the way. We didn't move every day, but close. And always advancing. Never gave up ground, but kept moving forward. Always.

Robert Allen, an intelligence officer at Third Army headquarters, describes the advance this way in his book *Lucky Forward:*

There were great deeds of daring, skill, and endurance, breathtaking breakthroughs, and slashing envelopments. Above all, there was vaulting *esprit.* Cockily, Third Army men were confident nothing could stop them; that soon they would "run out of France" and be racing through Germany to final victory.

They had every reason to believe that. In three weeks they had advanced 400 miles, liberated over a third of France, captured over 75,000 PW [prisoners of war], and were roaring full blast on the heels of a shattered enemy.

Rampaging Through France

Colonel Robert Sharon Allen, deputy G-2 officer at Third Army headquarters, was in a good position to witness and understand the full impact of the remarkable dash across France. He writes in his 1947 book, *Lucky Forward*, that "Third Army men were confident nothing could stop them; that soon they would 'run out of France.' In three weeks they had advanced 400 miles, liberated over a third of France, captured over 75,000 PW, and were roaring full blast on the heels of a shattered enemy." A perceptive insider, Allen was also in a position to observe Patton's leadership style. Allen comments, "Throughout his life he completely dominated every unit he commanded. Yet in dominating, he did not domineer. Patton always led men. He did not rule them. This vital distinction explains many things about him. It explains why the troops called him 'Georgie.' Why his men and units always were the most soldierly, the most efficient, the most aggressive, and cockiest. Why he always got so much out of them."

◆

Patton's remarkable charge through France did not go unnoticed throughout Allied commands, and comparisons with other units were inevitable. As Patton planned out a sustained advance, the highest echelons of the British and American air units were planning ways to support it. American General William E. Kepner, commander of Eighth Air Force Fighter Command, was present for one such planning meeting in which one British officer dared to compare Patton's progress with Montgomery's in the presence of his British superiors:

An RAF vice air marshal by the name of Sir Arthur Coningham . . . was down with British forces in the Mediterranean. He got well acquainted with Doolittle and the rest of the American forces down there too, before he came and joined as deputy to Eisenhower. This fellow Coningham was sitting at the table—Jimmy Doolittle next to him and I was on the side of Doolittle. They were discussing how they were doing after the Normandy landing invasion from England. A four-starred air chief marshal was standing in front of a map and talking about our progress. We'd been there maybe 8 to 10 days.

He said we're doing very well. "We're quite on shedule"—that's the way they pronounced 'schedule'—"so we had much to be grateful for. And," he said, "Montgomery is here at the hinge of the gate and he's holding very well. Joe Collins and Simpson and some others in the group of Army are in there and they are all doing consistently well."

When he finished talking, this fellow Air Vice Marshal Coningham, RAF, stood up and said, "Air Marshal, may I have a word please?"

"Of course."

"I'd like to point out one thing" and he did, up on the map. "You say we're on schedule. Here's Patton ahead of schedule. Here's Montgomery who's been here four to five days. I don't know just what the schedule is, but I thought he's supposed to be out here, and here are the scheduled positions of other people. The only one on schedule is Patton, and we'd better be damned thankful for that."

He came back and sat down. Jimmy said, "It took a lot courage for you to say that."

"Yes," he said. "They are now looking for a replacement for me in Whitehall. [Whitehall being the equivalent to the Pentagon in London]. I won't have my job but a few minutes longer, but damned if I'm going to say that Montgomery is on schedule when he's not."

The Third Army seemed unstoppable—as though it would roll right up to Hitler's doorstep.

Chapter 6

Stalled at the Moselle

Late August–October 1944

Napoleon, one of Patton's favorite historical figures, is credited with the military maxim, "An army marches on its stomach." But armored divisions roll on gasoline—and Patton suddenly found himself with none in late August 1944.

The Third Army shuddered to a halt at the Moselle River between Nancy and Metz—100 miles past Paris and about that same distance to the German border. The remarkable drive ended when it was decided the gasoline would go instead to Montgomery to fuel Operation Market Garden in Holland.

"At the present time our chief difficulty is not the Germans, but gasoline," Patton groused. "If they would give me enough gas, I could go all the way to Berlin!"

As tanks ran low and one of his corps commanders came to protest the obvious, Patton directed him to keep moving forward "until the tanks stop, and then get out and walk."

Patton's units had been consuming an average of 350,000 gallons of gasoline a day. On August 28, Patton's allocation fell 100,000 gallons short. On August 31, it was reduced to a trickle. Major Stephen Conland served in the 5th Quartermaster Battalion, which was responsible for distribution of gasoline. He explains:

> The Third Army was halted along the Moselle River. They had run out of gasoline. The advanced elements got into Metz and then had to withdraw. The result was that a long stalemate started. Gas rationing was inaugurated. All units were severely cut.

Chapter Six

Patton's whole concept was a battle of motion. And when he couldn't move because we couldn't get supplies up fast enough, he was in tough shape.

We were a service battalion with 13 companies. We were with Patton, I think, from [this time] to the end of the war. We were responsible for the pipeline and for the railhead set up. We brought in the railroad cars and decanted them into five-gallon cans and distributed them to the troops.

[Before the gas supply was cut off] tank cars were shipped in and the 100-gallon per minute dispensers were used to dispense the gas into five-gallon cans. Domgermaine did a very large operation. The conditions there had been ideal. A ramp at freight-car-door height 350 yards long and 35 yards wide, a double track on both sides. Output was excellent, hitting a peak of 250,000 gallons in a day.

There wasn't much danger from air attack on us, because they couldn't find the gasoline dumps. We were so far back. Usually they were really trying to find ordnance dumps. So that wasn't the cause of the shortage.

All I know is that we handled the gasoline, and decanted it as fast as it came in. Endless job. If it came in, it came in. In later September and October, it didn't. And nothing could be done.

Of course, Patton was not one who readily accepted that "nothing could be done." He immediately pleaded his case with his superiors. Bradley writes in *A Soldier's Story*:

George joined me one day in a plea to Ike that he might retain his allotment of tonnage and thus rush on to the German frontier.

"If you don't cut us back we can make it on what we're getting," he said. "I'll stake my reputation on it."

"Careful, George," Ike quipped, "that reputation of yours hasn't been worth very much."

Patton hitched up his belt and smiled. "It's pretty good now," he said.

And if one could judge by the headlines, we agreed that perhaps it was.

But it didn't change allotments.

Without gas, Patton's troops were relegated to a large-scale defensive role for the first time during World War II. One of Patton's chief obsessions was to maintain the momentum of an advance. He preached that stopping or hesitating allowed the enemy to regroup and stabilize his lines. A delay invited counterattack in the form of infantry assaults, artillery barrages, and aerial bombing and strafing, which is precisely what happened at many points along the front at the Moselle River. American casualties were inevitable. W. King Pound of the 4th Armored Division remembers his first Purple Heart of the war:

We were near Metz, in an orchard, and bivouacked at the end of the day. It was still daylight. I had a reputation for always being so ready to hop up on the tank to fire the .30-caliber. My sergeant would say, "If you fire it, you're going to clean the goddamn gun." I usually chose to fire it.

In the orchard that evening, I was taking "a bath in my helmet." Suddenly, we heard a Messerschmitt and it passed low over, strafing as it went. I hopped up on the turret, naked as a jaybird, and started firing. I swiveled the gun around as it flashed by.

Of course, it was gone before you could get the first damn shot off, so I didn't hit a thing. Just before I fired, I was jarred by something on my leg. Didn't knock me down, but I had caught a ricochet in the side of the leg. It hit the bony part of my [shin]. The bone stopped it, because it was mostly spent after ricocheting. It didn't seem to bother me. I just put a bandage on it. And I didn't worry about it.

A couple days later it got infected. I was taken back to Cherbourg and was there for three months. I was offered a job back in the field hospital in Cherbourg by a doctor who had known my father—in fact, he had been taught by my father, who was also a surgeon back in the States. We became good friends, and he was in a position to offer me a place there. But I wanted to get back to the 4th. Strong allegiance to the guys.

Pound would return to the 4th Armored Division on December 12, just before the Battle of the Bulge.

◆

Walter Unrath's half-track battalion came to a halt outside Metz, an old citadel on the Moselle. He describes how the Germans took advantage of an opportunity to zero in on them with a devastating weapon.

German artillery was trying to hit the XX Corps headquarters, located about 15 miles to our rear. To accomplish this, the Germans in Metz had a huge naval cannon (believed to be a 280-mm cannon), which fired a projectile containing over 600 pounds of TNT. The gun was on rails and would be moved out electrically from an underground tunnel, fired and then retracted. When the shell, and several had already passed overhead in our area, rushed by it would sound like a freight train in the sky—a tremendous whooshing sound. At any rate, I commenced to dig my foxhole and about 1:30 a.m. I crawled into my sleeping bag in the foxhole to get some needed rest.

[I was suddenly awakened when] I thought my foxhole was on fire, and I was desperate as I couldn't get out. I struggled and struggled to no avail. Suddenly, I found myself on my hands and knees with that terrible odor of burning gunpowder in my nostrils. I knew from experience that whatever hit us was extremely close. I rose to call my platoon sergeant and get a report on the damage—but no sound came forth. Instead, I could taste the saltiness of blood and felt its warmth caressing my face and my neck. I knew I had been hit. My hand moved to my face to check for damages, but didn't have the courage to touch my face as fear spread that my face had been ripped off. I bent over so I would not choke on my blood. By this time, the platoon sergeant appeared with a blackout flashlight. By his face, I could tell he was deeply concerned. The front of my uniform and my trousers were soaked in blood pouring from my mouth, nose and ears. My first question was the condition of my face, to which he informed me that it was okay. In my headquarters CP half-track, with lights on, they couldn't find any wound on my head, neck or face. I reached up with my right arm to check my head and couldn't move my arm—shrapnel had hit my right shoulder. I later learned that the edge of the crater was a mere 20 feet from the edge of my foxhole—a crater resulting from 600 pounds of TNT exploding.

My jeep driver took me on the road to a clearing station, which served as an interim medical base before getting to the field hospital. About four minutes from my CP, a shell hit the road in front of the jeep, turning the jeep over in a ditch. The driver rolled clear and I was thrown to the side of the road. My driver, who had been with me since the States, was totally beside himself. Instead of taking care of his wounded lieutenant, he hurt him further. Actually, other than my wounded shoulder and some bruises I was uninjured.

The clearing station was a delight as the doctor on duty, after determining that I wasn't still bleeding and my wound was not too serious, gave me a shot of whiskey, to my joy. (Apparently this was a treatment for all wounds, other than to the stomach.) The doctor, after learning what happened to me, stated that I was unbelievably lucky, in that 600 pounds of TNT, so close, should have reduced my entire body, bones, and vessels to the consistency of a jelly, in that the close explosion would have contracted, expanded and repeated the process, destroying me totally.

Stalled at the Moselle

The railway gun also seemed to be zeroing in on Third Army head-quarters. Major Frank Pajerski, air liaison in Lucky Forward G-2 section, says:

Near Nancy, the Germans were hitting us with a railroad gun. During the day, they'd hide it in a railroad tunnel, which there were plenty of. Then they'd take it out at night, take an hour to set up, and they could hit us about 14 times before they'd have to dismantle it and get it back in the tunnel before daylight, because that's when our Air Force would be up trying to find it.

We didn't believe it, but artillery and ordnance said the Germans were trying to hit Third Army headquarters. At this point, Patton's headquarters was a big house in the middle of a town. And ordnance and artillery had plotted every shot, and every one was in direct alignment. But every one was either over or short.

Well, one night, a shell went just over his headquarters and hit the house across the street. General Patton came in the next day and said, "Take care of that thing!"

Lieutenant Colonel Daniel Kennedy of Lucky Forward's engineering section took responsibility for locating the railway gun so it could be destroyed, and he finishes the story:

My boss, the Third Army engineer, came back from a briefing and said that this was the second night the Germans had bombarded the area where General Patton's house was—and that General Patton was awfully mad.

He asked, "What the hell can we do?"

I said, "That's what I was sent here to do." I went to work. The Signal Corps was intercepting German figures. But each army used a different set of mathematics for coordinates of the earth. I understood the German system and could calculate the location of the gun, based on the figures the Signal Corps was intercepting.

Once its location was known, the artillery and the Air Force bombardment silenced the railway gun.

After the railway gun was silenced, Kennedy received a Bronze Star personally from Patton. Patton solely credited Kennedy, who says in a personal interview:

When General Patton came back from the next meeting, I opened the door for him at the exit. I turned and faced him.

He said, "Kennedy, you did a good job."

And he pinned a Bronze Star on me. The Bronze Star, in itself, isn't a very high medal, but the fact he put it on me made it so.

Chapter Six

◆

The standstill gave Patton more opportunities for surprise visits all along the Third Army's front. Emil J. Schmidt, who rose from private to major by war's end, became company commander of the 39th Signal Company, 26th Infantry Division. Schmidt tells how Patton turned up unexpectedly and became a familiar visitor while his unit was stationary:

We were in a small town just to the south of Metz. The signal company always stayed close to division headquarters because we gave them 24-hour service for radio, wire, and code equipment. So Patton was often in the area and one day he visited and wanted something to eat. Fortunately, I had a helluva good mess sergeant. He'd been a cook on a riverboat on the Mississippi River and under his guidance we had some very good food. Somebody had told him that the signal company had hot meals. He came into the area and asked someone if we had C rations or K rations. He was told we had our regular mess hall going. So he came into the mess tent and said something to the first guy he came to. I don't know what he told the guy, but he scared the living daylights out of him.

The first sergeant and I were at what we called the orderly room at this time. Who appeared in the doorway but General Patton. Not his aide, but Patton himself. As I remember it, he had a few curse words and asked, "Is there anybody around the goddamn place?" That was Patton. A lot of that was showmanship on his part. When you talk to him, he wasn't that swearing, cursing guy that he was talking to the fellas or talking to you in the field. GIs were known for swearing, so he'd impress the boys and fire them up. That's what I think.

He stayed and had dinner with us. We had appropriated French dinnerware that had been in a house, and after he got his belly full, he got out by the doorway, he was leaving, and he turned to me and said, "goddammit, Captain, be sure that those dishes get back to wherever the hell your men got 'em from!"

When Patton got going, there was never anytime to set up a mess tent. Then we ate off the backs of trucks. But near Metz, we stayed put for a while.

Patton would travel in an L-5, a small observation plane a lot like a Piper Cub. He would land outside a division area, like by an orchard. Ordnance guys would have his jeep all ready for him—a jeep all set up with the flags with stars and that bar he could stand and hold on to. He'd get out of the plane and get right into the jeep and tour the area with a couple MPs in front of him and a couple MPs in back of him. He'd come riding into town, standing up and holding on to that bar. People would say, "Jeez, wait a minute. Two hours ago he was in Sariunion. How the hell did he get up here in Metz?" Then we figured out he was flying around in a plane. We in the Signal Corps could keep pretty good track of where the rascal was. Sometimes people would think, *If he's just starting out now, he won't be here until tomorrow morning.* But the rascal might show up 45 minutes, an hour later, because the rascal flew!

Soon we learned to start passing the word between units, "Watch it at your outfit. He might be coming up there." That was common practice to alert another unit that the general was coming. It was unofficial, of course, and frowned upon. That could alert somebody and maybe a sniper could be waiting for him. But you get a bunch of GIs together and they're going to work some system out! Talk about imagination. If they spent as much time doing the work they were supposed to do instead of working, well—

A second time Patton came up to eat with us. This time, I had been tipped off he was coming. As company commander, I came right up to him. The men were standing in line in the rain and I told him he could come up to the front of the line. I did that because I thought, *He's a general. He would want to head up the line, eat, and get out of there.* Boy, did he light into me.

"Hey, we eat after the men eat!" Patton yelled. He was loud about it. He did it for the GIs, you know. He did it to impress them that he was a regular GI. He was a great showman. And the GIs did like him!

He then proceeded to stick his nose into every pot in the field kitchen. I don't think there was a pot he didn't stick his nose in and snoop into. I don't know if he could tell what he was looking at, but it sure made a big impression. Again, it showed the GIs he was a regular GI and he was looking out for the food they were getting. Quite a showman. A lot of what he did was just showman tactics. Not that he wasn't a nervy bugger—he was. He didn't find anything to comment on with the food in the pots, so it must have been okay for him. And he wasn't one to hold anything back. If he had something on his mind, you knew about it shortly.

As always, we waited until after the enlisted men had their food before getting into the chow line. And by golly, he did the same damn thing. He got his food and, with his two aides, he sat down with the rest of us officers. We were so damn scared, we didn't talk very much. It was tough to eat when you're that nervous. You didn't need [a laxative] after you ate either! Then again, maybe it was the coffee that did it.

Patton emerges from a mess tent nibbling on a carrot. On visits to unit mess halls, he went out of his way to make his presence known, "to show the GIs he was a regular GI and he was looking out for the food they were getting," according to Emil Schmidt of the 39th Signal Company. **Patton Museum**

Lieutenant Colonel Leslie H. Cross, commander of the 43rd Reconnaissance Squadron, also had a personal visit from Patton while stalled at the west bank of the Moselle. Cross remembers anxiety and excitement:

It was in September 1944 that the 43rd Reconnaissance Squadron moved to a Nazi youth camp in Bettembourg, Luxembourg. We had been given a mission of occupying a 25-mile front along the Moselle River. The reconnaissance troops were out in front manning observation posts not far from the river in the daytime and then moving to listening posts at nightfall. The squadron headquarters was some 10 to 12 miles from the river in approximately the center of the sector.

I was notified that General Patton, Third Army commander, accompanied by the group commander, Colonel James Polk, was on his way to visit the squadron headquarters. They arrived in the middle of a pleasant morning so far as the weather was concerned. The leading jeep drove up and one got the impression of chrome trimmings, flags flying, and emblems blazing. Upon coming to a rather abrupt halt, two majors, looking like ex-pugilists, leaped from the jeep with their Tommy guns at the ready and ran to a corner of the building that offered cover and observation of the road leading to the camp.

A tall big man, easily recognizable as General Patton, got out of the jeep rather briskly. I advanced promptly to report to him. "Colonel Cross commanding the 43rd Reconnaissance Squadron reports to the Army commander."

He returned my salute, extended his hand and said something like, "Not a bad place you have here." He wore a well-tailored uniform with a pearl handled pistol. I hadn't realized how tall he was, standing a full head and shoulders over me. After some small talk about parking jeeps, he said, "I'd like to see your situation map."

I led the way and after entering the building and upon opening the door to the operations office, I called attention loud enough to make the windows rattle. He seemed pleased, or at least, not displeased. After he was seated at a table and had the situation map brought to him, I thought that he might have trouble seeing, since the table was away from and facing the window.

So I said, "Sir, maybe you'd like to move over so that you can see better."

But he said, "I can see well enough."

After studying the map for a while, he pointed to the location of the squadron headquarters on the map and said, "You're pretty far back from the river."

I explained that we had a very broad front for a force of our size and that one had to stay well back in order to defend the sector properly by allowing sufficient maneuver room.

After a short tense-filled delay, "Believe you're right, believe you're right."

I began to feel the tension in the room as my officers and soldiers waited to see whether they or I would catch hell for something or other or come through the meeting unscathed. All the while General Patton was studying the map. I felt my mouth go dry and I wished we could get on with it.

Finally he spoke again: "I know where every German division is on my front but one. Do you think it could be over there?" he asked, pointing to a wooded area across the Moselle River. What could I say? The tension in the room rose like a rocket. My officers and soldiers wondered what I would say or do. I was really on the spot. The thought that raced through my mind was a lieutenant colonel in my position wasn't being paid to answer that type of question. I looked at the map, studied it and thought of the actions we had been through in the past few weeks.

Chapter Six

The place was quiet as a morgue when I said firmly, "No sir, I don't think it is there."

He immediately asked, "Why not?"

I thought, *Oh hell, I might as well tell him exactly what I think and let him make the most of it.* With the tension still running high, I replied, "Sir, the road net does not appear sufficiently extensive to facilitate supporting a division there, and further, of the numerous prisoners we have captured in the past few weeks, all have been from units previously identified."

"I don't believe it is there either!" he said as he started to get up. With that tension was relieved, almost audibly. He stood up to his full six feet plus, looked at everyone in the room, pointed to another map on the wall and said, "I was here in 1918 and if you are going to be attacked, they will come right down that valley (pointing again) and I expect you to whip 'em!"

There are few wartime "grip-and-grin" photos with Patton. Lieutenant Colonel Leslie Cross tells how he found himself in one: "The visit was over and as we moved outside, the chaplain approached and asked General Patton if he (the chaplain) could take his picture with me. 'Happy to do it,' the general said, straightening up to his full height and extending his hand to indicate the picture should be taken with us shaking hands. During the interval the jeeps were being lined up, and he mounted and moved out with everyone saluting and feeling very relieved as he departed." **Patton Museum**

◆

A break in the action gave the replacement depots a chance to catch up with the line units and refill the ranks of units suffering attrition. Two stories of replacements follow.

Al Elliott joined the 5th Infantry Division at Metz. As a private first class, he was put in a corporal's billet as a gunner on an 81-mm mortar. He tells of his baptism by fire soon after arrival:

Stalled at the Moselle

I was a replacement in H Company, going where I was told to go and doing what I was told to do. I was trained as a gunner for an 81-millimeter mortar in a heavy weapons company. I was with Patton in the Third Army at Metz and stayed with him all the way after that.

At age 24, I was one of the older guys in the unit, but I remember a man from Oklahoma 12 years older than me; he was a replacement too. Most of these guys came from Tennessee and Kentucky, and I was from New England. So I was different. When I first came in as a replacement, we stayed in one spot just outside Paris for about 15 days. During those couple weeks, it was clear what everyone thought, *Hey, if you had no experience in combat, you know nothing.* That didn't wear off until we moved out—and we were immediately ambushed.

We were going down a dirt road by a wall made of stones and were just starting up a rise into this meadow, this open field. First thing I know, I hear a machine gun open up. I'm in the sixth squad, way in the back, carrying ammunition. We see all these guys going down ahead of me and I got down too. Everybody was getting down, but not all of them made it. Some were being shot off their feet.

We were pinned down for four hours. This German machine gunner would fire every time one of us would move. We were digging as much as we could to get down below his direct line of fire. Our own artillery fired some smoke on us with the thought it would help us get out. We couldn't see the machine gunner anymore, but somehow the gunner seemed to be able to still see us. The smoke didn't come down low enough, plus the machine gunner had his gun trained on us, in a preset field of fire. Any glimpse of something moving and he'd fire. Even sticking your hand up caused him to fire.

Finally, someone got up behind the machine gun and tossed a grenade. Then we were able to move again. We lost quite a few men—hard to say how many. There were five or six men in a mortar squad, and the machine gunners and riflemen were up ahead of us. After that, I moved up to a number one gunner on a mortar.

From then on, I was recognized as an experienced combat man—just after that one ambush.

Another replacement who joined Patton in the vicinity of Metz was Angelo Peter Rosato, who found himself in Tank Company B, 37th Medium Tank Battalion of the 4th Armored Division. Assigned as an assistant tank driver and bow gunner, he tells about his self-described "introduction to hell" in a personal interview:

It was my first day in combat and it had never occurred to me before that day we were actually out to kill one another. A repulsive thought, to say the least. I thought, *Hey, I'm a nice guy. Why are they trying to kill me?*

Prior to nightfall, I was assigned to one of the outposts on a plateau. Because of the lay of the land, it wasn't difficult to see what would come over the horizon. We set up the post, me with one other man, well forward of our tanks.

Then, just before dawn, the creeping fire started—German artillery advancing toward us. Like spraying a garden hose immediately in front of you and sending the stream farther out.

We guards waited too long before pulling out and running for cover. By the time we moved, we had to run for our lives back toward our tanks and the only option was to dive under them.

Explosions were happening all around us. The concussion of the shells was so massive. The forces of the concussion blasting against my body caused me to feel nauseous and like I had been pummeled in the stomach. My hearing wasn't affected because we wore a crash helmet—a thick leather football helmet converted to accommodate headphones, and the standard steel helmet fit over the crash helmet. These ungodly headphones were against our ears though, and I say ungodly because instead of being nice soft rubber, they were hard plastic disks, and in the course of a day it was like having a telephone pressed hard against your ear for hours and hours. But I think that might have actually protected my eardrums from injury that day.

All we could do was stay put. Tanks are not moved at times like that since there's no way of knowing where the next incoming fire would strike. As it turned out, there were no hits on our tanks, but the plateau was scarred all around by the time the shells stopped. As I crawled out, I felt like I had been used as a punching bag.

Once the artillery barrage was over, dawn came and then full daylight. We mounted up and started moving toward our targets—some distant German tanks. We came out shooting. The enemy tanks had to be at least two to three miles away, because our shells couldn't penetrate their armor. I was able to see that as we were firing toward the other tanks. We made hits. We could actually see the rounds strike. I don't know if they were red-hot or what, but we could see them glancing off and flying to the side or up, but not penetrating. I knew what being hit that way felt like inside the tank. Noise is not a word that can describe it. You are jarred to the core.

Anyway, we're proceeding forward into battle with these German tanks. There was a big tree real close to us. The Germans sent a high explosive round, what we called an H.E. round. Our lieutenant was riding with his head out of the commander's hatch of the turret, which was normal, like he was supposed to. You didn't ride all buttoned up—couldn't, because that was a sure way to get into a trap. And son of a gun, if a round didn't hit a branch of that lone tree about 20 feet from us. The tree triggered the round, because on the nose of the H.E. round, about the diameter of a dime, perfectly flat nose, and the way it looked to me was a tin foil-like material on that nose covering the triggering mechanism. Now, with the rate of speed the round is traveling, the nose could hit a twig and trigger the round to explode in midair. I felt the tremendous concussion and the shrapnel from the shell just showered the area from overhead. From my position, I couldn't hear the explosion of the shell. There was so much noise, we were firing, and the engine was roaring, and you aren't able to sort out all the sounds.

I didn't see him when he actually slumped down, but I turned around to see the blood. We were all splattered and the smell was sickening. It was the weirdest feeling I ever had, me being naïve and new to combat. The blood was spraying out of his head. He had been struck through the bridge of his nose by shrapnel.

There's not a heck of a lot of room in a tank, but he had gone down into a kneeling position with his head slumped down. I knew nothing about biology at that time, and I was flabbergasted by the pumping action of the blood, which was splashing all over. My reaction was simple and immediate: *My God, Lieutenant Lockwood is dead.* Who would ever think our lieutenant would get it this way. He was new, too—a replacement like me and facing battle for the first time that day, too.

The tanks were on line moving forward. We stopped, and the rest continued. We had no choice but to stop because the lieutenant's body was blocking the gunner. He couldn't shoot because the lieutenant had the gunner pinned to his seat. Plus, we had no "eyes," because the lieutenant had been our eyes.

As the line moved forward, we all jumped out of our respective hatches to pull the lieutenant out to release the gunner. On the turret top, there was a large, round hatch that both the tank commander and the gunner would exit the tank. To the left of that, there's a smaller hatch that the cannoneer—the guy who operated the radio and loaded the gun and used the antiaircraft gun—got out of. Down on the bow end of the tank, we had a hatch on each side. We knew we had to get back in action or die there stalled. We reached down into the large, round hatch and tried to get the lieutenant out, which wasn't easy. I remember that we struggled with it. While we grabbed his shoulders, the cannoneer went back down his hatch and, since the gun was level, could go beneath the gun breach and helped push up. We called the medics forward in a peep. They were close by and came immediately to take the body away—it's torn me up all these years that this had to happen.

We saw the tank was not damaged at all. We quickly reorganized. The driver took over Lieutenant Lockwood's tank commander position, and I took over driving.

We went on with the rest. As darkness was falling, we found ourselves in a swamp that wasn't on the map, too small to be on the map. Maps usually showed us tankers a swampy area, especially when it was many, many acres. But every now and then, like on the farm where I grew up, there would be a nice meadow that would turn out to be muck in a low area, even though it looked like the rest of the ground. We drove the tank into one of those and couldn't get out. We were stuck in the swamp.

Every tank had one-inch steel cables with an eye at each end that would fit over the hooks on another tank. But there was no other tank close by to pull us out. Something else we did [on the farm] when we got stuck was to build what we called a "corduroy road," by laying down brush in the path of the vehicle. Once you got a grip, it's amazing how much weight a bed of brush could hold. I knew that from experience on the farm, where our meadow was soft in one place and the trucks would get stuck. While the truck was still moving slowly, my brothers and I learned to grab a hay tumble and throw that down in front of the driven wheels to keep us buoyant and not sink into the mud. Plus the hay gave a fibrous grip.

But this day, just as we started to try that, we were hit. This meadow was surrounded by trees and rocks, typical rough farm countryside, so we were completely taken by surprise and didn't see the enemy tank approaching. It blasted us from a distance and knocked the tank out.

An excerpt from Rosato's memoir finishes the episode.

The driver and one other crewman were to torch their own disabled vehicle if it had not [been destroyed]. I placed two phosphorous grenades on strategic points in the drive train; the other crewman did the same in the turret area. We had already removed arms and food and whatever else could be used by the remaining tanks that were already in motion. Thompson submachine gun in hand, we ran as fast as was humanly possible to get away from the furiously burning hulk and to catch up to [our] departing tanks. We leaped upon a small narrow ledge of sheet metal that extended over the rear area of each track and used it as a toe pivot so we could fall on our chests on top of the engine compartment. We were safely aboard.

We traveled cross-country along a rib of high ground in search of a large gravel pit shown on the map where we hoped to find safety for the night. We had not traveled very far when we spotted what appeared to be a small troop movement off to our right. The order was given to swing all guns to the right, prepare for battle, but fire only if fired upon. We "hitchhikers" dismounted in a hurry to avoid the projections of the revolving turret as all tanks came to a halt.

The moments seemed endless and nerve wracking. The troop movement seemed erratic. As they came closer, we suddenly realized that it was a column of American infantry, most wounded, some seriously and a few being carried. These men, bloody and exhausted, had been part of the battalion that had been in the valley town now in flames. We put all of them on the five tanks. There wasn't room left for even a mouse.

Those of us who had been riding on the tanks were now on foot running alongside. The light of the fires well behind us was dimming and it became more difficult to keep up with the tanks. The pace was pushing us to the limits of our endurance.

At long last, after perhaps four or five miles, we reached the gravel pit in spite of the darkness. We entered it from a riverside road. It was perfect. Two sides were close to 100 feet high with the second side tapering down abruptly to a comfortable 20 feet or so near the end. The third side, running from the end of the second, exposed a large, well-tended civilian cemetery for an affluent area, judging from the size of the stones. We helped all the wounded men off the tanks and placed them within the shelter of the greatest clusters of cemetery monuments where they would be reasonably protected from possible shelling.

We spent three days and two additional nights in the gravel pit. We were fortunate in that our enemy was too busy elsewhere to bother flushing us out. We were surrounded, nonetheless, and we were too deep into enemy territory to make a break along the river road. It was here that some of my favorite phrases originated. Since it was not unusual for us, as a spearhead outfit, to be inside of enemy territory and needing to boost faith in our own abilities, our expression was, "The poor bastards, they have us surrounded again." The second one was in response to a comment about how courageous we were. "The definition of courage is the ability to be scared shitless and not show it!"

We had food and water aboard the tanks and were fairly well stocked with arms for the tank guns and hand-held weapons, but were seriously in need of medical supplies. Some of the wounded were in dire need of more care than we could give them. So, very early on the morning of the third day, the captain sent out a volunteer scout to get a close look at an American six-by [2-1/2-ton truck] that seemed undamaged from about three-quarters of a mile away. As near as we could tell with the aid of binoculars, there was a small bullet hole near the top of the radiator and an angular hole through the top of the hood. In view of the worsening condition of the wounded, we had to get to that truck.

The company commander called us all together and asked for six volunteers to ride two per tank on the outside alongside the turret of the three tanks to be used to retrieve the truck. We sneaked out of the pit and turned right along the river road, the meadow to our right with its hump edge to hide us. At the last possible moment, the tanks hurtled the hump edge of the meadow and we raced for the truck very close by. One tank swung in front of the truck, one tank went up to stand guard at the higher ground, while Cockroach and I dropped of at the edge of a wooded area where we covered against attack from within. We held our Thompsons at the ready. The hitch was made, both men leaped into the truck. We guards remounted and we were on our way. The truck was guided over a gradual area of the hump while our tank covered the rear. We dropped over a higher hump of meadow edge and slapped down on the road none too soon, because a few rounds went over our heads.

Gravel flew as we powered hard left into the pit entry. Our tank took a position just below the cemetery with the guns pointing to the high lips of the gravel pit. The other two also took up strategic positions. We six volunteers dismounted rather hurriedly. Everyone in the pit was primed for the worst. But nothing happened.

We assumed that the front was thinning out and hoped that it may have passed us by, but in any case, we could not wait. We made a crude repair on the truck radiator and made sure water was available for cooling if needed.

We loaded the more needy wounded in the truck. They were crowded and uncomfortable. The rest were on the outside of our tanks. I think we all prayed a little as we left the pit. We swung left onto the river road and entered the shelter of the descending countryside, somewhat forested. The area was not practical battleground for tanks, and we hoped our enemy felt the same. A few miles downgrade, we discovered a good bridge to our right, which took us along a secluded road, over a small mountain— and to freedom.

Stalled at the Moselle

We were back on our side of the fence. Rain had begun to fall, and we were getting wet. Immediate contact was made with a medical unit, and it wasn't long before those suffering sick were on their way to a hospital and proper care. The rest of us sought shelter and rest in what was left of a few buildings that had been shelled a few days previous.

As the saying goes, I had been bloodied. I saw no end in sight, but yet I felt an overpowering need to see the war through to the end or as far the Lord would allow me.

Private First Class Maury Laws was not a replacement, but his 26th Infantry Division caught up with Patton later, near Nancy. Laws was a guitar player selected for the division's band, but who chose instead to stay with his company and go to the combat area. After arriving on the Continent on September 1, 1944, some of the musicians became MPs. Other musicians, Laws among them, were assigned the grisly duty of Graves Registration—picking up the dead on the battlefield. (After the Battle of the Bulge, he would become a reconnaissance scout.) He remembers arriving in the combat area:

Patton's units had bogged down because they cut off his gas supply. He stopped his dash, then we caught up and went into the lines. They had shipped our instruments overseas in big crates, all greased up so they wouldn't rust. We did not see those instruments again until much later. As we made our way across France, all was pretty quiet.

Then I started seeing a lot of dead people, so I knew we were getting close to the action. Strange things started happening. You'd see some tough 38-year-old guy who has a wife and kids back home. And he gets hit and yells, "Mama." He skips all the way back to when he was 10 years old. I saw that happen.

I knew we were attached to Third Army. It didn't matter. Patton was no big god. He was known as a son of a bitch.

My job at first was to pick up the dead. It started out that we crawled out at night to throw lime on dead Germans that started to smell bad. It was demoralizing to the guys in the holes. The Germans very well may have known we were out there doing that, but we sort of left each other alone, because they knew what we were doing.

Then I was thrown into this detail that went out in an open bed truck with a trailer on the back. We'd throw the bodies on the back. We picked up both Americans and Germans, but the priority was for the Americans. It was demoralizing for the troops to see them, so they needed to be picked up.

Chapter Six

I think the people back home envisioned that these people had been killed with a neat bullet hole to the forehead. It wasn't like that. I saw unbelievable things.

We were near Nancy, slogging along, and my old company—I Company—took a hell of a wipeout one day that almost obliterated them. They had sent the scouts out, but the scouts hadn't seen anything in the woods. So the company moved out into the woods, and the Germans were waiting. In the meantime the Germans had moved in tanks and just mowed them all down. I had to go pick them up. These were buddies. All the guys I had come to know so well in training. A great percentage of my old I Company lay there dead. It was very hard. I knew them all.

At first you feel lucky—you weren't one of them laying there. You feel like you survived for some fluke—because I happened to play the guitar and was put on Graves Registration. But then the guilt comes.

It was then that I realized you don't know when it will be you. You realize the way luck works. You can't have luck all the time. You know it has to run out sometime. They put you there and you tried to stay alive.

One day we were sent to get two wounded. The 88s had zeroed in on them and were still zeroed in on their position. Usually our job was to get the dead, but not always. Not this day. And this day my luck almost ran out.

It was raining as always, and these two were lying in the mud, delirious. I knew them. I went to say *Joe*, but it came out *Jo-Jo*, because I was so nervous.

You could hear the 88 shells coming in. You'd hear the shriek and then you'd dive for the ground, and then *bam*, the explosion would send shrapnel flying all around. We got them out, got 'em on the truck, going down the hill and to the aid station. The one I was with, I heard later, died shortly after. I recall that, as my 21st birthday.

Somewhere during that time, I tripped a wire, a booby trap. I remember feeling it on my ankle and I dove to the ground. My nose rubbed up against the nose of a dead German as I went down. He was laying on his stomach, head turned on a cheek so he faced me. The German had glasses on his face, but the glasses were askew and broken. He must have been there for two or three days at that time.

I looked back toward my foot and realized I had broken the wire. I was terrified as I tripped the wire. Coming face to face with a dead German was nothing so traumatic. I had been on graves detail for some time by then. We saw dead Germans all the time.

Stalled at the Moselle

But it does bring things to focus when you fall to the ground expecting to hear an explosion. Those things went off about waist-high and just tore you apart. But the "Bouncing Betty" didn't go off. *It didn't go off!* It was supposed to go up waist high and ruin you. Just lucky, so lucky. A moment followed when I just lay there, searching myself and becoming aware gradually that I was all right and that my stomach was still there, legs still there, and so on. You feel it much more powerfully than the words can tell it.

Maury Laws, 26th Infantry Division, carries an M-1 during training in the States. He was shipped overseas in September 1944 and was sent directly to the front at the Moselle River near Nancy: "I started seeing a lot of dead people, so I knew we were getting close to the action. Strange things started happening. You'd see some tough 38-year-old guy who has a wife and kids back home. And he gets hit and yells, 'Mama.' He skips all the way back to when he was 10 years old."

While the Third Army was stalled at the Moselle, Laws encountered a surprise visitor one morning. Although he explains it with offhanded casualness, there could have been dire consequences had Laws not been there to offer directions.

We were in the woods around Nancy, the Moncourt Woods, a couple hundred yards from the front. So close that we could hear the creaking of the wagons that they must have used to bring food up to the front lines and we could smell the sauerkraut. We were eating K rations cold. But here they were eating vats of sauerkraut. The line hadn't moved, and we stayed there for two or three weeks.

It was cloudy and had been raining. I happened to be alone that morning, separated from my squad, slogging along carrying a carbine, and this jeep comes careening down the path. There was a driver and a passenger. The passenger stood up, on the seat of that jeep. And I saw the stars—the damn stars on the helmet. He didn't say who he was, but I knew who he was. It was General Patton.

He just said, "Where are we, soldier?" It was a high voice. He had freckles, looked ruddy. And he was lost.

I answered, "We're in the Moncourt Woods." That's about all I knew.

"Where are the Germans?"

"They're right back there, sir." By then I remembered to add "sir" as I pointed in the direction of the German patrol I knew was coming.

"How far?"

"I dunno. Maybe a couple hundred yards."

He said "thank you" at the same time he was pointing a direction for his driver—opposite of the direction they were going, because they had been headed right for the patrol! They wheeled around and took off.

◆

An unexpected meeting with Patton also came for an American bomber crew that plummeted out of the sky over Metz. At dawn on September 10, 1944, the crew of a B-17 christened *Homesick Angel* had taken off on their 11th mission. They were airmen of the U.S. Eighth Air Force's 92nd Bomb Group, based at Podington, England. When they had hurtled down the runway that morning, crew members could not have conceived in their wildest dreams that this would be a one-way flight—culminating in an impromptu decoration ceremony with Patton himself presiding.

Staff Sergeant Jack Spratt, the ship's ball-turret gunner, recalls:

We were over no man's land in France. Our B-17 had been losing precious altitude ever since flak hit us over Germany. The pilot, "Spence" Spencer, had been nursing *Homesick Angel* along, but we knew we could go no further. If we were going to bail out, we had to do it now. We'd dropped to only about 600 feet when I jumped out. John [Houk—radio man] was right after me.

They had told us to look back at the airplane and count ten and pull the rip cord. But I just cleared the tail and pulled the cord. The little pilot chute came out on a tether cord [and was supposed] to pull out the full chest chute. The pilot chute came, but the rest didn't come out.

We could hear ground fire on the way down. I found out later that either the gunfire from the ground or flak from the 88-millimeter guns . . . went through the chute. A chute is fanfolded and accordion pleated, so that it easily pulls out and unfurls. The shrapnel or projectile evidently went through the chute and sealed the folds of silk together.

When I realized the rest wouldn't come out on its own, I started pulling it out by hand. Only parts of it were out of the pack and open. It never fully blossomed.

During those scant seconds, the subconscious seemed to come forward and you thought of things you had done and shouldn't have done during your life. Being a Christian, I started to pray, and then *BOOM*, I hit a 75-foot tree. Ever since then, I call it "the life tree."

I thought I had passed everybody going down, but that might have been my own imagination. Jumping out of the door and pulling the chute—the flashback stayed with me for years.

Radio operator John Houk had followed Jack Spratt out the waist door of *Homesick Angel*. Houk remembers:

The whole crew of nine and the crashed plane could have been contained in a hundred yard football field. I have to estimate that the pilot jumped at about 150–200 feet, and the rest of us not much higher. We landed safely but hard.

We had actually come down in a forward salient, abandoned by the Germans but not yet occupied by the Americans. There were German SS troops on three sides of us and the American Third Army in front of us.

The crew was hidden by a French family for a few days before being picked up by a Third Army patrol and taken to the Third Army headquarters. Houk continues:

While some of us were finishing breakfast, a messenger came running to gather us together because General Patton wanted to see us. Of course, we had no choice, and were soon waiting on the grass outside the War Tent, where the general had been briefed by the Air Corps liaison officer, a full colonel. The colonel told the general of our presence and the circumstances under which we were there. General Patton ordered that we be sent for as he wanted to talk to us.

General Patton . . . met each of individually. He was very reserved, almost shy. He seemed to not know what to say or do and we anticipated immediate dismissal. Then, Jack Spratt, always the brash one, asked, "General, will you sign our short snorter bills?" This seemed to put him in a jovial mood and he willingly complied. When he had finished, he said, "Colonel, go get me nine Bronze Stars." Whereupon the colonel tried to expostulate, presumably because the Bronze Star was then considered exclusively as a ground operation medal. The general became very much "General Patton" and repeated the order with obvious emphasis. The colonel fetched the medals, and General Patton then pinned one on each of us.

Spratt recounts it from his point of view:

To see a gentleman as tall as Patton, a big-boned stocky man, come down off those steps toward us was quite a sensation for me as well as for the other crew members.

What does a staff sergeant or lieutenant say to a man like this? Do we come to attention, salute, what?

He said, "At ease, be yourselves."

But then there was an awkward moment—kind of like meeting someone, and asking, "How's your day?"—and then no conversation after that.

I realized somebody had to say something, and I said the only thing that came to mind: "Sir, will you sign our short-snorter bills?" It was our custom. If you fly over a body of water, you get people to sign a dollar bill. I didn't have a dollar bill, but I happened to have a franc note out of the escape kit. Anyway, this broke the silence with laughter.

He said, "I'd be glad to."

After you got to talking with General Patton, he became just like an old country gentleman, a grandfatherly type you could easily converse with. We talked for 35 to 40 minutes. They took a picture of all of us lined up.

The colonel standing by said, "I'll make sure you all get copies of this picture." Then, the general said to go get nine Bronze Star ribbons. The colonel explained that couldn't be done, because it's a medal for ground personnel. Plus, we weren't under his command.

He repeated: "Go get me nine Bronze Stars."

Like all good soldiers do, the colonel obeyed. Patton pinned them on us and asked each of us where he was from, down the line.

He was the kind of leader that people just wanted to follow. The ground soldiers had told us, "Ol' Blood and Guts would tell us to take this town. If there was a river in front of it, and we said, 'How we going to get across it?' he'd say, 'I'll show you how to get across it.' Then he'd swim across the river, swim back, and say, 'That's how we get across.'"

As much as I admired Patton and his men, I never wanted to be in the infantry. Aviation was what I wanted. We might put 6 or even 10 hours in the air, but when we got back, we got a clean cot to sleep in. The boys in the infantry, in the Third Army, had foxholes.

The B-17 crew decorated by Patton himself. Left to right: Second Lieutenant Paul K. Bupp; First Lieutenant Horace L. Spencer; Sergeant John P. Hensley; Second Lieutenant Harry J. McCrossan Jr.; Sergeant L. G. Spillman; Lieutenant General George S. Patton Jr.; Staff Sergeant John L. Houk; Staff Sergeant Thomas F. Jenkins; Staff Sergeant Jack Spratt; and Second Lieutenant Sargent J. Abelman. **U.S. Army Signal Corps via Jack Spratt**

Homesick Angel tail-gunner L. G. Spillman echoes Spratt's and Houk's sentiments:

He was an impressive individual. His stature. His bearing. A tall gentleman with very broad shoulders. Appeared to be a very domineering individual, which I think he was.

He made us feel at ease though. At first, when we all came to attention and saluted, he said, "Just be at ease. I want to talk with you for a moment." We all stood at ease, like he said, and he shook hands with each of us. He addressed us as a group and thanked us for our contribution to his effort to overcome the Germans. The Air Force had done lots of bombing.

When the aide went to get nine Bronze Stars, it was quite a surprise. I thought about how the folks back home wouldn't believe this, and the guys back at the base certainly wouldn't believe it either!

I wore that ribbon with my Class A uniform always after that. Still have it today, mounted in a frame along with the Air Medal. That along with a write-up in the paper. Of all the experiences in World War II, that experience was the most memorable beyond all doubt.

Spratt's wish for a return to a clean cot at Podington's bomber base would not be long in coming. He says:

> We slept that night in the colonel's tent. The next morning he said, "I didn't know so many soldiers talked in their sleep." We had been dreaming about bailing out and all the events of that previous day. He heard comments like, "Beat the gun turret." What that came from was, we were trying to jettison the ball turret. Normally there's a wrench that you could use to loosen the four nuts to drop the turret and the column and all. But the wrench wasn't there. Desperate to lighten the load, we took the barrels off the waist guns and tried to beat that column. We did bend it, but didn't get it off.
>
> The general asked Lieutenant Horace Spencer, our pilot, how we would get back to our home base in England. Before Spence could answer, General Patton said, "I will provide the transportation back to England."
>
> We were flown in Patton's private C-47 to our own base at Podington. Patton's C-47 was like a Cadillac compared to a B-17. This was not like a '17 with the long fuselage, ribs running up the sides. The C-47 had rows of seats with a table you could sit at and a little galley. It was plush. There was even a case of cognac and champagne. The very first thing I asked when I got on was: "Where are the parachutes?"
>
> When we came in for a landing, the pilot gave his call sign and the tower recognized it as being for Patton. So they naturally assumed Patton was in the plane. And all these command cars and high-ranking officers came zooming out to meet him. Then this group of grungy sergeants and lieutenants came out. That was humorous.
>
> Once we were off the plane, the administrative officer said, "You're not allowed to wear that Bronze Star ribbon."
>
> I said, "Until General Patton tells me not to wear it, I'm going to wear it."
>
> Then they had to find a way to let us have it or take it away from us. So they assigned us administratively to General Patton's Third Army for three days.

Houk concludes the story with a stateside epilogue:

> I completed my assigned number of missions in March 1945. I was sent back to America in the full expectation that I would take some leave of absence and then be sent to the Asian Theater of War.

Stalled at the Moselle

At the receiving air base, I was assigned to in California, I was designated "war hero," and spent the remainder of my service commitment staying in hotels with other, perhaps bona fide, heroes and speaking at various occasions as arranged by the U.S. Treasury Department, essentially to help sell War Bonds.

On one such occasion, "Patton Day" in the city of Alhambra, California, I was introduced and sat next to Miss Anne Patton, the general's sister. She told me that the general had always wanted to be a soldier, and that their play was almost entirely that of a soldier—hero and enemy.

The *Homesick Angel* bomber crew is the only crew known to have been decorated with Bronze Stars for air action, and certainly the only bomber crew decorated by Patton himself.

◆

While stalled at the Moselle, Patton had cordial meetings with others outside his command. He made a practice of inviting Red Cross girls to dine with his staff, especially when dignitaries and VIPs visited his headquarters. Jan Bryson Curtis was a Red Cross hostess assigned to the Third Army. She talks about two occasions when she dined with Patton in France, and about serving GIs in the field in Red Cross clubmobiles:

When we were in the camps, his headquarters was right there. He would talk to our group leader and invite three of us at a time over for dinner. So we got to join him and his staff. The first time I went, Archbishop Spellman was there. We went to his tent for a glass of wine first, then over for dinner in the general's tent. I was awed by the archbishop. But I wasn't awed by General Patton. I was impressed with him though. He was "shiny." His helmet was shiny. His boots were shiny. His fingernails were even shiny—but maybe it was the moon shining. He had a dog Willie and he was always under the table, so you never knew if it was Willie or someone else!

The second time I met Patton was at Nancy. That time a whole group of us were there, because he came to "our place"—the château where we were stationed—to have lunch with General Eisenhower. General Eisenhower left his driver, Kay Somersby, in the car for some reason or she went somewhere and didn't come in for lunch.

We were taken into the dining room and all us Red Cross girls were seated around at various tables. They sat at the head table with the VIP Red Cross people. We were excused at some point after

175

dessert, and the generals and our VIPs stayed on talking. We went back into the living room and a couple of the girls looked up at the mantel, and there was General Patton's hat and General Eisenhower's hat. So they each put one on and were having a conversation:

"Well, George, what's your latest move now? What's the plan?"

"Oh, it's up to *you*, Ike."

"No, no, no, you do the *strategic* thing—"

We were all standing around laughing. Then we turned around and there they were—standing in the doorway. Fortunately, both had grins.

Patton could quote a lot of Shakespeare. He was very well informed about the Bible and Shakespeare. Being a great Shakespeare appreciator, he stood up at the mantelpiece and spoke one of the sonnets.

We'd see General Patton often, just driving through. He was very friendly. He didn't use any profanity with us. And he had a mild voice, not a booming voice at all. With the guys, of course, it was different. He could certainly chew somebody out easily enough. And you'd hear a lot of the GIs say, "His guts and our blood." Some resented it, but I think they were proud to be part of it all.

It was a wonderful experience serving the GIs. The troops were very friendly and glad to see us. From our clubmobiles, six-by-six trucks with a box mounted on top of the back, we served coffee and donuts. Even had cigarettes and gum at that time. They appreciated any change from the monotony of C rations and mud.

Patton regularly hosted Red Cross workers who provided "ammunition for the heart and spirit." **U.S. Army**

Patton dealt with a couple of health issues while static in France. Robert Allen observed that Patton:

> ... had to give up one drink entirely: chlorinated water. Three years' consumption of heavily impregnated chorine water finally affected his digestion and the medics proscribed it. To provide him with drinking water, one of them each day dechlorinated enough to fill several canteens.

Also, because he had a tendency to colds, the medics constantly urged him to ease up on smoking. An inveterate cigar smoker, when going strong Patton smoked a score a day. Occasionally he would announce he had "sworn off" and divest himself of his cigar supply. Whereupon the staff would bet among themselves on the duration of the abstinence.

The usual period was 2-1/2 days, although on one occasion, when Third Army was sat down in September 1944, Patton didn't smoke for a week. It was a tough week, for him and the staff. All concerned were greatly relieved when he finally strode in to the chief of staff's office, reached into the bottom drawer of a desk where a box of his favorite cigars was kept for such occasions, picked up a fistful, and walked out, without saying a word. A few minutes later he was heard scuffling with Willie, and the word quickly got around that "Georgie" was feeling good again.

Willie was very not-smoking conscious. When he master was off cigars, Willie was off his master. During abstinence periods, Patton was apt to be abrupt with Willie, so Willie kept his distance.

Coy Eklund of Lucky Forward confirms stories from the encampment at Nancy that became part of Patton lore:

> It is *no* myth that one Sunday morning, after attending church services as he always did, he stalked into my office in the Army barracks in Nancy, France, where I was the Sunday duty officer.
>
> "Eklund," he demanded, "do you know Chaplain So-and-so?"
>
> "Yes, sir," I replied.
>
> "Well get rid of the son of a bitch. He can't preach!"
>
> And we got rid of him.
>
> On one occasion I escorted a group of U.S. Congressmen, about a dozen of them—including Clare Booth Luce—visiting the war zone. I phoned him and then escorted them to his house trailer where a cordial visit ensued. When Luce noticed a Bible on Patton's camp table, she asked excitedly, "General, do you read the Bible?"
>
> "Every goddamned day," he replied.

Still speaking of myths and truths, Eklund adds, "It was a myth that he carried pearl-handled pistols. They were *ivory*-handled."

Chapter Six

The standstill gave unit commanders a chance to write up much-deserved commendations and recommendations for medals. When combat action was heavy, medals that should have been awarded weren't, simply because commanders didn't have time to write them up. Regulations imposed tight time limits, preventing later submission. Therein lies the hit-and-miss nature of combat medals. Lieutenant Colonel James Moncrief, G-1 officer of the 6th Armored Division, explains:

I considered myself a small cog, but a cog, in the machinery having to do with medals. They were initiated by unit commanders, reviewed by a board of officers, all of whom were combat wise, went up through the division commander, who personally had to sign them if it was anything above a Silver Star. He didn't have authority to give anything over a Silver Star. Above that, it goes up to Army. An Army headquarters has a board, and General Patton himself reviewed it.

I remember we recommended a man for a DSC [Distinguished Service Cross] to Army HQ. Administratively, you didn't have to go through a corps headquarters from a division; that was for tactical [matters] only.

This DSC recommendation came back with a buckslip on it. Penciled on the buckslip was: "This is either a Medal of Honor or a damn lie." It was signed GSP Jr.

I wish had kept that penciled buckslip, but that was an official communication. I could probably sell it now for a million. We immediately rewrote it and recommended the Medal of Honor. He was one of two who got them in our division. One was Gammon. The other was Briar. I'm not sure which of the men this was.

So much of all this depends on judgment. And language. If you got a recommendation by a guy fluent in the English language—somebody with a lot of good adjectives—then it got noticed. A good writer could submit something far better than some cabbage patch soldier company commander who could barely scratch. We had a lot of those, too, and when a man on the board reviewed it, he'd just shake his head. If the man with fluent English made it sound good, he couldn't turn that down.

There was no shortage of heroism during the Third Army's drive across France, and it resulted in much-deserved recognition and

Stalled at the Moselle

In his senior post as personnel officer at 6th Armored Division headquarters, Lieutenant Colonel James Moncrief was responsible for reviewing unit commander recommendations for medals. Moncrief remembers when his divisional board "recommended a man for a DSC [Distinguished Service Cross] to Army HQ. This DSC recommendation came back with a buckslip on it. Penciled on the buckslip was: 'This is either a Medal of Honor or a damn lie.' It was signed 'GSP, Jr.' "With this jotted note from Patton himself, the man received the Medal of Honor.

medals given in front-line units. But with so many requests submitted, Army brass had to draw the line somewhere. Carl Ulsaker, a company commander in the 95th Infantry Division, remembers the procedures and frustrations of awarding medals:

> One of the heavy administrative chores of a company commander is to write recommendations for awards for men who have performed beyond the call of duty in combat. The Army has a form for this and a procedure calling for signatures of witnesses to the heroic act. A regimental commander could award the Combat Infantry Badge, given for satisfactory performance of duty in combat at or below the regimental level, and any attending surgeon could award the Purple Heart, which went to anyone injured or wounded (or killed) as a result of a hostile act on the part of an armed enemy of the United States, but recognition for deeds of greater merit had to come from higher authority. A division commander could approve award of the Bronze Star Medal (BSM) and the Silver Star Medal (SSM), although he was limited by quotas imposed by the Army commander from

month to month. The theater commander had to approve any recommendation for the Distinguished Service Cross (DSC) and the Medal of Honor required the blessing of the president himself after appropriate review by the secretary of war.

The BSM had been devised by the Army in World War II to be given rather liberally to men for "heroic achievement" in ground combat. It also could be awarded for "meritorious service," a distinction made, I supposed, so that people who did good work in the rear echelons could get some recognition. The majority of the recommendations I initiated were for the Bronze Star. The SSM ranked higher on the scale of heroic performance, given for "gallantry in action." It could be won only for that; a rear echelon "commando" had to come up and get shot at if he coveted a Silver Star. A soldier or junior officer had to do something considerably out of the ordinary to get this medal. It was awarded rather liberally to battalion and regimental commanders on the premise, I guess, that their bravery was inherent whether or not they ever proved it. . . .

I also found that to get approval to award an enlisted man the lowly Bronze Star, I had to write it up to sound as if he deserved a much higher award. Where the recommendation just told the facts as they happened, the Division Awards Board would usually send it back marked: "Disapproved, line of duty." (The board consisted of a chairman, the chief of staff, and members such as the inspector general, the judge advocate, the chemical officer, etc., with the adjutant general as secretary.) Fortunately, I had always been a good writer; therefore, I personally wrote, or rewrote, all the recommendations for awards to men in my company. Once I learned what the Division Board wanted, I succeeded in getting approval in most cases. A couple times they knocked a Silver Star back to a Bronze Star, and the one recommendation I made for a DSC they reduced to a SSM.

I wrote up a citation recommending the Silver Star for all 14 of the men who had been either on the bridge or across the Moselle River. Ten of the proposed awards would be posthumous. To my amazement, my recommendations were disapproved by the Division Awards Board, with the comment that I could resubmit for the lesser award of the Bronze Star Medal. This really burned me up but I had no recourse other than to act as advised. Several months later, in March 1945, I read in the *Stars and Stripes* where some general had pinned Silver Stars on several engineers who attempted to defuse some explosives on a Rhine River bridge but had to abandon their efforts as the bridge was about to collapse. I clipped the article, attached it to a copy of my recommendation, and sent it to the

Awards Board with this comment: "My men crossed in the face of enemy fire and 10 of them died in the effort!" The Bronze Stars were promptly upgraded to SSMs. Occasionally, the good guys win one!

H. M. Trowern wasn't much for medals. And, of course, the decorations he won in combat were not worn there. But Trowern explains that one decoration was an exception:

I had earned a Combat Infantry Badge and the Bronze Star. The Combat Infantry Badge was the one that riflemen prized the most. We were prouder of that than the other medals. I'd gotten the Purple Heart and a recommendation for the Silver Star, but those things you get in a very quick action. You do something that somebody determines as brave, but you don't think about it too much ahead of time or afterwards.

One of the things you have to remember about medals is that the write-ups had to be made by an officer within three days of the action. We were short on officers to begin with and they had a lot more things to do than write up guys for medals. It depended on the timing. If you had an attack and you did something outstanding and there was a little time to rest after the attack, you could be written up by an officer. But other than that, a lot of brave men didn't get credit for what they did because of the paperwork that was involved.

In our outfit in the Third Army, we couldn't get a Combat Infantry Badge until we'd been under fire for 30 days. And that's a long time to be shot at. A lot of guys just didn't make the 30 days. So that when we did get our Combat Infantry Badges, we would wear them in combat.

I was a platoon sergeant, and after I got my battlefield commission, it was up to me to keep track of the men in my platoon as to how many days they'd been under fire, including the replacements. When I started to hand out these Combat Infantry Badges, the men started to wear them—in combat. We didn't wear other medals in combat. But these guys put on the badge as soon as they earned it.

I asked one of them one day, "Why are you wearing your badge, Dottore?"

He said, "We all do it."

"Yeah, I noticed that but I haven't put it on."

"Well, you should."

I said, "Why?"

"Because, when you get involved with other companies or even other platoons, we want to know who's had combat experience. You don't want to get stuck with a greenhorn replacement that's just been on the line a couple of days. You want somebody that knows how the

game is played, because that gives you a better chance of survival."
It made a lot of sense. And after that I wore mine every place.

Medals were welcomed and well-deserved recognition, but there probably was not a man in Patton's spearhead who wouldn't have given up his medals if it meant the Third Army could have maintained momentum without interruption to finish the job.

◆

The Germans were well aware of what good fortune it was for them when the Third Army stalled at the Moselle. Colonel Robert S. Allen discovered the writings of German Major General Richard Schimpf. As commanding general of the German Third Paratroop Division, Schimpf had battled the Third Army in France. He writes just how detrimental the halt really was for the Third Army:

> There is no question that if your Third Army had not been halted before Metz in September, it could have penetrated the Siegfried Line very quickly and been on the Rhine in an hour's time. At that time we were powerless to cope with the situation in that portion of the front. But when your Third Army was halted, we obtained the time to regroup, and we used that opportunity to the utmost.

As the stalemate dragged on for weeks, Patton's tanks needed at least enough gas to operate in a defensive mode, in which they at least could move around and not be sitting ducks. Stephen Conland of the 5th Quartermaster Battalion comments:

> We got vehicles from the antiair unit to haul gas. We diverted gas from Seventh Army in the north. I went up there a couple of times to the Seventh Army myself, since immobile tanks can be a very dangerous situation.

While stalled at the Moselle, the Quartermaster Corps did what it could in stopgap fashion to keep Patton's Army functioning. Then finally, the gas supply was restored. But by this time, in early November, the opportunity to barrel through Lorraine on the heels of the retreating Germans had been lost.

Chapter 7

On the Hunt Again

November 1944

By early November 1944, Patton's Third Army was flush with fuel and ready to attack again. Patton's flagging spirit soared. "Compared to war," Patton declared, "all other forms of human endeavor shrink to insignificance." He inhaled deeply. "God, how I love it!"

An all-out offensive was planned by the Allies for November 10. Patton's Third Army, along with the First Army and Montgomery's forces, was to launch a massive attack along the front. But the week before, word came from General Bradley that Monty would not be ready on the chosen date and, in fact, would not be ready for an offensive until the first week of December. Furthermore, Bradley said, the First Army would not have sufficient numbers to attack until reinforced by U.S. divisions then attached to Montgomery's forces.

After explaining the status of the other Allied forces, Bradley queried Patton about the Third Army's combat readiness. Patton gave an instant reply: "I will attack alone."

Patton was authorized to choose a date of attack, which was decided "unquestionably due to sentiment," according to Charles Codman, "two years to the hour and date since Patton's first attack in this war was made off the coast of Casablanca"—precisely at 0500 on November 8.

The attack delayed so long by the fuel shortage would kick off with a concentrated barrage of artillery. Then, seven infantry divisions and three armored divisions would begin the long-awaited advance.

The first hurdle was crossing the Moselle River. Lieutenant William Baker of the 989th Treadway Bridge Company remembers the challenge of assembling a bridge near Metz:

Chapter Seven

Crossing the Moselle was the worst experience we had trying to cross a river in the ETO. Crossings needed a good bridgehead set up by the infantry on the other side of the river. The 5th Infantry Division put a battalion of infantry on the other side of the river, but they were getting chewed up awful bad by artillery. Patton sent word down that the bridge was to go in at all costs. When the general speaks, you do. We did, but lost more men and equipment there than anywhere else in the entire war.

We were trying to cross at a place where the Germans had an artillery [officer] school. So they knew every inch of their terrain. And, they had plenty gun emplacements there—the kind that would come up out of the ground and go back down. This day they must have been training their young officers "on the job." We had air support, but they weren't able to take the guns out.

The artillery hit our air compressor right off—killed the man and the machine. We pulled out our spare, but the artillery kept coming. They were looking at us. Right at us. So every time we put in a section of bridge or try to, they would take it out. This was direct fire. So direct in fact, it was like aiming a rifle.

Since we couldn't get a bridge across, we set up a "ferry service." The Moselle was about 250 feet wide here, and we used two sections of bridge that we could load two or three vehicles on and our power-boat would pull it to the other side. But they were so accurate in their fire that they made a direct hit on that powerboat. We never found the operator. The only thing we found of him was some flesh embedded in the side of that boat when we pulled it out of the river later. It just blew him apart.

I was with the company commander right on the bank. They had a big levee there to keep the river in its bounds. We had gotten caught there and shells were coming in at a rate of one a minute. There were tree bursts, airbursts, ground bursts. We were lying on that levee just scared to death. Shells were raining in there all up and down the levee. We were there, just trapped. A lot of the men from the platoons got under their trucks—that was as safe as anything, because an eight-ton truck could withstand a lot.

After several attempts and all this shelling, the decision was made to cease operations and bring in a smoke company. Smoke. That's all these guys did. They had little smoke generators and could fog the whole area. Then we had to move the site, because the Germans would have had us zeroed in still. While that was happening, we had to go back to a depot 20 miles to the rear to get a complete new load of bridge. All our bridge parts had been destroyed. We found a new site—a place with a good enough road leading up to it to handle all the heavy equipment, but not necessarily a main road that would be such an obvious place for the Germans to zero in. Finally, after two or three days, we got them across.

Just as at the Normandy breakout, Patton was everywhere—but mostly where somebody happened to be doing something wrong. He berated any officer he saw who masked his rank insignia, growling menacingly about infecting his troops with fear: "Do you want to give your men the idea that the enemy is *dangerous*?" He yelled in his high-pitched voice for the troops to keep rolling and again directed traffic himself to keep his divisions moving.

At a newly erected bridge on the Moselle, Patton's jeep was blocked by a traffic jam of tanks and trucks. A lone MP stood directing traffic at the bridge. Bill Jennings, a staff sergeant MP in the 819th MP Company of XX Corps, remembers the sensation of suddenly seeing the general in a shiny star-studded helmet emerge from the darkness.

This was early November 1944 at a small town called Thionville. We were trying to put the 10th Armored Division across the Moselle River. The engineers succeeded in getting a pontoon bridge across the river, and we were trying to get an armored division across so it could face its first combat. We were getting hit with occasional artillery.

To keep the bridge from being overloaded, my job was to keep them spaced and allow only two units on the bridge at one time. One tank and one jeep at a time, or whatever. The units were bumper to bumper, and everyone was anxious to get on the bridge first.

I was at my wit's end, as they all tried to bulldoze through, when out of the darkness came a voice asking if I needed help. Without knowing who it was, I answered in the saltiest language I could muster that these troops weren't listening to us.

It turned out to be Patton. He was suddenly standing there, ramrod erect and shining with his helmet and pistols.

He took over. First, he went to the closest jeep where he asked who was in charge. An officer on the passenger side said he was. Patton asked him who the hell he was, and the officer responded, giving his rank. At that point Patton blistered him for covering up his insignia with tape and painting it over with green. Patton told him, in even saltier language than I used, that if he didn't take off the goddamned tape immediately he would be a private. He ordered him to get his unit spaced like it was supposed to.

It took about 10 minutes for things to get better. Then Patton finally asked me, with surprising humility, if there was anything else

Chapter Seven

he could do for me. As he walked away he muttered, "If those bastards don't behave, let me know."

I admired his total disregard for danger of the incoming shells
and for his bearing and genuine helpfulness to do a job, regardless of
who I was.

Traveling along with armored and
infantry divisions were companies of
MPs, among them Staff Sergeant Bill
Jennings of the 819th MP Company. One
of Jennings' frequent MP duties was
directing traffic—a major task when
hundreds of vehicles needed to quickly
pass through a confused network of
roads. Patton himself was known to jump
in as traffic cop. Jennings: "I was at my
wit's end, as vehicles of the 10th
Armored Division all tried to bulldoze
through, when out of the darkness came
a voice asking if I needed help. Without
knowing who it was, I answered in the
saltiest language I could muster that

these troops weren't listening to us. It turned out to be Patton. He was suddenly standing
there, ramrod erect and shining with his helmet and pistols. He took over. . . ."

A replacement assigned to the 90th Infantry Division, Al Teclaw
alludes to the "worm's-eye view" of the foot soldier, who never saw the
big picture. He saw only what lay directly in front of his foxhole. He
rarely even knew where he was. For him, the Moselle River crossing was
a notable exception, because shortly after he experienced his first combat and witnessed a buddy's death for the sake of a souvenir.

I never knew for sure where we were. Except at the Moselle River.
That river crossing was one thing I knew. I remember being amazed at
how the engineers got the pontoons and steel across to make the bridge.

The 90th had a lot of replacements, so there were a lot of inex-
perienced soldiers. We did miles and miles of riding on tanks to catch
up to the Germans falling back after the Moselle River crossing. I can
remember one incident when we were going down a hill on those
tanks and we got pinned down by an antiaircraft gun firing point-
blank at us. We jumped down into a ravine. Dirt and stones were

flying above us and falling on us, but we weren't hit. That was my first encounter of someone shooting at me.

Once we knocked out that antiaircraft gun, we went down into a town. We were fired on again, and got down into a bomb crater. That's when I saw my first buddy killed. Everybody was getting souvenirs from captured German soldiers and he was anxious to get a souvenir. The Germans put out a white flag to surrender. He got up and ran over to get to them and somebody else opened fire from a different direction. Killed him instantly. You didn't dwell on that. The medical people came by and got him. Strange thing—nobody mentioned him again.

Lieutenant Eileen (Courtney) Biersteker was a nurse who had landed in England only a month before, in October 1944, and was sent to the Third Army straightaway as part of the 65th Field Hospital, at the time Patton went on the offensive again.

We were the first ones to cross the Moselle River on the pontoon bridge. After we crossed, we set up our hospital right there near the bank, because there was a lot of fighting around there.

We'd get the soldiers straight off the battlefield and their arms and legs would be blown off, and many chest wounds. We were divided up in platoons—each with five doctors, six nurses, and 60 enlisted men. The platoons were spread out with the infantry divisions. We worked 24 hours a day, and our surgeons worked 24 hours a day if needed. There really weren't shifts; we worked as was needed.

Artillery was going over us all the time. We were that close. It was constant while we were working. Like thunder all the time.

It was so very sad to see the wounded as they came in. They seemed so very young. I was 25 or 26 at the time, and many of them were 19. When I saw the war wounds, I had to wonder, *Is it all worthwhile? Is that what should be going on?* But we were happy to be there because we knew we were doing something. Really doing something. You had a very good feeling about that. I suppose that's the way a lot of our soldiers felt about what they were doing, too.

But it was difficult dealing emotionally with all the death. While I was still in France, my brother was killed in the Air Corps. For some reason, they weren't able to contact me about it. I heard from my own family before I heard from the Red Cross. It was my younger brother.

When I saw these many young soldiers carried in, I would see his face in their faces. I found myself wondering, *If he had gotten this far, would I have seen him like this?* The last I saw him was in the States in uniform. He was still in training to be a fighter pilot. My other brother was a navigator, but not overseas either. So when my family saw the telegram delivered, they assumed it was about me. Me—over in Europe in the field hospital. And they assumed the worst. But it was my little brother instead. That was difficult to get over for all of us.

The greatest fear I had was at night, when we'd hear the bombing. In the daytime, it didn't seem as severe as it did at night. It was more frightening when we weren't on night duty.

There were nurses that were killed over there. Planes would come over at night and strafe our hospital, even with the huge red crosses on the tent. I don't know if they could see the red crosses or not. We would all go for cover. Never any advance warning from anyone—just all of a sudden you could hear it diving down. Even when we were in an abandoned farmhouse, we would always spread out a big red cross on the roof. They were not supposed to fire on that, because of the Geneva Convention.

Patton reviewed us once or twice. So I saw him with his pearl-handled revolvers and his little dog. Of course, we had heard about Patton before we saw him. From what we heard, we knew he was a very strict man. And used profanity quite a bit. But he knew what he was doing. He was a very, very splendid looking man. Stood straight, tall and imposing. Had a riding crop in his hand all the time. I remember his little pep talk. He said, "Keep going. You'll see daylight."

At some point we were given a three-day leave in Paris and General Patton ordered that all nurses, really everyone in the Third Army, were to wear helmets all the time. So no matter where we went, we had to wear those helmets. We were very upset, because all the Red Cross girls could go dressed up, and here we were in the glamour of Paris, in the clubs, wearing combat helmets on our heads. But I think a lot of us were very happy to be in the Third Army under Patton. I know we were. He was a good general.

After crossing the Moselle, we were always on the move. We'd set up in tents, in abandoned farmhouses, or we'd set up in schoolhouses, and kept moving forward as the front moved forward. We'd have to leave on a moment's notice on our 2-1/2-ton trucks. When we would have to leave, our patients were taken over by another group of doctors and nurses called a holding company, which means they would hold the patients until they could be evacuated. Eventually, they would transfer the wounded back to England.

As Patton prepared to move against Metz, there were regular visits to his headquarters from Bradley's staff. Among the frequent visitors was Colonel Chester B. Hansen, who kept a remarkably detailed diary throughout the war. Although on Bradley's staff, Hansen encountered Patton often and, in the privacy of his diary, writes about him frankly, with a critical eye and sometimes curious amusement.

Brad arranged to visit Patton today, acquaint him with the details of the revised plan, which gives us greater chance of success and chance for greater concentration. Drove down to Patton's HQ at Nancy with General Kibler, the G-3.

Patton in good spirits, anticipating great success in his attack around Metz toward the Saar. He is inclined to be overoptimistic, to dismiss supply difficulties too readily, but lacks no temerity. He is not timid and he expects division and corps commanders to function with equal aggressiveness.

Offered us drink before dinner which everyone declined, and took us in, chatting merrily all the while—good soup and Patton told the story of how his place was shelled the night before when the enemy bracketed his house with three 280-mm shells, all of them falling within 50 feet of the place where he was living—breaking the window, smashing the doors and dislodging the ceiling. It was an ugly place anyhow. Horribly ugly.

Patton was amusing in telling the story: "goddammit, that was once when I was really scared."

Talked of Monty; I don't believe he has ever forgiven Monty for the alleged snub on the road to Sfax when the Brit and American troops made union with the Eighth Army on the road east of El Guettar and Monty declined to come over for a meeting with Patton to symbolize the meeting of the two Armies.

Finished the business there shortly and took off for visit with Milliken, the commander of III Corps, which had just arrived that day in Etain. . . . Patton not too sold on Milliken, not because he does not like him but simply because he feels that corps commanders would be selected from among experienced and successful division commanders. Feels that it is bad for morale to put new corps commander over a battle-tried div commands. Pumping hard for corps for Pete Wood who is an irascible fighter but who would not be regarded too highly in the old man's [Bradley's] estimation, I believe, for command of a corps. Success as a division commander does not necessarily mean the man can command a corps. The remoteness and the longer range view of a corps necessitates a superior commander and the general has often said there are few good potential corps commanders among the divs.

Patton's stature has increased immeasurably in this campaign and everyone has a far higher regard for him than they did in Sicily.

Chapter Seven

Combines the aggressive instinct that makes him good with a more realistic moderation. General Bradley acts as the leveler here and figures out the combinations and tactics necessary to make the Armies move with such perfect coordination.

Patton, too, is less bombastic—appears to have fitted himself well to General Bradley's authority. Everyone appears quite happy in the current command organization. General Hodges has a giant pair of shoes to fill when Brad left but he appears to be doing satisfactorily in his command of the Army there. Meanwhile, Brad has slumped into greater obscurity than ever before as a result of his remote command in the group.

Back in 1925, Patton is supposed to have said, "Hell, a division commander doesn't have to know anything. He can be as dumb as a son of a bitch as long as he's a fighter."

Most generals agree that Patton puts too much stress on a fighter and is less concerned about sound tactics in the management and administration of a campaign. Bradley has to constantly exercise some control on Patton's proclivities, else he would have a group of senior corps commanders and whatnot that would know nothing whatsoever.

◆

During the long period of immobility, there had been lots of time to plan. It enabled various division headquarters to hand down meticulous plans for a series of objectives around Metz. Objectives for the 95th Infantry Division were Semecourt and Woippy, stubborn strongholds buffering Metz. By this time, the American infantrymen were seasoned fighters who succeeded in taking objectives even if things didn't happen as planned, as Lieutenant Waverly Green writes:

At times, detailed plans and preparations are made for an operation and nothing works out as envisioned. Such was B Company's attack on Semecourt.

The plan of attack for the battalion was A Company to make it through a gap to the rear of Fort DeFeves and attack it from the rear. C Company to the left was to clear out a body of woods across from the origin of the attack and then seize the town of Feves. Then B Company was to move into the woods that C Company was supposed to clear and use it as an assembly point to attack the town of Semecourt. Semecourt was the regiment's first objective. The main objective was the high ground above Woippy, a town just outside of Metz.

On the Hunt Again

I had the Weapons Platoon at the time. Light machine guns and 60-mm mortars. . . . The 2nd and 3rd platoons had already begun to move into the assembly area, a wooded area on a ridge overlooking the enemy's position in front of us. The company commander, Captain Schoonover, had told us as much as he knew.

As usual, there was a steady rain, and we were cold and uncomfortable. It was constantly raining while we were in the province of Lorraine. The ground was soft and muddy. In the woods, fallen leaves made footing most treacherous, and in the fields we were mired down in mud.

Our area was in the woods, just off a paved road. Everything was soaking wet, the trees, the brush, and leaves on the ground. The platoons settled down in the assigned places, placed security and tried to get as comfortable as possible. Using shelter [tent] halves, raincoats, or anything available. Most munched on K rations, which was their evening meal.

When it became dark, Schoonover got the platoon leaders all together to go back to the battalion CP and get the orders for our attack. By then, it was a steady rain. The four of us, plus the driver, crowded into a jeep and started off. The windshield was down because of the danger of the glass being shattered and causing injuries. Only blackout lights were used, which meant little illumination on the road. And the rain, because of the windshield being down, was blowing right into our faces. If you bent your head forward to protect your face, water from your helmet poured down the back of your neck. The ride took about a half hour during which time we were most miserable.

Arrival at the battalion CP, which was in a well-constructed house, meant welcome relief from the elements. The battalion commander, his staff, the company commander, the artillery liaison officers, and the doc (battalion surgeon) gathered around a long table. The rest of us sat or stood in the background. The place was warm and had the odor of wet woolen clothing.

It seemed like a long time that the battalion commander looked over maps, studied papers, and talked with those around him. Finally, he stood up and greeted us with "Gentlemen." Then he covered the typical five-paragraph field order:

1. The enemy situation as known by our forces.
2. The station of the troops.
3. Our mission.
4. Supply and evacuation.
5. The CO position and means of communication.

Chapter Seven

He had little to add about the enemy. We already knew that he was well positioned in Fort DeFeves, the town of Semecourt and surrounding area. The strategy for our attack was like something from Robert E. Lee. The most likely approach to Fort DeFeves was a short distance hitting its right flank. For several days, our service companies were moving into a likely jumpoff spot to attack in this way. They also scrounged all the .50 caliber machine guns, antitank guns and whatever other weapons were available and set them up along the front they had created. Just prior to the jumpoff of our attacking companies, they were to let loose with everything they had.

We bundled up in our jeep, made the wet, windy ride back to the company area and rejoined our men. By then, the bed rolls had been brought up for the men and they were trying to get as comfortable as possible, using shelter halves to shield themselves from the rain and trying to find a spot that was level and free of rocks, roots, etc. But comfort, no way. It was still rainy, cold and miserable.

Schoonover stretched out on one of the medic's litters and made out as if he was relaxed and sleeping. Afterward I found out that this was an act to appear relaxed and unconcerned.

I got little sleep that night, just dozed a few times, and was up and going long before the battalion was to attack. I went along with the machine gun section, until they joined up with C Company and stayed with them as long as I could.

Just before the attack, the [diversionary] forces in front of Fort DeFeves let loose with everything they had—.50-caliber machine guns, BARs, rifles, mortars, and a heavy artillery barrage. A and C Companies then jumped off. A Company reached Fort DeFeves and in spite of heavy losses, managed to take it. The platoon commander, Lieutenant Frogh, led a "marching fire" attack and was wounded. For this, he received a Silver Star.

The road where the company was regrouping was under the cover of woods. Between it and the wooded area where we were to organize our attack was an open space of about 100 yards with several rows of barbed wire traversing it. The company had assembled along the road and then moved into the assembly area.

When the company was well within the cleared area, we received heavy automatic and small arms fire. I saw several men go down.

Green looked at the scenario with the same eye for history that Patton might have:

The company's reaction to coming under fire would certainly have pleased General Patton. You talk about the Union attack on

On the Hunt Again

Missionary Ridge in Tennessee during the Civil War. Well, I don't think it was any greater than B company's rapid advance and closing with the enemy. Instead of hitting the dirt, most of the men opened up with whatever weapon they had and delivered a heavy concentration of fire. In addition, they moved rapidly forward.

I marveled at how we got through the enemy's fire. I looked back and saw "Flat Top," a real character, coming up the slight rise with his M-1, blasting away. He had a most fierce and determined look.

I had been firing my carbine and running rapidly forward. Just before reaching the woods, several mortar rounds landed nearby. Those of us in the area hit the ground when they exploded and I felt something warm lodge in the left side of my neck. Blood began to run down the front of my field jacket and I ran into a railroad cut that was an excellent shelter. One of the company aid men was nearby and with the use of our first aid packets, he stopped the bleeding.

When I looked around, I saw a German soldier waving a white handkerchief from a bunker that had been dug on one side of the cut. One of our sergeants, Batista, covered me when I moved to check the enemy. He was a German medic and had several wounded and sick soldiers in the bunker. Batista and I realized that they could have shot us in the back, but apparently the German medic was right when he said that they were unarmed. I told him to make his way to the road running the direction of our attack and that our medics would pick them up.

I then rushed to catch up with the company and came across Sergeants Greer and Harmon lying on the ground, each with a foot blown off by mines they had stepped on. A miracle for me that I had passed that area without stepping on one. Sergeant Greer was most disgusted after 18 years in the Army and knocked out so soon. I checked with our medics, who said that stretcher bearers were headed for the two.

The company had continued its rapid advance, with delivery of heavy volume of fire that pinned the Germans down. A number of them had been killed and several began to surrender.

When I got with the company again, the 1st Platoon on the left was still in the woods. This 3rd Platoon was in the open. Sergeant Oberleitner and I ran together and we got between the two to keep them from running into each other.

We continued to charge towards our objective, Semecourt. Men were yelling, shouting, several were crying.

The German artillery opened up. At first their fire was behind us, because they expected us to hit the ground when we were first fired upon. If we had, they would have butchered us. But our rapid advance kept the enemy artillery from doing a lot of damage to us.

Oberleitner and I were yelling constantly at those we saw in 1st and 3rd Platoons, trying to keep them separate. We came to a cut in a road with a machine gun firing. Along either side of the road were mines. The machine gun position was quite visible—in fact, somewhat exposed. We decided to go up the road and risk machine gun fire rather than taking a chance in the mines.

Both of us fired on the machine gun. When the machine gun fire seemed to slacken, I ran the length of the cut while Oberleitner covered me. Then I covered him by firing at the machine gun. Both of us experienced bullets snapping by us, but we got to where we could be under some cover along the road. We continued our fire and opened up on the machine gunner. Suddenly, we saw him rise up and run away from us. He wasn't hit and was able to get to cover.

By then, most of the resistance before Semecourt had been wiped out and we occupied our objective. Semecourt had been shelled so much that now a few walls and occasional roofs were all that was left of it, except for some well constructed bunkers along the edge of town. We captured the soldiers in them and used the fortifications for our benefit.

Mines, the so-called *Schu* mines [*Schuhminen*—an antipersonnel mine with deadly steel balls housed in a glass or wooden container (making them hard to find) that would spring up and explode at waist level], had caused many of our men to be wounded. Stepping on one meant at least the loss of a foot, at times a leg, at times castration.

Colonel Olivier ordered B Company to continue the attack to seize the main objective, the high ground above Woippy. We advanced again, using marching fire. Most of the enemy before us were small units of infantry or artillery batteries. The size of attacking force and volume of fire made it possible for us to overrun them. We eliminated two batteries of 88s and took the high ground above Woippy and dug in. The number of enemy killed was high. We moved into the dugouts that the enemy had been using and helped ourselves to sausage and other edibles.

But we were now in a precarious state. We had driven well beyond any of our other forces. The men lost no time digging in. We had not been in our position long when there was a counterattack. I don't know the size of the force, but they came from a wooded area to the left, charging wildly and firing rapidly. From our dug in positions, we delivered a heavy volume of fire and they fell back, leaving several dead, among them a major.

On the Hunt Again

Then the artillery rained down on us. It seemed to be coming from every direction. Thank goodness we were well dug in. We owed this to the fact our position had been occupied some time before by the enemy, and there were a number of foxholes that only needed some additional digging.

The German battery had been horse drawn. The horses had broken out of their stable and were running from one place to another. They were magnificent, large, gray draft animals. No one had the heart to shoot them. Darkness and cold came in. Talk about feeling cold, isolated and afraid. You huddled in your hole, moving little. It was quite eerie.

The enemy continued to shell us. Our own artillery let loose at times. It was like we were marooned on a spot catching it from all around. Plus, the horses were still running around. Several times they came close to my hole. If one had stepped into my hole, I would have been crushed.

A lieutenant colonel, who must have come from well in the rear, stopped his jeep and told Schoonover to move the company into the woods. I think Schoonover's words were: "Colonel, you can tell those men to move into the woods. I can tell them to move into the woods. But they will not move into the woods. Enemy artillery fire is still heavy around here and tree bursts from it would probably wipe them out."

I was wearing only a field jacket and had become quite cold. To get warm I dug more on my hole. After getting warm, I would try to rest but would become cold again and start shivering. Then I would resume digging. By morning I had a very complex hole, quite deep in places with firing steps so that I could stand and be protected.

Morning came. The artillery firing stopped. We were really tense and on edge, wondering if we could hold on. From the same woods, we could hear sounds of an impending attack.

During the night, Schoonover had been very active with our radio, trying to get our location to our battalion artillery liaison to deliver some fire to protect us. I thought it was a result of their efforts, but Schoonover later told me it wasn't. Anyway, a heavy artillery barrage landed among our would-be attackers and broke up their formation.

What was so fascinating about the attack at Semecourt is that nothing that occurred was planned. The company met opposition and obtained victory by its heroic response.

Also in the 95th Division attack near Metz was Captain Carl C. Ulsaker, a West Point graduate and recent company commander. He

Chapter Seven

remembers the attack and a visit from Patton:

That afternoon and night all units moved into their designated positions and prepared to attack a pillbox. The second platoon under Skowronsky would furnish the assault team. I put my observation post in the attic of a three-story house. From a window there I had a clear view of the entire area of operations and could direct fire over phones installed in advance. Around midmorning we were ready and began the attack. About the same time, my first sergeant brought a new replacement second lieutenant to the attic and introduced him to me. I told him to stand by, observe the action, and I would assign him a duty later when I had time. Next, I received word from Colonel Kelly, the regimental commander, that General Patton was visiting the division and wanted to come watch our show. Apparently, it was the most interesting thing happening that day in our sector. Soon, the great man arrived accompanied by Kelly and General Don Faith, the assistant division commander.

As soon as the VIPs arrived, Kelly asked me to report to General Patton. The latter interrupted, however, and said, "Never mind the formalities; I can see the captain is very busy." I couldn't help but note this consideration on the part of the controversial leader who had the reputation of being unusually hard on subordinates. He then stood in the area behind me, talking to the people there and observing all that took place.

Fortunately, our attack progressed according to plan and within a few minutes I ordered Skowronsky to dispatch the assault team. As luck would have it, the man carrying the beehive was hit by a small arms round apparently fired at random through the smoke by some German rifleman, and he dropped the charge. Skowronsky observed this from his post, only a few yards away, and without hesitation personally led a second team to the embrasure, saw that the beehive was successfully emplaced, and returned to cover on the north side of the pillbox. The charge blew with the usual heavy *crump*, the assault team chucked in some WP grenades, and in a minute or so white flags appeared at the embrasure and at the underground entrance. In quick succession the 2nd Platoon rounded up the prisoners, the engineers placed their charge, the demolition blew, the roof of the pillbox rose slightly in a kind of slow motion, walls bulged outward, and the entire structure collapsed into a heap of rubble under a cloud of dust.

I ordered all supporting weapons to cease fire and turned to report to General Patton. He said, "Congratulations on a successful operation, captain, but I'm not entirely satisfied with what I've found here."

Puzzled as to what might be wrong, I replied, "What's that, sir?"
"I've been talking to this lieutenant and he tells me he hasn't killed any goddamned Germans yet," indicating the new replacement who had been standing by throughout the proceedings.

"Sir, he reported for duty just before you arrived and I haven't had a chance to put him to work yet."

"Oh, I see. Well, captain, I am giving you a direct order, bypassing the entire chain of command. See that this officer kills lots of the sons of bitches. Understand?"

"Yessir," I responded, saluting as the generals and Kelly departed to return to their respective posts of duty.

At the earliest opportunity, Ulsaker spoke to the lieutenant and gave his standard new-lieutenant orientation, as he did for all new replacement officers:

The lieutenant who had reported for duty just before General Patton's visit was an earnest young man named Hill. As soon as possible I gave Hill his introductory briefing. A main point that I stressed with all newly assigned lieutenants was that I expected them to motivate their entire platoon to fight. Generally, I stated it something like this:

"I see you recently graduated from the Infantry School's Officer Candidate Training. What's the motto of the Infantry School?"

"Follow me, Sir," was the inevitable response.

"All right," I would continue. "I want you to forget that 'Follow me' stuff beginning right now. If you get out in front of your platoon and cry "Follow me," you know what your men are going to say."

"Nossir."

"They'll say, 'Go right ahead, lieutenant,' because they know from experience that the man most likely to get shot in combat is the one in front. Your job is to get the entire platoon to fight. After all, 20 or 30 rifles firing at the enemy equates to a hell of a lot more firepower than one officer's carbine. I'm not looking for heroes. I want leaders. As a matter of fact, I want *pushers*. Your place is behind your men where you can control them, not too far behind but close enough where you can kick someone in the tail if he lags to the rear. Sometimes I think the Army should redefine 'leadership' and call it 'pushership.' "

In spite of my harping on this point, inevitably some eager beaver shavetail would get out in front, wave his arms, shout, "Follow me, men," and get shot. The company table of organization called for six officers: a captain as commander, a lieutenant as executive officer, and four lieutenants as platoon leaders. In six months of combat,

Chapter Seven

Company I ran through 19 officers. The casualty rate for lieutenants was nearly twice that of enlisted men.

After I briefed Hill, a runner guided him up to the platoon he was to command. The route to the platoon led through a maze of backyards, alleys, mouse-holed buildings, and a place that had been a clothing store. The runner came back laughing. He told me that as he led Hill through the store, the lieutenant remarked on the amazingly realistic dummies dressed as German soldiers. The runner had to explain, "Them's no dummies, lieutenant. Them's dead Krauts that we haven't gotten around to removing yet." Since the winter temperature served as a freezer, the bodies did not decompose, therefore, we took our time about policing them up. Our own dead we removed at once for obvious morale reasons.

◆

A constant danger in newly secured towns was from snipers and other stragglers left behind by the German army. Emil Schmidt, company commander of the 39th Signal Company, 26th Infantry Division, recalls the sudden strike of a sniper.

I felt safer on the front than in the rear. In the front, you knew what was going on and you were going as a unit. In the rear, there were so damn many stragglers. I was scared several times.

The first sergeant and I were standing in the doorway of a ruined house. I was looking out from the doorway and the first sergeant—big Polish fella taller than I was—was in back of me looking over my head. Suddenly a bullet came from nowhere. Scared the hell out of me. I swore and we jumped back into the house. Some damn sniper shot, and the bullet hit the doorframe. Splinters and varnish hit the back of my neck. The first sergeant got some splinters on the face. He went off to the first aid station and got a Purple Heart. I didn't go to the aid station. I later got the French *Croix de Guerre* . . . so I guess that was supposed to make me feel better.

We had good firepower coming out of what was left of the house. A couple of .50-caliber machine guns and a bazooka team. But we never knew where the shot came from to start with, so there wasn't another shot fired. They didn't know where to fire. Did it come from the first floor, the second floor, halfway down the block? We didn't know. Never did find out. We never went down through the neighborhood to ask where the sniper was (laughs). But boy, it was time for a drawers check after that!

On the Hunt Again

Ulsaker's company also faced the problem of snipers. It was his job to clear them from Metz in the aftermath. He writes about an attempt to silence—or at least intimidate—what the GIs named the "Main Street Sniper."

My company stayed in place while K Company moved up to the tracks in the area to our immediate south. With no operation to supervise, I decided to do something about the damned "Main Street Sniper." On the north side of the street the building adjacent to the railroad tracks was a larger structure than the other ones in the immediate vicinity. It appeared to be a combination *gasthaus* (beer hall) and meeting place, most of it being taken up by a spacious room that could hold a couple hundred people. Vertically, the room extended from the ground floor to the roof, which was flat with some raised skylights in the middle. Just under the skylights some steel beams ran from wall to wall. At the west end of the building were two floors of offices and stairs that led to an exit on the roof. I decided to climb up there with binoculars and an M-1 rifle to see if somehow I could locate the sniper and zero him out. Still smarting over the loss of his platoon sergeant, Lieutenant Reilly volunteered to help me.

Once on the roof, I flattened out on my stomach and crept to the edge where I could observe most of the area east of the tracks. Reilly placed a helmet on the end of a stick and thrust it into the street from behind the *gasthaus*. The sniper fired. Through the field glasses I searched the houses up the street in vain. "Try again," I shouted down to Reilly.

Bang. The sniper fired again. I looked in every window, door, or other spot from where I thought someone could shoot, but I saw nothing. After several repetitions, I finally decided to give up. The German's use of flashless, smokeless powder had made it impossible for me to locate the target. Moving back to the west edge of the roof, I looked down to see Reilly waving a red Nazi flag from his protected spot behind the building.

"What in the hell are you doing?" I called down.

Reilly looked up at me. "I'm giving him Maggie's drawers. The lousy Kraut bastard fired seven times and hasn't hit the helmet once!" "Maggie's drawers" is the slang term used by American soldiers on the practice firing range to denote the red flag waved by the scorer in the pits when a target is missed completely.

◆

Chapter Seven

After taking Metz, Emil Schmidt remembers the dash for the French-German border, and a gruesome discovery of mass atrocities en route.

We were ready to go on the line, and then Patton broke through. He took off like a bunny. We traveled like hell for the French border. Tough to keep up with that rascal.

At a town near the border, we had an experience. At this small town, we moved some people out of their houses, and commandeered them. A little lady of the village had been given my name and she put two-and-two together. It's a German name, so she thought I might speak German. She started talking to me, in German, about something outside of town.

We went there, and the Germans had buried a bunch of Frenchmen there in a mass grave. They dug a hole, about the size of a kitchen room, and just dumped the bodies in there. We got a hold of the German burgermeister and his flunkies. We made them dig up the bodies. The Quartermaster Corps came with heavy wrappings and we made them wrap the bodies in these wrappings. The engineers dug a long trench for us. We laid the bodies in that trench, side by side, body beside body in that long trench. Probably 40 or 50 of them. I have pictures of that.

The lady who told me—I never knew if she was French or German, but she could speak fluent German. In some of the occupied areas, the people were forced to speak German even if they were French. She knew it wasn't right that these many men were buried that way, but at the time it happened, of course, she couldn't say a thing about it. She had kept her mouth shut until we got there. I have pictures of the burgermeister and his flunkies. These bodies hadn't been there long. I suppose they had been lined up and killed as the Germans pulled out. That had happened in a number of places that had been occupied.

Unfortunately, there were atrocities on both sides—although on the Allied side they were isolated and stopped by superiors when known. Carl Ulsaker remembers a GI's crime:

Prisoners of war began to form between men and the forward elements of the battalion. As I approached a spot where the Weapons Platoon of L Company rested awaiting orders for further deployment, I saw to my horror one of our noncoms plucking Germans at random from the POW column and sticking them in the belly with his bayonet. Several of the wounded Krauts lay groaning in the ditch. I accosted the man and instructed him in no uncertain terms to stop this mayhem, warning him that as soon as

I saw his company commander I would see that he was placed in arrest and charges preferred for court-martial. I pressed forward and found Captain Sundberg, L Company Commander. After consulting with him about supporting fires for the assault across the canal into Metz proper, I brought up the matter of the offending noncom. Sundberg agreed with me that this was serious misconduct and promised to bring the man to justice. As I returned the way I had come to rejoin Kelly and the command group, I again passed the L Company Weapons Platoon, now moving forward. Not seeing the noncom who had been stabbing prisoners, I inquired about him. The platoon leader informed me that a few minutes earlier they had been shelled by the guns at Plappeville and that the noncom in a question had been severely wounded and probably would lose a leg. Apparently, a higher court had seen fit to pass sentence.

Desperation in battle evoked other dishonorable behavior, such as desertion and SIWs (self-inflicted wounds). Patton made it clear that such acts would not be tolerated. After visiting a hospital where he found three SIW cases, Patton stated: "I told the chief of staff to get out an order that all who receive self-inflicted wounds will be tried on two counts before leaving the Army area; first, for self-inflicted wounds; second, for negligence. On the latter count, they can get six months. They should get life, the yellow dogs. . . . In my opinion, there is nothing lower than a man who, in order to save his own self, maims himself and leaves to his more heroic comrades an extra duty to perform." Ulsaker writes about his experience with SIWs:

It was one unpleasant problem that all frontline commanders had to deal with . . . From time to time a soldier, desperate to get out of combat, would shoot himself, usually in the foot. As a matter of fact, the Army required all foot wounds to be investigated as possible SIWs. I had one poor soul in Fraulautern who thought he could beat the rap by putting a neat little hole in his hand. One night while on guard duty he placed the muzzle of his M-1 rifle under his hand and pulled the trigger. He did not reckon on the tremendous muzzle blast generated by the cartridge designed to propel a bullet at a speed nearly three times that of sound. Instead of a neat hole in the center of his hand, he wound up with a mangled mass of shredded flesh, blood, and tendons.

Chapter Seven

With the lifeblood of gasoline fully restored, Patton was bulldozing through the Saar River Valley region of southwestern Germany, building momentum as he had through northern France. But after the river crossing, some fueling challenges remained. Stephen Conland of the 5th Quartermaster Battalion writes:

There was a great deal of work as the Army kept setting up reserves all the time. These varied from 100,000 to 400,000 gallons. These were constantly being moved.

On the other side of the Moselle, practically all hauling was done by truck. The dumps were put in railroad stations for hard standing, and the gas trucked in, because the rail system on the east side of the river was in shambles. Decanting operations in Domgermaine to Nancy and Mousielles were kept up.

Patton became obsessed with regaining the momentum, even if it meant personally driving out past a defensive perimeter in front of troops who had become accustomed to digging in. Vince Gish, demolitions expert in the 6th Armored Division, says he saw Patton in the farthest forward combat areas more than once, as they moved into the forested hills of the Saar Valley. He describes one such sighting.

We were really up on an edgy situation, knowing some Germans were down off the backside of a hill in a woodsy area. We were in the Saar Valley, the coal region. We were out in front of the tanks, even the infantry, clearing mines. And coming across the field, here comes General Patton with a driver and a jeep. And he had that damn gilded helmet on, and ivory pistols at his sides, and had his foot up on the side runner of that jeep as if there was nothing to it. Really, like a movie.

Someone turned and asked, "Where the hell is he going?" He passed us while we were digging in to escape the shrapnel of artillery coming in. The shells were going over us at the point and we got down. We didn't know what it was hitting in back of us. But here comes this son of a bitch past us, heading right for where we knew the Germans were.

We never knew if it was his appearance that scared them away or what, but the Germans must have moved out because he came back a little while later and said, "Move out. There's nothing down there."

The Third Army was lumbering into the Saar basin, but what happened next would break its stride again.

Chapter 8

Battling the Bulge

December 1944–January 1945

In a famous episode of Patton lore, General Eisenhower's lieutenants were called together and asked how fast they could respond to a new German counteroffensive in the Ardennes— Hitler's last-ditch effort, later named the Battle of the Bulge. Patton replied without hesitation: "On December 22"—in three days.

Some officers at the meeting shifted in their seats and stifled incredulous laughter. It meant disengaging an entire Army from an eastward advance and turning on a dime northward. And the grand design for a mighty strike on the Saar basin would be instantly discarded.

Colonel Paul D. Harkins knew his boss spoke in earnest and that hyperactive days would follow. As deputy chief of operations, he had joined Patton at the meeting. Harkins recounts Patton's response, and what ensued.

General Eisenhower told him that he'd have to call the attack to the east off and attack north, on the southern edge of the Bulge, because the Germans had already reached Bastogne. Bastogne was an important road . . . center—a very important position. The 101st Airborne was already there. They were pretty well surrounded by this time. So, when Ike asked how soon he could attack, General Patton said, "I'll make a meeting engagement in three days."

That brought a bit of a chuckle. Ike's staff didn't think that was possible. General Patton turned to me and said, "We can do that," and I said, "Yes, sir." There wasn't much else I could say.

So, he went to Luxembourg from Verdun and I went back to Nancy, to brief the Third Army staff. I told them what we had to do and got things moving.

I left that afternoon for Luxembourg to join General Patton, and I arrived there after supper. He wanted to know where the hell I had been, and I said, "I've been fighting divisions, moving up this way. It took quite a while through a snow storm."

He said, "Well, here's what I've done." And he turned to his driver, Sergeant Mims, who had been with him all day and the only one with him. He asked, "Didn't you take notes, Mims?"

"No, sir, I didn't."

"Well," he said, "I'll try to remember what I did." And he started telling me this and what my orders were.

I went around the next day to see if everything was in order. The units were so broken up after they got hit by the Germans. Antiaircraft units were mixed up with infantry, etc. There were tanks mixed up with antiaircraft and nobody seemed to be in command. Well, General Patton just went up there and got them all together and formed little task forces out of them. He said, "You are in command and you are now known as a task force . . ." He named them using the name of the commander: Task Force Gregory or Task Force Jones.

I don't think if you sat down in Fort Leavenworth and tried to figure out how you save that thing, you could have done better than he did. He just had a knack for what should go together and what they should do.

Patton lore also has it that this 90-degree turn was launched by a single telephone call. True in the strictest sense, according to Harkins. But what that doesn't divulge is that the change in direction was actually planned *before* the meeting with Eisenhower (and perhaps Harkins wasn't fully aware until after "the call"). Patton had already directed Hap Gay in Nancy to prepare to move the armored and infantry divisions, battalions of artillery, tanks and tank destroyers northward. Gay explains:

Patton told me to bring out that corps which was facing the Germans on that northernmost side, and . . . start them down right away, down into there, and he would go see General Eisenhower.

Eisenhower asked him when he could attack and Patton told him December 22. Eisenhower said, "Don't be absurd. You know better than that. You know you can't move those troops out of the one direction, and move them down there and do it again." But of course, General Patton never told him he had *already* given the orders, and they were on the move down there right then (laughs).

General Patton believed there was only one way to fight a war and that is to go after it and get it over with. Such was the case when the Germans made the breakthrough.

Personally, I recommended to General Patton he let the Germans go, for two to three days, and then cut in behind them and end this war. But Patton said, "No sir, we're going after them right now. I'm going down to talk to them, the troops, and you pull out two divisions which are now facing the east and pull them back, ready to go into there."

Warrant Officer Fred Hose, of Lucky Forward's G-2 section, casts more light on Patton's foreknowledge and the deft move northward.

The Third Army was poised for a big kickoff. There was to be a tremendous bombardment on the Siegfried Line. There were to be 4,300 planes coming over in waves, the fighters and the medium bombers, followed by the heavy bombers. Generally, with that kind of bombardment, if it didn't kill the enemy, it would leave them shell-shocked. And the armor would be standing by to roll right on through them. That's what had happened during the breakout at Normandy. The infantry punched a hole through and then the armor rolled. That was all expected to happen in the latter part of December. Then the Battle of the Bulge started.

Colonel Koch of the G-2 section had been warning that there was a build-up in the area. It was not just a hunch. Advance warnings were out. But, higher headquarters ignored both the G-2 of the First Army and G-2 of the Third Army warnings about a build-up. One reason they ignored it was because Hitler never put out a general order over the Ultra [coding] machine that would be picked up by the British in England. So there was no confirmation of it. And higher headquarters poo-pooed that the threat was as big as they said. When Colonel Koch warned General Patton, General Patton said, "We'll keep our eyes open, and if it happens we'll be prepared." His confidence must have been strong enough, because he pulled the 4th Armored off the line [after being readied to charge the Siegfried Line].

We had an OSS man, a major in the Marine Corps, who dressed like a peasant and went back and forth between the lines. Up around Trier, he reported, there were all these trains coming in with armor, that there was this build-up there. So Colonel Koch learned first about it that way. General Patton was briefed every day as to what was going on. He had a big map in the war room that showed all the German dispositions—what units were in action, on the move, whatever. So he knew about all this.

Every morning I'd go up into the operations sections, and I knew the night duty officer well. I went in on December 16 and asked him, "What's cooking today?"

Chapter Eight

He said, "We got something big going on. So big that VIII Corps had to pack up and get the hell out of there." Now we knew the intelligence was right, and everybody started getting scared. But Patton knew that the 4th Armored Division was back, getting ready to move north. That's when Eisenhower asked Patton how soon he could get moving to the north, General Patton just said, "Where's the telephone?" And Patton made the call to turn us loose north.

The fact was that we were already packed up and all ready to move out for this all-out attack on the Saar basin to the east. Hell, it didn't take us long for the quartermaster to get us trucks to move north instead. In that respect it was easy. They made decisions about which divisions would stay on the line to hold the line, while the other units turned north.

The conditions became terrible for movement, of course. It became snowy and icy, and all the roads become clogged with vehicles. The roads in vicinity, even today, leave something to be desired.

Most people don't think about what that change of direction meant for logistics and the engineers. The job was phenomenal. The Signal Corps had laid all these lines getting ready for this advance eastward that never took place. They had to pull it all up and reroute it to the north. Quartermaster dumps had to be established. Ordnance dumps had to be established. The logistics to keep an Army on the move is tremendous—something people don't think about.

But we got to Luxembourg and Lucky Forward was established at an old folks' home. The next morning Colonel Koch called me and told me to deliver an envelope personally to General Seifert, G-2 of the Twelfth Army Group. I went and got a driver, found out where the Twelfth Army was located, still in Luxembourg. We drove over to it. Never saw anything like that. There were sandbags out in front, a water-cooled .30-caliber machine gun with gunner behind, sentries at the door. They asked for the password at the door; I gave them the password and they let me inside, where an officer was sitting. This officer asked for my A.G.O. card—the only time in service I was *ever* asked to show my A.G.O. card. I told him I needed to see General Seifert, and I was met by a colonel who said he'd take the envelope in to the general. I said, "I'm sorry, sir. I'm under orders to deliver this personally to General Seifert." He said okay.

At that time I didn't know the contents of the envelope, but I was to learn this was the G-2 reports bringing Seifert up to date on what was going on. Colonel Koch later wrote in his book that G-2 provided all this intelligence for Patton, primarily to exonerate G-2 from the blame that was heaped on him. It was said there was no knowledge of the build-up, and the people who were supposed to be in the know weren't aware of the troop build-up, which was crap.

At headquarters the next day, General Patton announced to the staff what the situation was, and that we'd need to get moving right away. Patton announced very matter-of-factly what we were going to do, and that we were going to kick the shit out of the Germans.

Was he excited about it? This was right up General Patton's alley! He was in hog heaven. Hog heaven! This was just the kind of situation he was looking for.

This man, his thinking was prolific. Like any really intelligent man, he was two steps ahead of everyone else's thinking. I've often thought that if it wasn't for the slapping incident, Patton would have to have been given charge of the Twelfth Army instead of Bradley. And then I've wondered what course the war would have taken. Perhaps ended earlier. On the other hand, then the Third Army would have been commanded by Bradley, and would Bradley have handled the Third Army the way Patton did?

At the end of that meeting, I heard one of the war correspondents asking General Patton about meeting the German counterattack. Without batting an eyelash, he said to the correspondent: "If von Runstedt wants to stick his ass in the meat grinder, I'll be more than happy to turn the crank."

Citing the old "lead, follow, or get the hell out of the way" dictum of the military, Major Frank Pajerski, air liaison in Lucky Forward's G-2 section, recalls a subsequent meeting in which Patton let everyone know the bold charge northward would be impeded by nothing—the weather, the enemy, or his British counterpart, Montgomery.

One briefing I remember well was on the Continent. General Patton didn't believe much in night attacks. So we'd have the briefings at night in order to plan everything for the morning. At a briefing, you could expect to get news from home, the weather, the G-2 situation and G-3 information, and so on.

At this particular briefing I remember Patton was sitting there quietly through all this. Then a British liaison officer from Montgomery's headquarters gave a briefing on the British situation. Of course, Patton didn't give a damn for Montgomery. And this major made the mistake of asking General Patton: "Do you have any message to pass along to General Montgomery?" This was during the Battle of the Bulge.

He thought awhile, flicked his cigar, and nodded. When Patton nodded, everybody shut up and waited, because we all knew he was going to say something. Finally, he said, "You tell Montgomery that the Third Army is attacking north and for him to get out of the way, because I'm going to run the German army up his ass."

Sometime later, he saw that same major again. Patton asked, "Did you give General Montgomery my message?"

This British major hemmed and hawed and stuttered out, "Bub-bub-bub, yes sir."

"Well, what did he say?"

"Bub-bub-bub, I-I-I would say, sir, h-h-he was not h-h-highly amused." I'll never forget that.

◆

Patton's III Corps was indeed ready to attack the morning of December 22, as Patton had promised. Maury Laws' 26th Infantry Division, which became part of III Corps, was one of the first three divisions moved north to confront the German breakthrough. He remembers the sudden change in plans and action in the Battle of the Bulge:

We'd been slogging through mud for six weeks. Now finally, we were here at Metz, where we were supposed to clean up and get some R and R. It must have been 10 o'clock at night and we were billeted in some buildings—one was an old stone building, maybe a school. It was to be the first night of sleep in a building since we hit France. We were in there to take showers and bed down for the night, even get new clothing, but then word came through to get on the trucks. Word was that the Germans had broken through—the start of the Bulge. That was December 17, my grandmother's birthday.

When we got off the trucks, we were told we were in Luxembourg. We began slugging our way through those woods, getting shot at, while shells were coming in. One landed so close I got tossed up in the air, but—not a scratch. Every tree around me had bark torn off from shrapnel. But again, not a scratch on me. That was where my friend John Sipiletti disappeared. Just disappeared. He was going from one hole to another and simply never got to the next one. I looked for his body but never found it. I didn't find out until after the war he had been taken prisoner and survived. He still sends me Christmas cards.

The Bulge just ground on. One day after another. It was very cold—and the snow! There hadn't been snow at Metz. It may have rained. The snow happened first in Luxembourg, and we began to have to chip the bodies out of the ice. The bodies would be warm right after death and melt the snow or ice where they fell, then it would refreeze around them.

We went through the mountains with our truck on a narrow road with no lights at night. Two of us would walk in front of the truck to tell the driver how to steer. We had to go out in front of the lines in a truck to pick up bodies. We were on a hill, and with only a valley between us, and the Germans on the next hill over, I thought this was suicide. But they didn't fire on us. We put out white flags and they knew what we were doing.

It was snowy, rainy or foggy all the time, it seemed. It was Christmas Day and the sun came out. It had been overcast almost all the time. Now, the weather was finally good enough for our planes to fly. And by then the Germans had no planes to put in the air. So here's this brilliant sun and silver U.S. aircraft gleaming in it. Now we knew things would change. You could see the power in the sky. There must have been a thousand planes in the air—a beautiful sight!

We took prisoners, too. We learned something from them about how we were driving them crazy without even knowing it. Our mortar men were doing it to them. Here's something I remember vividly— like a scene out of a tough-guy movie—that will tell you how:

One day, our chaplain was talking with one of the mortar men. He was a wonderful Roman Catholic chaplain. I am not Catholic. But the father, Father Bob—everyone loved him—he'd come up and ask you how you were doing. He did that with everyone. Everybody's friend. Always a smile on his face. A guy comes out of his foxhole. He's got a cigarette hanging out of his mouth. He's wearing no helmet, just an olive drab cap. He grabs two or three mortar shells, then turns to head back to his mortar.

The chaplain smiles and asks in his Irish accent: "What pattern are you firin', son?"

The guy just says, "Screw 'em, father." In other words, no pattern. There was no pattern that fired one or two every five minutes or anything that regular.

The Germans couldn't *stand* that. Couldn't stand it. The Germans might send two 88s every three minutes and a mortar shell every four minutes. You could time it and run from building to building.

We captured Germans who had a nervous breakdown because they couldn't figure out the firing pattern. Because there *was* none.

We noticed other differences in the way Germans thought, too. For instance, if their leader was killed, the Germans would often surrender. If that happened to the Americans, some guy from South

Carolina or somewhere would jump up and yell, "C'mon, let's get 'em!" He would jump up and become the John Wayne of the moment. The Americans were much more individual in their thinking. So often, I found myself glad to have some guy from Georgia and others from the South, because those guys seemed to do more of that. They had great resourcefulness.

◆

When Patton vets talk about the Battle of the Bulge, they naturally recall the ferocity of the German counterattack. But in the same breath they mention the other punishing foe—the worst winter to descend upon Europe in years. Later in the Bulge, during January, infantrymen trudged through deep drifts and tanks skidded off the icy roads. German mines, always a threat, were even more easily laid—tossed loose into the snow and quickly snowed under. Heavy snowfall and unusually cold temperatures had dramatic effects on men in combat, inflicting frostbite and worse: Not only did they endure teeth-chattering cold, but the dazzling white blanket of fresh-fallen snow made them stark targets in their olive-drab uniforms.

H. M. Trowern describes the effect of weather and what his unit did to overcome it. Enlisted at age 17, Trowern was a squad leader in the 2nd Platoon of G Company in the 2nd Battalion, 345th Infantry Regiment, of the 87th Division, which was set to attack the Saar basin when sketchy news about the German counteroffensive spread through the ranks. The word in his squad was simply: "The Germans had broken through up north." His battalion's sudden assignment became to attack the town of Moircy, Belgium, and then go on to clear Libramont and Recogne, all in the vicinity of Bastogne. During movement northward, he saw rain change to snow, as temperatures plummeted.

What I remember most vividly was the cold. I had grown up in northern states of New York and Massachusetts, so I was accustomed to winter, but this was really cold when you had to sleep outside all the time.

The Belgians kept telling us it was very unusual weather, but that struck me as a phrase that some hotel manager would tell you when you went to a resort, paid a lot of money and it rained all the time. He'd say that it was very unusual weather. Years later, I found out that this *was* unusual for the Ardennes. The bitter winter was the worst they had had in 80 years. We just happened to be stuck with it.

After a while we learned how to adapt to the severe conditions. Snow is a good insulator, so when we'd dig a foxhole, we take some tree limbs, or branches, put them on top of the hole and cover those with snow. That kept the hole warmer and it also was good camouflage. The problem was that we didn't stay in one spot long enough to really get comfortable in a hole. We'd dig it, spend maybe one night in it and then move out on the attack again.

Being part of Patton's Army, we fell under his strategy of attacking continuously. We learned the hard way, earlier on, that if you let the Germans dig in, they were much harder to break through than if you kept them running all the time. So as far as we were concerned, it was better to attack every day and every night if necessary. Bear in mind most of us were very young. I was 18 and there probably wasn't anybody in my platoon that was older than 25, except for one or two. We were young men, so we had a lot of energy and we could recover from fatigue more quickly . . . Older replacements that we got just couldn't recover very well and they kept getting progressively more fatigued.

One of the concerns we had about the cold, particularly when we were on patrols, was that if we got hit or wounded and we couldn't move and they didn't find us right away, we'd probably freeze to death. And there were several instances where we found men from our company who had gotten hit. Either we didn't know about it or we didn't know where they were and by the time we'd gotten to them they had frozen to death. And we stayed out in the cold for so long. . . .

We sort of adapted to the cold, or at least we learned different ways to improve our conditions. And one of them was to walk behind our tanks. When our tanks were in a column or they were moving forward, they didn't go very fast. They were capable of higher speeds than the German tanks, but they would usually move along slowly. And we'd walk behind them. If you got up close to the engine the exhaust would keep you warm. And the engine itself felt warm. So we'd walk behind the tanks.

Whenever we got the chance, we'd sneak up on the back of the tank where the tank crew would have these ten-in-one rations. They were much better than the K-rations that we got. Ten-in-ones were much more varied and they tasted a lot better. We couldn't carry them as infantry soldiers because we didn't have enough room in our packs. But the tankers could put them right on their tanks. They had them strapped or tied down at the back of their tanks and we used to sneak up when they weren't looking and take these rations and eat them for ourselves. We thought we were getting away with what we called "scrounging." But actually what I found out after the war when I was talking to guys in various armored divisions was that they would put that food out there on the back of their tanks because they *wanted* us to stay near them. They knew that it would hurt our pride if they gave us food, so they let us think that we were stealing it and fooling the tankers. They were putting it out there so that we would hang around them because tanks need infantry to protect them. Particularly our tanks, because the German troops could get behind our tanks if our infantry wasn't around to hold them off. They could then set fire to the tanks because we had gasoline engines. The tank's machine guns couldn't fire to the rear, and the Germans could take their time and just destroy our tanks. Our tankers knew this. Therefore they wanted us, their friendly infantry, to hang around to protect them. And one of the ways they did it was to put food out for us. It was like baiting an animal. But it worked.

As the snow kept getting deeper and deeper, it was not only hard for us to walk through the fields and woods, but we stood out more because of the contrast. Everything was white except our uniforms. We were in olive drab that made us very obvious. We noticed that the Germans were wearing white snowsuits. So we started to look for bed sheets, anything that was white to use as some camouflage. I remember one time this little Belgian village. There was a nuns' convent and a clinic. We went into the convent and when I saw there was a clinic there, I asked one of the sisters who was in charge (I think they were Sisters of Charity) if we could borrow some linens, bed sheets so that we could cover our uniforms with camouflage, snow suits. We used their habits as sort of capes. And because they were wool they were warm as well, so we really lucked out.

The Battle of the Bulge, you know, lasted for over six weeks and this was about the first week in which we'd gotten these nuns' habits to wear and we got other bed sheets from other places, but when the snow started to thaw in February, the snow suits became a liability because they made us stand out when there was not much snow. We didn't want to stick out against the dark trees or the dirt, so we decided to get rid of the snowsuits.

I remembered that this nun had asked if we would return the habits when we were finished with them. I didn't think there would be any chance of that at all. But when the guys who were wearing the habits got hit, we would take them off and give them to somebody else. So, most of the habits were still around. They were pretty dirty and some had quite a bit of blood on them but they were still in one piece . . . I found a Red Ball Express driver who was going back near that village and we loaded these habits . . . he took them back to the mother superior, and she wrote us a thank you note. Of course it was in French, so I had to get somebody else to read it to me.

Harold Madsen, also in the 87th Infantry Division, had his baptism of fire in the snow on his very first day as a replacement in the division.

We were in the Ardennes area of France and Belgium. We had skirmishes with the Germans in the woods. There was a lot of snow. Two feet deep. We tried to burrow into the snow, because we were out in the open. It gave no protection, of course. Since we couldn't dig trenches, at least we could dig into the snow to stay out of sight. We didn't have much air support during the Battle of the Bulge, because it was snowing so much.

As a private first class and mortar gunner in the 5th Infantry Division, Al Elliott remembers the unique challenges for a mortar squad in the Bulge's weather conditions:

In Luxembourg they were expecting a breakthrough, so we were sent there. We were in a jeep when shells started coming in, and we drove it right up into the woods. Then we started getting tree bursts—artillery shells exploding right against tree limbs with shrapnel raining down instead of the shells exploding on the ground—so we jumped off the jeep and headed further into the woods, which was the worst thing we could do because of those tree bursts. When they let up a little bit, we made it out into an open field on the other side, which was better than facing the tree bursts.

In the open field, we tried to set up the gun, but in December the ground was too cold. A foot of frost in the ground. Plus it started to snow—4 or 5 inches that day.

That night, we started getting what we called "Christmas Carols" that the Germans fired off a truck. And we got the order to start firing our mortar. We didn't know where our jeep went and there were 30 or 40 rounds loaded on the trailer. So all we had was what we were carrying—three men with maybe six rounds each.

The mortar had a built-in compass, so we knew what direction we were firing. We started firing, but the guy at the OP [observation post] who could see where the rounds were landing, called us on the field phone and told us to move right, left, up, down, or whatever after we fired a few rounds. This time he called to say we were firing way short. We were firing off of frozen ground and couldn't dig it in. We tried to hold the base plate down, but it was difficult. The whole thing would come up off the ground and you'd have to set the whole thing up again.

They called to say to stop firing, but we had fired all the rounds we had anyway. They discovered afterward that we were on target. But the German shelling coming from the *other* way was what they were seeing and assuming was short fire—"friendly fire" on our own positions. The riflemen and machine gunners were up ahead of us. We were ordered to make a hasty withdrawal because all of us were short on ammunition. They also told us at the time that, no matter what, don't get captured because the Germans weren't taking prisoners here. Great to hear.

We got out of there, south by jeep. Four guys could travel in the jeep and two guys would have to ride on the trailer on top of the canvas covering the ammunition. We were at the tail end of the convoy. We came down the road in this jeep and couldn't stop on the ice, so we steered off the road to miss the jeep ahead of us. I also remember traveling in the dark, last jeep in the squad, and tanks running on blackout lights. Every time the convoy stopped, I would jump off the jeep, and all I could see were these blackout lights on this tank and the sound coming so close. So we were worrying not only about the Germans, but our own tanks driving up behind us.

We would always try to get into a house to sleep. Or since most of them were destroyed, at least down into the cellar.

We'd stay in vegetable cellars, made of concrete and with a rounded roof. Vegetables were pretty frosty in there, but you could stay in there. Some were big and you could fit more than just our squad.

We'd have to post a guard around the clock, of course. If we were out in the field, sleeping in foxholes, we always had two guys in a foxhole, and the shift would always work out that with the six-man squad, you'd have to do a two-hour watch. I was out there one night on my two hours, and I kept hearing noises. I didn't want to discharge a weapon, especially if I didn't know what I was firing at. So I'd make mudballs and tossed them to find if I could hear anything. If the noise would keep on the same, I would assume it was okay. But you could see these fence posts out there, and I swear, the more you look at a fence post, the more you'd think somebody was out there moving! My way of dealing with it was mudballs.

The next morning, after a night of throwing mudballs, I found that there had been these cows walking around in the night, eating. Shrapnel had hit some of the cows and half of their guts were hanging out. I remember being with Dale Sugg, from Illinois. What I remember best is that Dale chewed snuff and had a little Bible that he would read every day. He was the most panicky guy I ever saw. I thought he'd shoot someone or leave, but he made it through somehow. He was one guy who wouldn't fall asleep even when he wasn't on watch. He must have had to sleep during the daytime. Somehow I would sleep through it all; they'd have to shake my arm hard to wake me up.

We never got a chance to rest. We were so exhausted. If we stopped, another unit would move up through us. Then another unit up ahead might stop and we'd move up through them. It was constant action. We were never far back from the front lines. Patton wanted us to just keep on going!

We saw Patton once. He was in a jeep with his aide. I remember seeing him get out with his pearl-handled pistols. He waved as he left, but we were all so cold and miserable, it didn't leave much of an impression. We would have much rather have seen a chow truck pull up with hot food!

George W. Knapp was a young chaplain in the 4th Infantry Division who had landed with the division on D-Day at Utah Beach with the First Army. His division was transferred to the Third Army on the day the Battle of the Bulge began. He remembers being reassigned to Patton's command and the time leading up to Christmas 1944:

When the Battle of the Bulge happened on the 16th of December, the 4th Infantry Division was in Luxembourg. The powers that be—Eisenhower—called up the Third Army from the south where it had been, and they came up and took us over and from then on the 4th Infantry Division was with the Third Army until the fighting was over.

On December 16, we had been fighting in the Hertgen Forest. We'd been there for weeks by then. It was terrible. We had many casualties and the weather was terrible. Normally, there were 15,000 men in the division and 15 chaplains—one of them Jewish because proportionately there weren't many Jewish men, about eight or nine Protestant chaplains, and the rest Catholic. That was proportionate according to the number of the men. There were three chaplains with the 12th Infantry Regiment, because we normally had 3,000 men. Two Protestants, of which I was one, and one Catholic.

We were down to about 50 percent of our men and 50 percent of our equipment. That's why we were sent down to Luxembourg, because that was the quietest part of the front at the time. Even though the Germans were right across the river from us, there wasn't much activity. The civilian houses where we stayed even had electricity still. Then on December 16, all of a sudden the artillery shells started coming in from the east, across the river.

I'll never forget our battalion first sergeant was hit in the shelling that day. Seriously injured. He was walking out in the open between buildings. I took my belt off my trousers and used that as a tourniquet to stop the bleeding. The medics came almost right away and took him away in an ambulance. I don't know how I ever held my pants up after that, because the belt went off with him. I didn't see him again for 20 years. He had been slender and redheaded, a young guy, maybe 20 years old. Then in 1964 or 1965 we had a reunion in Pittsburgh. And he was so happy to see me. I might have saved his life with that belt, I don't know. He was chubby and had nearly no hair left. I hardly recognized him.

I didn't have many young men approach me to discuss their fears around that time. Everybody thinks they're going to be the one to make it all the way through. I thought that, too. Even though the 4th Division had the highest rate of casualties that fought in Europe: 400 percent casualty rate—they kept replacing our dead and wounded. But I remember a platoon sergeant, great big guy, who had been in charge of his platoon from D-Day on. He was close to me, one in a quartet that always sang songs at my services. One day he said to me, "I feel terrible because I'm leading these men into battle, but whenever I fire my gun, I fire high enough that I know I'll never hit anybody. It really bothers me and I know I shouldn't do it. I don't know what to do and I could be court-martialed for it. I just can't kill anybody!"

I told him, "I know the commandment says, 'Thou shalt not kill.' Another way to put that is, 'Thou shall not murder.' And you're not murdering anybody. You're doing what you're supposed to be doing—picked by our government to protect our country. If somebody dies because you hit them with a bullet, it's not murder. It's different than if you were a civilian who, in anger, killed someone."

He said with great emotion, "I still can't." He knew it was wrong for him to be leading his men and not fighting that way himself.

The sergeant went to his battalion commander, a young replacement because all the originals had been wounded or killed, and told him how he felt. The battalion commander liked this sergeant and said, "I'm not going to do anything as drastic as you thought I might. But I'm going to bust you down from staff sergeant down to private."

He lost his leadership role and pay. And he had to write to his girl back home and his folks to tell them about his decision. Now, instead of carrying a gun and shooting, he worked in the outfit that carried food, water, ammunition and clothing up to the front.

He went on singing in the quartet for services that Christmas, although the quartet was soon reduced to a trio when one of the other members was captured by the Germans. I don't even know the name of the little town, but we had services on Christmas Eve. I can see the inside of the church as clearly as if I were standing in it right now. The church had been bombed, so the roof was gone. On the altar—this was a Catholic church—were the big chancel candles. We took them down the street to this little stable right in the middle of town. We lit the candles for a Christmas candlelight service. We had Jewish men there, we had Catholic men there, we had Protestant men there, we had men who had probably never been to church before. And all during the service, we could hear the trucks going by on the way to the front. Replacements for our own men in the 4th Infantry Division who were now facing the big German counteroffensive. The foxholes were nearby on the west side of the Ruhr River facing the enemy on the other side of the river. These were all replacements just brought in. I felt so glad that some of our boys were going to be relieved, but I felt bad that these poor young replacements, who had just a couple days before been in the United States or Paris, were put up there in those foxholes—on Christmas Eve.

The next day, Christmas Day, we were sent back to Luxembourg City. That day, I had six services, all in a bowling alley. Many of those men who had been relieved from the foxholes the night before were there, with their gas masks and everything. The bowling alley was only a two-lane bowling alley, so it was very narrow and long. Here we had our services. These guys were just so glad to be out of there, and on Christmas. It was really a special Christmas for them.

The trio sang. And my assistant—a big six-foot Southern Baptist fella from Jacksonville, Florida—was always there with me, playing the organ. It was a portable organ that folded up into a big suitcase. He would play by pumping his feet. He was somewhat of an experienced organ player before the war. But the chaplain's assistant also did the typing and driving of the jeep.

There were many letters written from the people back home who wanted to know what happened to their loved ones. Those letters were turned over to the chaplains for answering. The letters would come to the company and regimental commanders. We'd go to personnel—our personnel sergeant would have information telling if someone was KIA or a prisoner. He'd have whatever the medics sent down about how a man was wounded and how long he lived. I'd draw off these records [to respond to the letters].

At first, I got emotional about it. It got the best of me. I remember going over to another place, away from everybody, sitting down in the weeds and having a good cry. But that got it out of my system. I thought about how I had volunteered for this job, and that I better just buck up and do it. So that was my way of stepping away from it emotionally. From then on, I would just keep on going and do my job no matter what it was. Otherwise I would have been sent home or sent to the hospital with battle fatigue.

Those letters took most of my time when there wasn't fighting. I'd be sitting in my jeep with a typewriter on my knees typing letters. Through all these years, I've kept all the letters I received from families during that time.

Patton's armor rumbles through a snowy town in Belgium or Luxembourg around Christmas 1944. Patton writes in his diary for December 25: "A clear and cold Christmas, lovely weather for killing Germans, which seems a bit queer." **U.S. Army**

Private W. King Pound had a Christmas Eve of a different sort. After spending three months in the U.S. Army hospital at Cherbourg, Pound returned to the 4th Armored Division just in time for the Battle of the Bulge. His reintroduction to combat is described in part by a citation that awarded him a Bronze Star: "Private Pound exposed himself to intense enemy artillery and small arms fire, crawled several hundred yards over snow covered ground to reach the wounded man and removed him from the burning town." He describes it this way:

We were on the Arlon-Bastogne highway on Christmas Eve. Our platoon sergeant was called to a meeting with the company commander and others. So we moved off the road about 11 o'clock at night. Orders were coming down from the Third Army to make a night attack on this little town called Warnach about 10 miles outside of Bastogne. But my platoon sergeant and company commander were against it, because night attacks were not exactly what you wanted to do with tanks. But a one-star general sent down from Third Army headquarters insisted.

With us was a platoon of infantry, 26 guys. It was close to midnight when we started across the snow-covered fields. We saw the quaint little town in the distance—thatched roofs and all. The tank commander told me, as gunner, to aim the .30-caliber at those roofs to set them on fire so we could see what the hell was going on. That's what we did, and the roofs started on fire. I didn't see any enemy vehicles at all.

All of a sudden the tank commander hollers down to me: "Get the hell out, Pound! We've been hit!"

I was so engrossed in the targets I hadn't even felt it or heard anything in the confusion. An enemy shell had gone in on the driver's side. I hadn't felt the impact. It had ricocheted around inside and exited back out the front. So we got out and started running. Didn't even have my grease gun or anything. But all hell was breaking loose from the village. Then I realized, after I'd run 50 yards through small arms fire, that I had left the turret turned so the driver couldn't get out of the driver's hatch. I went back.

The driver's name was "Squirrel," Squirrel Hayden, and I called to him by name.

He called back: "I can't get out. I think my foot's been shot off."

He wasn't able to crawl over the transmission to get out of the escape hatch on the bottom, because he was injured. The bow gunner had gotten out that way. I climbed in and centered the turret so the hatch could open. I climbed and reached down to help him out. He climbed on my back piggyback style and we headed for the tree line to avoid being seen and lay down in snow that was about a foot deep at this time. By that time, everyone else had disappeared, so we were alone.

I heard motors, so I turned to Squirrel and said, "Shermans." And I started toward the sound.

But Squirrel, a Kentucky boy, recognized the sound better and said, "Hell, not Shermans. Not even one of ours. It's one of theirs!"

We lay down again. A minute later, a German patrol pulled up in half-tracks to capture us. They stopped about 20 feet from us in the tree line. We could see them, but they couldn't see us. I had a hand grenade, but figuring the odds quickly I thought, *Throw it and we're dead heroes.* So I kept it. But I knew I hadn't wanted to be captured. A couple of our guys had been captured and we found one of them the next day, bound up in ropes on the floor of a barn. He was dead. I don't know if he had been left there alive and our own fire killed him, or if the Germans just killed him outright. He had been shot. Anyway, they didn't see us and climbed back in their half-track.

Then we went another half mile to get back to our lines. I collapsed about 50 feet away from them, and guys from our tank came out to help us the rest of the way. They took Squirrel and I never saw him again.

Pound encountered Patton a short time later in the Battle of the Bulge:

The most memorable time I saw Patton was when we were driving to Bastogne. We were all buttoned up in our tank because of the heavy artillery fire coming down on our position and I looked through the periscope and saw him driving through the snow, standing upright in his jeep, and assessing our position. Crazy bastard. But inspiring.

◆

Lewis Ingalls, a field artillery captain, took part in Patton's thrust across the Ruhr River. The advance was met with ferocious German blocking forces that left many GIs bleeding to death on the riverbanks. Ingalls reflects on his feelings in the midst of the carnage:

There's something about being in combat, you become a different person—like a third person. You're standing outside of you and telling you what in the hell to do. Most people in that situation would tell you the same thing.

That's how I felt in battle when the Germans made that damn Bulge movement before Christmastime. Their idea was to cut off our salient that was headed toward the Ruhr Valley. They hoped to go through to Holland and cut us off. Our division spearheaded that and we lost a lot of people. It was a mess.

They were bombarding the hell out of the river and the river was real fast. There were reservoirs upstream and the Germans broke those reservoirs to make the river a mile wide in some places, and just flooded us. Where we crossed, it was about 100 yards, but real fast. We had a hard time as we tried at first to cross the river in rubber rafts. Lost a lot of people. Christ, I saw people on top of people. It was as bad as some of the pictures I've seen of the beaches at Normandy. It was a bugger, because there was only the one place we could cross and they could zero in on it. To start with, there was German infantry firing rifles at us at the same time we were getting shelled. But that quickly went away, because we had a hell of an artillery preparation. For a while you couldn't hear yourself think because the artillery pieces made it like there was constant thunder rolling.

Battling the Bulge

You don't have fear at a moment like that. You just sort of freeze. There's no place to go. It's just like anything else that happens to you. If you were in an automobile accident or something, what are you going to do. You're not going to lay down and quit. And to see the bodies stacking up on the shore, even though it was like they were your brothers dead, you had to keep going. You busy yourself with the things at hand and there was plenty of them. We just poured the artillery in, then lifted the artillery a little bit at a time—shooting a little bit farther so you don't hit your own men. Then the German outposts gave up easily.

The engineers were trying to put in a footbridge so the infantry could get across. Hell, they were shelling the hell out of things. They just got one bridge in, and the Germans bombed it out with aircraft. I was too confined to see the big picture and sure didn't question the decision of the commanding general.

◆

Patton's fast-moving armored warfare made logistics a nightmare. Yet expectations were sky-high for Patton's quartermaster, Colonel Walter "Maud" Muller. In supply circles, Muller became well known for his extraordinary knack of delivering just what was needed when it was needed during Patton's charge across France. Some of Muller's magic was witnessed by Major Wilbur Ash, quartermaster for the service command of the Eighth Army Air Force, based in England. Ash remembers a meeting that gave some clues to how Patton always seemed well supplied, even during the sudden German counteroffensive known as the Battle of the Bulge:

Colonel Mayberry and I, from the Eighth Air Force, flew over to Paris in General Jimmy Doolittle's plane for a meeting of the quartermasters in the European Theater. It was an unusual meeting called by the Quartermaster General Littlejohn, because of the Battle of the Bulge.

They were really concerned for the lack of supplies, especially because of the terrible winter weather. The troops over there had urgent needs, like blankets, overshoes, and overcoats.

General Littlejohn wanted to get an idea of what items we were actually short of. Every major unit over there had a quartermaster at this meeting to represent them. General Littlejohn went around the room calling on the various commands and asking, "What are your needs?"

Chapter Eight

General Littlejohn was an impressive looking guy, kind of built from the ground up. Very military. Looked very much the part. Short, cropped hair. Stocky.

He went down the line, asking each quartermaster what was needed. Through the various commands, always asking the same thing. Bradley's quartermaster needed blankets, overshoes, and warm clothing, exactly like most were saying. No one was really prepared for the Battle of the Bulge, the weather, or all that fighting.

He went through more, hearing much the same. Finally he got to General Patton's quartermaster, Colonel Muller, a leathery looking guy.

Littlejohn asked, "Colonel, what does General Patton need?"

Patton's man stood up ramrod straight at attention, and said, "Not a thing, sir."

General Littlejohn blinked, because everybody had needed something. Littlejohn said, "Come again?"

The colonel repeated, "Not a thing, sir."

Littlejohn paused and said, "How is it that everybody else needs something, and General Patton doesn't need anything?"

Implying he couldn't wait for meetings like this, he replied, "Sir, when General Patton says he needs something, I go get it."

According to Robert S. Allen, "Patton never asked Muller how and where he got supplies and equipment, and the latter never bothered Patton with needless details." When supplies were diverted, as they inevitably sometimes were, the result was "irate outcries from other quarters, but . . . they were viewed as merely the disgruntled wails of envious malcontents."

The Quartermaster Corps that served Patton's forces so well was not exempt from combat. Attrition among combat troops on the front lines had ramifications in the rear areas. Major Stephen Conland of the 5th Quartermaster Battalion found his staff dwindling and greater challenges in fulfilling the huge drain on supplies during the Battle of the Bulge.

On December 16 and 19, two gas company commanders were transferred to the infantry. The front-line divisions had become so short of men that 10 percent of all service units' personnel were transferred to the infantry.

On December 22 we moved to Fontoy. All divisions were pulled out of the line to hold the southern flank against the German attack. By the 22nd there were practically no troops except a little artillery and some reconnaissance units between us and the Germans.

Our quarters in Fontoy were quite cramped. We were next to the railroad station. One hundred yards on the other side was a quarry with ammunition stored. There was 200,000 gallons of gas stored in the rail yard, and this was, unfortunately, an excellent target.

On several evenings, planes came over. On December 25, they tried to bomb the gas. One 500-pounder fell in the cemetery 100 yards away. Small bombs fell in the street outside the house. We had wooden shutters on the windows and the pieces came into the room in which we were living.

That is as close as we came to getting hit, but it was close enough for me. Later they came over and strafed the ammo. It was most annoying as they were over practically every night. They constantly dived down to get a better view. This was the last big effort of the German Air Force.

◆

As casualties mounted, front-line units throughout the Ardennes were screaming for replacements. It was Coy Eklund's responsibility at Lucky Forward to find replacements and get them to the front.

While in Luxembourg during the Battle of the Bulge I was looking for 800 replacements for the 80th Infantry Division. They had been in heavy combat a day or two before. They were critically short of 745s [infantry riflemen]. I was a major then, and my job in the G-1 section of Third Army headquarters was keeping track of casualties and arranging their replacements as promptly as possible. The replacements were shipped in from the States, across the ocean to the landing area, then by train or by truck to the replacement depot, which sat behind Third Army headquarters.

So I called Colonel Brown at the replacement depot and told him we were desperately short of infantry riflemen. He said, "We had a truck company—50 trucks—come in this morning with 1,000 infantry riflemen. Twenty on a truck."

I asked, "Where are the drivers now?"

"In the mess hall having lunch."

"Good! When they get out, let's get 800 loaded up and moved this afternoon right on to the 80th Division."

"Major," he said, "These 50 trucks that came in here are from the Replacement and School Command in the rear, near Paris. I can't take them."

I said, "Colonel, in the name of General Patton, I'm commandeering those trucks."

He said, "Major, do you know what you're doing?"

I said, "Yes, sir."

"Okay," he said. "We'll do it."

I knew what I had to do immediately. I had to go tell General Patton what I had just done. Otherwise he was going to hear it from someone else, and they might not tell it in the way I would.

As I approached his office, his door was ajar, and I saw he was looking at something on his desk. Always working, you know. So I stepped in, clicked my heels and saluted him as he looked up at me.

I said, "Sir, I just commandeered a truck company in your name, sir."

He looked at me again and said calmly, "The hell you say."

I was probably trembling at that point, but explained, "Yes sir, the 80th is critically short of 745s, and they were there at the depot. And there were 50 trucks there who brought 1,000 of them in today. So I just took it upon myself to commandeer those trucks in your name, sir."

"Oh," he said. "That's goddamned good."

I saluted, clicked my heels, and left quickly.

Lieutenant Colonel Coy Eklund, Lucky Forward's G-1 (personnel) section, had responsibility for reporting casualty counts to Patton on a daily basis and finding replacement troops to fill out dwindling ranks—a particular challenge with the heavy casualties during the Battle of the Bulge.

Lucky Forward remained in Luxembourg through most of the Battle of the Bulge. Warrant Officer Fred Hose remembers with humor an incident while Lucky Forward operated out of a large old folks' home commandeered there as its headquarters.

We had a duty officer named Helmut Gerber, a refugee from Germany valuable for his ability to translate. One day, Gerber was in the operations office by himself and the telephone rings, and he hears, "This is General Patton and I want to be briefed!"

Captain Gerber thought this was a very poor imitation of General Patton—a trick being played by one of the other officers. And he made some flip remark on the telephone. General Patton was calling from within that same building, but a good ways down the hall, and this time Gerber could hear General Patton from that other office without having his ear to the telephone receiver.

"Godammit! This is General George Patton and I want to be briefed!"

This time, he answered, "Yessir, yessir." He was certain he'd be transferred before the sun set. When Colonel Koch came back from lunch, Gerber told him what had happened and that he made a terrible blunder, and that he was sure this was his last day with headquarters. Colonel Koch told Gerber he should see General Gay, the chief of staff, and apologize. So he went to General Gay and apologized, and General Gay said, "Okay, but *don't* let it happen again." He wasn't transferred.

Patton is quoted as saying, "A good solution applied with vigor now is better than a perfect solution applied 10 minutes later." Paul D. Harkins saw the principle applied by the headquarters staff particularly during the confusion and upheaval caused by the German counteroffensive, as he explains:

I'll say one thing about General Patton's staff, although he didn't stick to the book sometimes, he wanted people to get things done and when he wanted something done, the staff were the doers. It was a great bunch. There were no prima donnas, and they worked very closely with each other. They all knew what General Patton wanted, and they just saw that it was done.

One thing about his staff was that he insisted that somebody from the staff go forward every single day. When General Gay, chief of staff, didn't go up, I'd go up, or take some of the other staff officers and we'd just visit. At first, the corps and divisions didn't think much of having the Army staff come up and bother them, but then they found out we went up there to find out what they needed and that we would get it to them. They changed 180 degrees and they were all heart.

My job was to see that the staff coordinated and cooperated all the way through. That wasn't much trouble in Patton's staff because they all wanted to get things done and they wanted to get it done quickly, because as General Patton said, "The quicker you do a thing the more lives you save." That was true.

Chapter Eight

I wouldn't sit in the office and read a lot papers. I'd go down to the staff sections and tell them what we had to do and when we wanted it done, it was usually the day before yesterday. It was just a matter of getting across the idea of what the general wanted. He preferred a *good* plan rather than a *perfect* plan. Because a good plan, well carried out, would do the job just as well as a perfect plan, only delayed a few days longer.

I went around with Patton quite a bit, just to find out what he wanted done. Then it was my job to go back and see that it was done. Later he always would come to me and say, "Now, we want to change this or change that." I'd understand what he meant and go out and tell the staff and have it redone. I was getting it done in the quickest possible time and saving lives, and he appreciated that very much.

◆

A new and devastatingly efficient weapon—the proximity fuse—entered the arsenal of Patton's artillery units during the Battle of the Bulge. Major Martin Miller was the chief of the fire direction center of the 492nd Armored Field Artillery Battalion, 11th Armored Division, when proximity fuse shells first reached front-line units.

We were just west of Bastogne, when we used them for the first time. The proximity fuse was a brand new invention to us. We had to be more careful, because these fuses were more fragile. This was really a little radar set that sent out a beam. We couldn't set the fuse; it was set automatically to explode about 10 or 20 meters from something like a building, or anything that would reflect back. That caused the shell casing to explode in midair and splinter, sending its jagged parts flying and hitting somebody or something, and just rip through it. It could go through a human body without any trouble. The proximity fuse was really one of the reasons why the war didn't last any longer than it did.

We used the proximity fuse primarily on soldiers in the open. It gave kind of the effect of a tree burst, which infantrymen spoke with such fear about. But trees didn't have to be around and, in fact, you wouldn't want trees around. We didn't use proximity fuses in wooded areas, because the fuse would go off as it approached a tree. And you would never use it on a tank—it wouldn't go through a tank. But it was devastating on people.

The people manning the howitzers didn't see the targets. In the battalion, we had 18 self-propelled 105-millimeter howitzers on M4 tank chassis. There were three firing batteries, and each had six of these howitzers. The gunfire is adjusted by forward observers on the ground or in tanks, or from the air. Each battalion had two aircraft, with a forward observer in each plane. And we had forward observers on the ground with the armored infantry and the tankers. We were talking with all of them on various channels. They'd radio us with direction, either coordinates on an aerial photo or a map, a crossroad, and then they'd adjust after the first round hit. They'd say, "200 right, 200 short." Then we'd adjust the guns right or left, up or down. When we got a good adjustment, then we'd use those proximity fuses. We'd hear them saying, "You hit the target! The men are on the ground."

We had to rely on them telling us what was happening since the fire direction center was in back of the guns, and we didn't actually see men fall. But we were in constant contact by radio with the observers who *did* see it. We'd move forward after a barrage of proximity fuses on an open area and see the damage.

All our artillery battalions began using them at this time: the self-propelled units like ours in an armored division and the other artillery weapons in an infantry division that were pulled by trucks.

The fire direction center determined the number of shells, based on what our forward observers saw. It depended on how many and how dispersed they were. We could adjust each battery so we covered a fairly large area. If they were dispersed in the open, the proximity fuse was the weapon of choice.

We also used timed fuses occasionally for buildings, because the shells could go into a building and explode inside. Time fuses had been around a long time—used in World War I. That was the difference between the two fuses. The proximity fuses were really best for people in an open area. That's what made them best for the type of fighting that we saw in the Battle of the Bulge.

◆

Nothing is more fierce than a soldier defending his homeland. As the tide turned in the Battle of the Bulge and Patton began pushing German forces back into the Fatherland, the casualty lists grew. H. M. Trowern sustained a serious wound, although not the "million-dollar" kind that would send a man home.

Patton wanted [the German village of] Olzheim, because he wanted to take out the communications. He wanted the village desperately, and that's why we were sent to get it. As we were ready to attack, a guy from intelligence, they called it G-2 at battalion, came over to me. He knew I would be leading the attack, so he came over to me and he pointed out the village. He showed me on a map the area we were going to attack. Then he said, "It's very lightly held. There's hardly any enemy troops down there."

Well, I had been watching these German half-tracks coming into town. . . . I saw about seven of them come in and he's telling me it's "lightly defended."

We started the attack and you don't run, but you move rapidly. We were coming down a hill. It was a lousy place to attack, because there was so much open ground before you got to the village. The Krauts started to shoot at us with small arms fire, for the most part. Then they started giving us some mortar fire. We were getting closer and closer to the village. I guess I was about 100 yards or less from a farm house that was on the edge of the village and I could see Germans in there firing at us. They shot a couple of guys around me and then it felt like somebody hit me with a baseball bat on the top of my head.

It turned out I had been shot in the head but I don't think I was knocked out very long. Maybe a minute or two. When I came to, I put my helmet back on and I crawled over to behind a little stone wall to get out of the field of fire because I realized I was still out in the open . . . Then I took the first aid packet that we carried. It had sulfa powder in it, and I put that on top of my head. I couldn't see the wound but I could feel it and I put the sulfa powder on top to stop the bleeding. It stopped a lot of it. Of course with a head wound you bleed like crazy. Then I looked at my watch, I don't know why I did that. But it was about 3:30 in the afternoon. Then I got to thinking, *Gee, if I've been shot in the head but knew enough to get out of the dangerous area, put sulfa powder on my head, and I knew enough to interpret what the time was, my wound can't be too bad . . .*

A couple of guys came by and wanted to know if I needed any help. I said, "No, you'd better get into Olzheim. Don't stay out here. It's too exposed." So they did. I still had my rifle, and one guy, Roy Curtin, came by and stopped because he saw I was wounded. He asked if I needed help, and I said that I was okay. I didn't want to keep him exposed out there. I said, "Get into town and help the other guys."

He asked, "Where are the guys that shot you?"

I pointed at this farmhouse and said, "There's about a dozen of them in there."

And he said, "Oh yeah, I think I see one, yeah. I'm going to nail them." So he picks up his rifle and he goes to fire it and a German bullet came right through his receiver. The receiver is the part of the rifle where the action is held. It knocked the rifle right out of his hands.

Without even pausing, Curtin looks at me and says, "Hey Joe, can I borrow your rifle? Mine's busted."

He took my rifle when I said, "Here, you might as well keep it. I can't use it."

So I laid there for a while. We were losing a lot of my guys coming down that draw. We took a real bloody nose that day. I don't how many in my platoon were killed. I think it was something like 10. Ten out of 30 men killed and maybe another 15 wounded. That was a real heavy casualty day. But they took the village. Not my 5 guys who were left, but our battalion took the village that day. They secured the objective. They got hold of this communications hub and tore it apart and reported back to Patton the mission was accomplished. My battalion received the Presidential Unit Citation for taking Olzheim.

Later that day, Trowern was evacuated to a field hospital. There, his head "was stitched up" and he was back in combat with his platoon five weeks later—after the Battle of the Bulge was over, but in time to later attack Koblenz.

Nurse Eileen (Courtney) Biersteker was a short distance behind the front lines, and the first to see the wounded after combat medics brought them from the battlefield.

I have a picture in my mind of what we went through at the peak of it. The Battle of the Bulge was the worst. I saw more casualties during the Battle of the Bulge than anytime. This was January 1945 and there was deep snow. So deep. And cold. The medics would carry in the litters.

We set up in what had been a beautiful, exclusive girls' school. The windows were blown out and there were big holes in the ceiling from the artillery. As soon as we got there, we had to hang up blankets over the windows. There were beautiful crucifixes and statues. Up in the attic we found lovely crocheted bedspreads and linens, which told us the nuns and students of the school left in a big hurry.

We had an area set up for the incoming. The doctors would quickly make a determination about which would go immediately into surgery and which would stay behind. Our corpsmen were very efficient. They were trained to give blood, and they often did so.

If a leg had been severed on the battlefield, it was just bound up in a tourniquet or just rags to stop the hemorrhaging. If the tourniquet was still on, it would have to be released every 15 minutes. And there were a lot of chest wounds. And a lot of amputations. Some head wounds.

Chapter Eight

I was in the unit before they went to surgery. We would try to get their clothes off of them. We'd cut them off with scissors.

Some were brought in already dead. We'd then take the dog tags off of them and place one with the little chain on their big toe to identify them. And we'd turn the other one in.

For the survivors, the dog tags were important because it had the name, religion, and crucial for us, blood type. We'd get them ready for surgery. And if they needed blood, we'd look at the tags and one of us would give the blood if they didn't already have it. The doctor would prescribe the blood. There was always one or two doctors in this area. We would give plasma ourselves right there.

We worked automatically. Weren't affected by what we saw. We went from one to another, and they would be so mud-caked. We had to get them clean for surgery, and water was a scarcity, and we would go clean them with water from a helmet. We'd have to bathe them, but water was difficult to get. The medics would have to chisel the ice and snow, and all we'd have was the melted snow in our helmets to wash these boys. I remember we had a German prisoner with his face blown off. And so many of our boys with their legs blown off. We'd go from one to another washing the dirt off of them. It was all so very primitive.

One nurse was sent home because she couldn't take it. I think it takes a certain person to deal with all that. It was a terrible thing to see, but you didn't think about it. You had a job to do.

The most troubling thing was that they were so young. They almost always asked us to write home to their parents, and that was probably as heart-rending as anything. It was hard to have to write and tell them what had happened.

But there were times when we laughed, too. The enlisted men were quartered on the school's third floor in little cubicles once occupied by the nuns—the Notre Dame nuns, we were told. One of the enlisted came down all exasperated because he had opened the closet in his cubicle and said he was never so startled in all his life. A nun's habit had been left hanging full length there—looking much like someone standing there in the closet.

One Sunday morning, we were allowed to go a little Catholic church in a village nearby. Alongside of it was a building, a warehouse, and I decided to look in there. And here were our American soldiers who had been killed. Bodies filled the place. This was winter and they were frozen, still clutching their guns. Corpses clutching guns. It sent a chill down my spine.

You never knew what you would see. In another warehouse, we came across yarn—a warehouse filled with yarn. Our doctors liked that. After we found that treasure, you'd see the doctors, between surgeries, knitting scarves for their wives and things. They said they were taught knitting in school to keep their fingers nimble for surgery. I had never seen doctors knitting before. It seemed funny that they were knitting like that. We nurses were busy knitting with all this yarn. For us, it was something to do. That's a fond memory—sort of a calm in the middle of the storm.

Field hospitals moved forward on the heels of the frontline troops. Outside a canning cellar that also served as a bunker against air attack are nurses Lieutenant Eileen (Courtney) Biersteker and Lieutenant Helen Gosz (background), both of the 65th Field Hospital. About treating GIs just taken off the battlefield during the winter of 1944–1945, Biersteker recalls: "We worked automatically. Weren't affected by what we saw. We went from one to another, and they would be so mud-caked. We had to get them clean for surgery, but water was difficult to get. All we'd have was the melted snow in our helmets to wash these boys."

After a great sacrifice of life on both sides, the Germans were losing the hard-won ground of the Bulge. As Germany's last reserves of men and equipment dwindled, German Field Marshall Model pleaded with Hitler to allow complete withdrawal from the western Ardennes. He finally received permission, opening the way for Patton's men to continue advancing toward the Rhine.

As the Battle of the Bulge concluded, some units were transferred out of the Third Army. Carl Ulsaker writes of a memorable sendoff of the 95th Infantry Division by Patton himself:

> [T]he 95th received orders transferring it to the Ninth Army in the area between Liege and Maastricht. Thus, in early February, we

terminated our association with the Third Army. Patton had driven us hard. But, as he explained it, "Remember men, you may be tired moving forward, but think of how much more tired the Nazi bastards are moving backward!" For all the publicity about Patton's posturing and bragging, I found him to be a practical leader who understood what motivated soldiers and who put it to them in terms they could understand. An excellent example of this occurred during one of our road marches during the early days of the German counteroffensive in Belgium. We had stopped for a break during a light snowfall. Most of the men were sitting on the ground resting by the side of the road. A small group of us officers stood nearby talking and smoking. A procession of vehicles moved along the center of the highway and we took little notice until someone said, "Look, there goes Lucky 6." Lucky 6 was the radio code for General Patton. Sure enough, his jeep was passing by with Old Blood and Guts sitting in the right front seat behind a machine gun mounted on the dash before him. Suddenly, the jeep braked to a halt and backed up to a point opposite where we stood.

My God, I thought, *We failed to salute and he's going to bawl us out.* We popped to attention and saluted tardily.

Patton dismounted and approached us on foot, head thrust forward and face set in his famous scowl. Gesturing with his right hand, in his high-pitched voice he said, "Man, von Runstedt's nuts are in the meat grinder and I have the handle in my hand."

Not waiting for comment, he changed his expression to a broad grin, waved airily in response to our salutes, remounted and drove away, disappearing rapidly in the cloud of swirling snowflakes. Maybe you think this bit of calculated drama didn't lift the spirits of the men. As the word passed up and down the column, one could see clearly in the posture and expression of every soldier that any previous doubt of the outcome of the Battle of the Bulge had been summarily erased. We had them licked, by God. That pistol-packin', swaggerin', Hun-killin' son of a bitch had just said so in unmistakable terms!

Chapter 9

Through the Siegfried Line and Beyond

Late January–May 1945

A t the end of January 1945, Patton's Third Army stood poised at Germany's doorstep, ready to slash through the border defenses of the Siegfried Line. Patton sneered, "Maybe there are 5,000, maybe 10,000 Nazi bastards in their concrete foxholes before the Third Army. Now if Ike stops holding Monty's hand and gives me the supplies, I'll go through the Siegfried Line like shit through a goose." Supplies came, and Patton's four corps charged into the line between Saint Vith south to Saarlautern (now Saarlouis).

Operating under the command of the VIII Corps, Lieutenant Colonel George Godding was a 24-year-old battalion commander in the 90th Infantry Division. His battalion would be the first to breach the Siegfried Line. Godding recounts an extraordinary, almost bloodless operation.

On the night of 5 February, we received word that we were to move against the Siegfried Line. My practice with the battalion was to start my attacks early in the morning. I figured the enemy would still be sleepy and everyone is scared of the dark to some degree, so it would all act to our advantage. Action started at about 2 a.m. when I sent out a patrol headed by my S-2 [intelligence officer], a lieutenant named Oscar Drake.

The patrol had to slog through mud, because the weather had changed dramatically right after we closed up the Bulge. We had gone from fighting through 3 feet of snow to fighting our way through mud when it all melted at the Siegfried Line. Drake led his patrol to a road crossing that had dragon's teeth and iron bars across, and I-beams that had been welded over—anything that could keep

233

tanks from going through. They walked up on the side of that road and found a German soldier asleep at the crossing. He was immediately taken prisoner and sent back with one of our men, while the rest proceeded on.

They approached the hill with the first pillbox and saw the apertures oriented toward an oncoming enemy from the west. But no one was keeping watch out of the apertures and in fact they were closed shut. Around the back of the pillbox was a big steel door. The patrol went around to the door, pounded and called out. The Germans opened the door and found themselves face to face with Lieutenant Drake. To say the Germans were stunned was an understatement. Here they were, in the middle of the night, in the safety of a big network of pillboxes. They were evidently so surprised that they didn't know what to do.

Drake was from a Jewish family that had been in Germany and had immigrated to the United States. So young Drake knew German very well. I can give you the essence of his conversation with the stunned men inside this first pillbox: "I want you to surrender. If you don't, we will destroy you." This conversation lasted just a few minutes before they surrendered.

Lieutenant Drake brought his patrol back and then we started more of the troops going in. We took four more pillboxes the same way—approaching the big steel door in the back. I had several others who could speak German fluently and they talked to them essentially the same way as Drake had. We didn't have a fire fight—didn't even fire a single round. The Germans were just so startled that it worked. They had not even seen us approaching, because those apertures were not even opened. And no local guards posted around outside. We captured 30 or 40 more Germans and sent them back.

Suddenly, we found ourselves 100 yards into the Siegfried Line! I didn't expect it to come like that. We just capitalized on a situation presented.

I posted some foot soldiers around those pillboxes. Then we started with the process again right after daybreak. I organized teams, each led by a man who could speak German. Each team had a man with an automatic rifle and another man carried a satchel charge and another carried a radio.

By now the artillery had pulled up. They prepared for what was called direct fire, where they would pull the breech block down and look right down the barrel to sight in on the target, an aperture of the pillboxes. The targets were only about 1,000 yards from our 155-mm howitzers, so they would have been shooting with very little trajectory.

As we went down the valley and up the next hill to the south, my teams followed the procedure of going around to the backs of the pillboxes and calling out in German, "Hands up or we'll blow it up!" Many gave up, but some of them didn't. When they didn't surrender, the team would pull back a little way, and by radio, tell the artillery to fire. Then the artillery would put a shell right into an aperture, causing enough concussion to kill anybody in there. This same procedure would be used by the other regiments going through. In the end, we had few casualties in the battalion.

We were ordered to hold what we had and not go forward. The rest of our 359th Regiment joined us. The other regiments—the 357th and 358th—came forward, too. Then Patton released his armor and the tanks moved through us.

Patton had frequently visited the front-line units in the area, and Godding was not surprised when several generals, including Patton, came to his headquarters. He continues:

Patton came to talk with us about 48 hours after this episode with the pillboxes. He wanted to know what had happened and asked how things were going. Standing there alongside the regimental commander and division commander, I was very much the junior member and didn't say too much unless a question was directed to me. In the presence of four stars and two stars, you don't say too much. But when asked what happened, I told General Patton about my method of always starting before daybreak, before the other battalions started out. His reaction was essentially that it was my prerogative. In other words, how you fought the war down at the battalion level was up to you.

At the battalion level, he showed only appreciation for what you did as long as you kept things going. It may have been different for division command. Based on my observation, I think that at the two- and three-star level, he was ruthless if the mission wasn't accomplished to his standards. I base that on the number of commanders the 90th Division had. I saw at least a half a dozen relieved. The original commander, Major General Terrell, and his assistant commander that landed with the division on the Continent didn't accomplish what he thought they should have. Terrell was relieved soon after. The assistant took over for a little while but also was gone. Then came a major general direct from an assignment in the Aleutian Islands. He lasted, if I remember correctly, 10 days. He didn't do what he wasn't supposed to do, but I won't go any further than that. At the time of the Siegfried Line, General Van Fleet was in charge and was not relieved like his predecessors. He was in Patton's good graces, so later got a third star and took over a corps.

I felt fairly confident talking with General Patton, because I knew I had been doing a good job, and knew better probably then anybody else what was going on there. Speaking with him in the combat area was very informal. None of this ranting and raving that a lot of people attribute to him. There was nothing antagonistic. No intimidation or trying to impose his four stars on me. He talked man to man.

General Patton had an ability to talk with people on the ground and always bring you back to the basics of infantry. Not only in one-on-one conversations, but when he would assemble the corps commanders and their staff, and the division commanders and some of their key staff from operations and intelligence. It would include the regimental and battalion commanders sometimes, too, so I attended several of those. We'd sit on bleachers set up in a clearing and he would stand beside a big map, explaining the Army's next objective—to take over this complex of towns out here or to get across this river or whatever. The intermediate objectives are thus and so. He would go through it all, lay it out clearly so everybody knew where they were going. He might explain some special operation, like if some unit was to hit from the side.

Then, after 30 or 45 minutes, after explaining the mission at hand, he would always return to some basic tactic. *Always*. Whether it was how to attack a fortified village, how to take a line of pillboxes, how to make a river crossing. Right back to a basic textbook explanation of how to do things. He had been an instructor at Fort Benning and other places. He was probably the most learned individual of military history that there was. And a great admirer of the old German general staff. He ended up sounding a lot like a teacher talking to his students. I remember him saying, "These wars aren't won by me up here. They are won by tactics of the regiments and battalions." And so he loved to talk about tactics at our level of operations, speaking extemporaneously about the basics you simply can't violate if you're going to accomplish your mission. Patton also once said, "Do as I have taught you, and you will stay alive." Of course, we listened closely. There was intense interest by all present, because he had proven himself. This man's leadership was why we were where we were. We had a lot of confidence in him.

And, as you left these assemblies to go back to prepare your unit, you felt confident that you'd get what you needed in the way of support. If you needed artillery to further neutralize the enemy, you could get it. He saw to it that you got it. Those material things for the combat troops that helped us prosecute the war—they were there in the amount they needed to be. I attribute that directly to him. This was his philosophy all the way.

He said, "If anybody lacks food, if they need anything in the way of clothing to keep warm, any ammunitions, any fire support, *you will get it.*" Amazing given the circumstances. But this went back to when we were stopped just outside of Metz, where Eisenhower or whoever made the decision that there wasn't enough gasoline for us to go on after we had been rolling so well. Patton had to tell us we'd get no more gasoline and to stay right where we were. Supplies had gone up north to Montgomery. He wanted to make sure that we weren't slowed down like that again.

Godding would later retire as a major general, after a distinguished career that included commanding the Army Security Agency in the 1970s.

◆

Captain Lewis Ingalls was an artillery officer assigned to the III Corps. He found that corps' intelligence had done a remarkably thorough job of mapping the Siegfried Line's defenses, but he would discover that the tiniest of misnomers on a map could have cost him his life. He also found that "cordial" German pilots passing overhead couldn't be trusted.

This just made you know the good Lord was watching out for you. We were a third of a way into the Siegfried Line. I had a map that showed 93 pillboxes in our sector. S-2 had the boxes all numbered on the map marked like little goose eggs. Our division front had two regiments on the line and one in reserve; each regiment would have two battalions on the line and one in reserve. Some nights we'd get one box, some nights two, some nights none.

Those boxes were set up so that they could fire on one another (for protection) and had connecting trenches between. At night, the people in the boxes had sentries out in the trenches. In the trenches they could hear and they could see any patrol we had coming. They'd just dive back in the box and burn the hell out of anything with their crossfire.

One of my lieutenants in A Company, 405th Infantry, had been in one of the captured pillboxes about four days and had gotten sick. He called me on the field phone to say he was sick. So I told him I'd come out to him. He gave me the number of the box—number 4— where he was. I started to go to this damn box through the creek bed.

I no more than got started going and the mortars started popping. Somebody must have seen me and thought there was a group, a squad or more, because they never would have thrown that much at just one guy. When it quit, I kept on going.

As I walked, I finally came to these pillboxes. They were covered with earth so they just looked like a bump in the ground. I walked by one and walked near another one about 50 or 75 yards past the first. I walked right up to the box thinking I could turn to my left and get to this box number 4, about 50 or 75 yards over, where the lieutenant was waiting. Anyhow, as I'm coming to this box, I see this aperture and this machine gun moving back and forth a time or two. I didn't think anything of it, because that was our box. I walked right in front of the box so I could use that as a cover.

I walk right up to the damn thing and see two sets of eyes looking through the aperture at me. I gave 'em a wave, gave 'em a highball, and turned to go to the other box. Of course, the door was on the opposite side so I walked around it to get in. I come in and find my lieutenant with a face as white as snow.

"What the hell is the matter with *you*?" I asked.

"Holy Christ, you walked right up to that Jerry box."

"What do you mean? That's our box."

"No, that's *their* box," he said.

Our maps were haywire. I was within 20 feet and waved, but those guys with the machine guns probably wondered what the hell was going on—the audacity of it—and so never fired.

Later I was looking for one of my lieutenants who got killed one afternoon. I wanted to find his body and make sure his affects got to the correct place. This was behind a position we had just taken. There wasn't a soul for a half-mile around me. Just corpses. A couple hundred, both German and ours. All at once, here comes an airplane. Just like one of our Piper Cubs, but it was German. I knew by the sound of the motor.

He wasn't more than 100 feet over my head. He came right over the top of me and rolled to give me a wave. He had a white scarf, black helmet, and goggles on. So I waved back at him. He kept puttin' past me, *putt-putt-putt*, way the hell past me a couple miles. Five minutes went by, then I hear this *putt-putt-putt* and he's come back over me, this time heading back toward German lines. As he comes over low, he rolled her up again and dropped something—a sack. He dropped the thing right over the top of me, and something told me to get down. I no more than hit the ground on my face and *ka-boom*, an explosion no more than 8 or 10 feet from me. The concussion went right over me. If I had stood and waved again, I'd be there still today.

Through the Siegfried Line and Beyond

━━━━━━━━━━━━━◆━━━━━━━━━━━━━

Lieutenant Walter Unrath served in a battle-hardened half-track battalion that had been a part of Patton's Third Army since it landed on the Continent and began its remarkable drive across Northern France. After the Battle of the Bulge, his battalion was reassigned to the 94th Infantry Division, which was new and untried. The division's baptism of fire at the Siegfried Line did not impress Patton. Unrath recalls Patton's unhappiness with 94th Division leadership:

The 94th was entering a vicious area called the Siegfried Switch of the main Siegfried Line. It was where the Siegfried Line was anchored onto Luxembourg. It was the thickest portion of the Siegfried Line, kilometers thick, complete with dragon teeth intended to trap tanks and many pillboxes ingeniously designed and placed so that each pillbox covered another, making it difficult to attack one without being constantly under fire from one or more pillboxes. Early in November 1944, the 10th Armored Division, 90th Infantry Division and 3rd Cavalry had failed to penetrate and destroy the Siegfried Switch. This entire area was hilly, with a huge ridge running its length and heavily wooded in places. This hostile arena was to be the place where the 94th Infantry Division was to receive its main baptism of fire.

When we initially met with the 94th people, it was all too apparent they were extremely "green" and had much to learn about the Third Army, General Patton and the nature of combat. Of course, they had the typical attitude and arrogance that they knew most things and didn't have to be told anything.

The 94th Division almost immediately commenced to attack in the Siegfried Switch area with moderate success. Apparently the Germans recognized this new division was directed at Trier, which the Germans could not permit to fall into American hands. As a result, the 11th SS Division, an elite crack German division, launched a counterattack on January 19, which produced heavy fighting—truly a learning experience for the 94th. The battle raged for several days and the 94th lost territory it had taken earlier.

A priority message was received by our battalion directing that available officers would report to the town of Perl, about 10 miles to our rear, for an important meeting of all division officers with the Army commander, General Patton. Upon arrival at the huge meeting hall, I made certain that I was seated in the rear of the auditorium, knowing that I did not desire to be within questioning or sight range of "Old Blood and Guts." A sharp shout of "Attention!" rang through the hall as we jumped to our feet at attention. General Patton, complete with pistols on his sides, cavalry boots and breeches, stormed down the center aisle heading for the central stage. On the stage was an officer to introduce him. Patton physically moved the officer to one side, grasped the microphone and commenced to direct his comments to the officers present. I was amazed as General Patton had a high-pitched voice, different from what I had expected, but cultured in tone. He vigorously informed all present that the division had suffered too many casualties, both combat and noncombat; entirely too many prisoners had been taken by the Germans; battle objectives had not been taken by the division; and that the battlefield conduct by the division was not to his liking or expectations. His entire talk to this point was interspersed with choice words normally associated with the colorful language of the stables of a cavalry troop.

General Patton then commenced to provide battlefield lessons for the division, such as, if you move twice as fast, you lose half as many men; if a hill cannot be taken from the front, take it from the side or the rear; the sight of a general or a high-ranking officer on the front line, under fire, can only inspire the GIs and let them know they are not alone. At the end of his 20-minute talk, General Patton slowly moved to the edge of the stage and, with icy eyes staring at the front row which contained the generals, regimental commanders and battalion commanders, made a very positive announcement. He informed these commanders that the division will receive new objectives within the week and that if these objectives are not taken, "this entire front row will be empty the next time I meet with this division."

General Patton stood glaring at the front row for what seemed like an eternity and then vaulted off the stage, as he had vaulted onto the stage a short while earlier, and stormed out of the auditorium amid the shouts for attention. It was an experience for all officers present, but I am certain it was even more impactful and memorable for those officers who occupied the front row. My battalion stayed with the 94th until we took the city of Ludwigshaven on the Rhine River in April 1945. I must observe that it was a changed division after Patton's lecture. I suspect they moved twice as fast, took hills from the rear and regimental commanders and generals were seen more frequently at the front lines.

Alvin H. Kruse was an infantryman in that new and untried 94th Infantry Division being flung against the Siegfried Switch. He writes of a single encounter with Patton that astonished him at the time and still astonishes him today. Patton himself said, "Do everything you ask of those you command." This anecdote demonstrates a bold characteristic of Patton's leadership: When he growled his expectations to the generals in the 94th Division about being up on the front lines to "inspire the GIs," Patton was not expecting anything of them that he himself would not do.

I know that the legends about Patton's policy of being with his men on the front lines are not exaggerated. Patton was a guy who believed in getting up there where the action was, to see firsthand how the battle was going. Many times he was within 50 feet of the enemy.

This took place on February 22, 1945, as I Company of the 94th Infantry Division crossed the Saar River at Seirizg and broke the Siegfried Line.

On the day Patton almost got shot, we had captured a German village, but there were still some German pillboxes that we hadn't taken out yet.

A mortar sergeant and I were in one of the houses and I was guarding the door when the door opened and Patton came walking in. He had come into the house to check on the progress. Before the door could swing shut, a German machine gunner put about 12 rounds of fire through the door. They missed Patton by no more than a foot.

He looked back at the door and then came over to me. He said, "That was a close one, wasn't it?"

I said, "Sir, it's been 'close' here all morning."

Then he asked me where Captain Donovan, our company commander, was. I told him he was in the third house up the street. He looked back at the door with the machine gun holes in it . . . Before I could do anything, he turned around and walked out the door where the bullets had hit. This was the first and last time I saw General George S. Patton.

As his unit pounded through the Siegfried Switch with the 94th Infantry Division, Walter Unrath issued a routine order to one of his troops in a foxhole—just like a hundred such orders he might issue on any given day at the front line. But this one would haunt him for a lifetime, causing him to vacillate between self-reprieve and regret.

For two weeks the battles raged and the Campholz Woods was reached and dozens of pillboxes cleared and captured, all by February 15. The entire division was to smash forward, breaking through the Siegfried Switch. In order to do this, other troops were required to hold the flanks. Reconnaissance by me indicated that my numerically small unit was to hold a line formerly held by a reinforced infantry company, normally numbering in excess of 300 men. In order to hold the position reasonably, I would be able to occupy only every fourth foxhole and place machine guns on the flanks. . . .

The path to the front line was outlined with a narrow white tape, laid by the engineers to indicate a safe path through the mind fields. *Schuh* mines, an invention of the Germans, were terrifying and relatively small; when triggered by a foot, it would spring up to almost waist level and explode, doing horrible damage to the groin area, many times emasculating the wounded party.

Nights in combat are so very dark that they represent a pitch-black velvet, another factor of terror. Periodically, when posting the line, the Germans hearing noise would send up flares to check whether a patrol was approaching their lines. When flares burst in the sky, all stand perfectly still to avoid detection. . . . It is at this time that you stand motionless in the bright light of the flare with a tingling in your body as though in anticipation of a bullet striking you.

As I progressed along the front line, placing my troops in appropriate foxholes, several flares slowed my progress. After placing my entire group in place on the line, I returned along the same line to double-check that all required positions were occupied. I came to one of the foxholes where I had placed a corporal, an excellent soldier. He was not in that foxhole, but was in the next foxhole. I chided him and told him to stop the nonsense and get in the proper position. He told me he was scared and didn't want to go in that foxhole. Impatient and angered, I ordered him back into the foxhole I had assigned as his combat position, as each provided a maximum field of fire in the case of an attack. I returned to my command post and informed my executive officer that I was going to catch two hours of sleep, not having slept for two nights, and to awaken me then. Sleep blessed me instantly.

Someone grabbed my arm and was shaking me. I grabbed my carbine and lurched to my knees. Above me was one of my track commanders with blood over his face and his field jacket splotched with blood. He shouted, "Lieutenant, they're hitting the line hard. We've got dead and wounded on the hill." My stomach sank and rose again as I felt sure I was going to be sick. My thoughts were a wish that this was not real, that I was not a commander, that the responsibilities were not mine, and that I wanted to be home safely in bed. But the instant of wishful thinking passed, and I knew that I alone was in command.

When I got to the hill with my sergeant and aid man, it was apparent that we had suffered direct hits from mortar fire which had now ceased but was followed by machine gun fire from the Germans on our right flank. The aid man was working on one of my gunners, whose arm was hanging on several strings of sinew. A rapid check indicated that several others were wounded and one KIA. As I walked down the line after ensuring that the wounded were being evacuated, my stomach sank again that night, as I saw my corporal sprawled over the front of his foxhole with an ugly bloody hole in the back of his field jacket where shrapnel had ripped into his back. He was dead. A little over an hour earlier, he had begged me not to put him in that foxhole, as though he had a premonition of a pending disaster or death. Why had I ordered him to stay in that foxhole despite his pleading to me? Would he be alive today if I had not insisted? Was the field of fire that critical? To this day these questions keep cropping up in my mind.

◆

Following orders is one thing; following a commander into the jaws of death is another. Glenn Doman, a company commander in the 87th Infantry Division, was horrified that he must order his men to charge up the Gold Brick Hill, a fortified bastion within the Siegfried Line.

Gold Brick Hill was 700 yards from the bottom to the top. It was completely devoid of the slightest cover and on its top were seven pillboxes with eight-foot thick concrete walls. The pillboxes were mutually supporting and the hill commanded the entire front. Gold Brick Hill had to be completely neutralized before my division and the Third Army could advance.

A captured German captain, under some pressure, talked. In the seven pillboxes were 200 crack German troops and seven officers. Gold Brick Hill, he boasted, would never be captured by direct assault. It could only be captured by being surrounded and its defenders starved out. This process, he estimated, would take two months . . . To add to the difficulty a light snow had begun to fall, which would silhouette and outline us, making us beautiful targets.

The battalion was far under strength. My company, normally composed of 187 men and 6 officers, now had 30 men. I Company had 35. L Company 50. These were the rifle companies of the 3rd Battalion. The order was unfortunately quite definite. It said that the 3rd Battalion would seize and hold Gold Brick Hill. It did not say "if possible." The colonel gave us his attack order. There would be a 10-minute artillery preparation starting at 0300, Company I on the right and Company K, my company, on the left would cross the line of departure, a woods at the foot of Gold Brick Hill, at 0105 while the artillery was still firing. We would be preceded by five tanks.

This announcement was met with sarcastic laughter. All our experiences with the tanks did not lead us to believe that they would attack. The colonel assured us they would not run away. As we approached the top of the hill the artillery would lift and we would take their position.

With a heavy heart I returned to my waiting company headquarters and platoon leaders. The accomplishment of this job seemed virtually impossible, but the orders were quite clear. We would seize and hold Gold Brick Hill. No one said "or die trying." That we understood.

I tried to keep my voice steady as I gave my attack order. When a company attacks it maintains one of its three rifle platoons and its weapons platoon in reserve. My entire company, cooks, clerks and all had less than one platoon. If by any turn of fate we took this position it would have to be by an all-out effort and ignoring many of the basic laws of the military. We would attack, cooks and all, without any reserves, on a 200-yard front. Every weapon in the company would be fired at the pillboxes, as fast as they could be fired. The BARs would fire at 200 yards to the front. Riflemen 100 yards to the front. The light machine guns, in movie fashion, would be fired from the hip and while moving. The rocket launchers (bazookas) would fire directly on the pillboxes.

The roar of an infantry bazooka round is difficult to tell from an artillery round. We hoped that the Germans would never know when the artillery stopped firing. Men armed only with pistols would fire at 50 yards to the front. Everybody would shoot low and fire whether or not targets appeared. We would try to get ricochets, which when coming in your direction, sound extremely dangerous. We hoped they would sound that way to the Germans. The one consolation was that we would have the cover of five tanks in front of us.

Covered by trees, we heard our artillery give the message "on the say" and soon fierce firing landed on the hill to our front. I looked at Gold Brick Hill and had a sinking sensation. It was worse than I had pictured it.

While the artillery prevented the meatheads from leaving their pillboxes, it could do no harm whatsoever to the Germans inside. I was somewhat surprised to hear the tanks moving out of the road that led to our position and was cheered by the fact they did. In front of us the tanks fanned out and started up the hill. I stood up and waited to give the signal to move out. As I did the tanks turned and came back down the hill. In all honesty I admit I was delighted. Now of course we would not be expected to attack. The tanks were leaving. The colonel came running toward the position, swearing violently at the tanks and threatening to shoot the tank commander at sight. Grimly he told me to move out quickly in the attack before the artillery stopped firing. My stomach did flip-flops.

"Colonel, it is impossible, you know we cannot . . ."

The colonel swore, "I said *move out*." He meant it. My mind raced.

Surely, surely no soldier would go up that hill. Getting killed is bad enough, but getting killed while accomplishing nothing was useless. I loved and admired my company, but I had no right to expect they would go up that hill. In a few seconds a thousand thoughts raced through my mind. To explain them is extremely difficult, perhaps embarrassing. I hope you will try to understand how I felt. My men were excellent soldiers, the very best, but nobody had any right to expect them to go up that hill. They were there because it was their job, but few of them had asked to be there. Somebody else had made this war, they were simply fighting it.

To this day I am firmly convinced that if I were a private no one could have gotten me out of that woods. I think perhaps I am not a very brave man but I did not enjoy the same immunity these soldiers enjoyed. This was my war. I had asked for it. Even sought it. I wanted to wear [officers'] pink pants, be called "sir," eat in the officers' mess, sleep in the officers' quarters and be saluted. I had asked for this. Deep in the heart of every infantry officer lies the realization that some day he may have to pay for all these privileges. He may have to pay with his life. I was now in this position.

I did not expect the men to go and I did not blame them a bit. I agreed with them but that was it. The men were watching me for orders. I waved my arm forward and tried to pretend that I expected them to come. Scared almost motionless I walked out of the woods. My only hope was that the Germans would fire quickly and would wound me while I was close enough so that the men could drag me back into the woods. When I was 10 yards out of the woods I stole a glance to my right where I Company was supposed to be attacking on line with us. I saw one man, Captain Swanson, commander of I Company. My heart sank further. I would have given all that I possessed to look back over my shoulder, but if the men were foolish enough to come, my looking back would show them that I did not expect them to.

When I was 20 yards up the hill and praying to be hit now, but only a little bit, I heard behind me a commotion I shall never forget. They were there, every single one. They were firing as fast as they could fire, exactly as the orders said. I shall never forget that moment. My heart soared. These were my people and in my mind's eye I shall see them always as they came shooting from that woods. Scared, cold, tired, even exhausted and they came shooting. I was never happier. It almost didn't matter if I got hit. This surely was the supreme moment for me. My boys were coming with me.

By the time we were halfway up the hill the men were charging wildly, screaming and firing. I have often thought that if that scene were made a moving picture, every soldier who saw it would laugh in disbelief. It just didn't seem possible.

As I went over the crest of the hill there was before me a German soldier outside a pillbox. In his right hand he held a rifle; on the muzzle was a white handkerchief; on the open palm of his other hand was a pistol which he held toward me as a souvenir. He had heard about the Americans. At my side was a little soldier, who could not have been over five-foot two. He was aiming at the German, 10 feet away with a bazooka. Had he fired it at that range we would all have been destroyed. I shouted to the German, who dropped the weapons and ran into the pillbox behind him. He led 22 Germans out of the pillbox.

With disbelief, my messenger and I entered the pillbox. On a table a telephone was ringing. My messenger, Henry Simmons, was a German Jew. His mother and father had been in Dachau. His grandmother and grandfather were still in Buchenwald. He had come to the United States when he was 16. Now at 18, he was back in Germany, having volunteered for a rifle company. Henry knew why he was fighting the war.

He answered the telephone. It was the German commander in Pillbox 3 wanting to know how we were doing. In flawless German, Hank told him we were doing very well and that he had better get out of the pillbox with his hands up very quickly. That news was something of a blow to him. He replied that they would never surrender, *never*. We went out and over the hill toward his pillbox. All of the others had quickly fallen to my soldiers and I Company, which had also attacked just as fiercely. We were met with a blast of machine gun fire from the German command base. We fired bazookas at the pillbox but did it no harm.

We had arrived at a stalemate which could go on indefinitely. We went back and phoned again to the German commander. He assured me again that they would never come out, *never*. I agreed that that was perfectly all right with me if that was the way he wanted it. I would even help him have his way. To make it positive, I would bring up bulldozers and cover up the pillbox and he could stay there with the rest of his officers forever and I hoped his coffin was comfortable. I gave him 30 seconds to think about it. He did. He came out.

Realizing the position was taken, the German artillery, without regard for their fellow German soldiers now taken prisoner fell heavily on our position. We got inside the pillboxes and called for casualty reports from my officers and I Company. The news was too good to be true. We had captured seven pillboxes, 200 Germans, six officers, and killed many. Neither I Company nor K Company had a single solitary casualty. No American had even been scratched.

War is an emotional time. I felt my eyes blur again. I was totally ashamed that I had ever doubted these men of mine. I felt that I did not deserve to be their leader. This I knew: Were we ordered to assault the gates of Hell itself, these American infantrymen would go. We had seized and were holding Gold Brick Hill. The 87th Division pressed onward. Much later my division commander, Major General Culin, said this to me. I have always considered it the supreme accolade my company received. "Doman," he said, "tell K Company this for me. I have been a soldier for 35 years. Hundreds of times in that 35 years I have wondered why. Now I know. I stood on Hill 29 and watched the attack on Gold Brick Hill. My 35 years in the Army were spent waiting for that attack. If I had a picture of those men going up that hill, I should carry it in my pocket forever and bury it with me. That attack was complete compensation for the past 35 years."

◆

Pillbox by pillbox, the Third Army broke through the Siegfried Line. Once the Third was past it, Hitler desperately threw what he had to stem the American advance. Patton's troops began to see evidence of the "secret weapons" that Hitler had promised in his rantings. Captain Chesterfield Smith, artillery battery commander in the 94th Infantry Division, was astonished to see jet aircraft—German Messerschmitt 262s—for the first time as his unit approached the Rhine River:

We broke out and headed for the Rhine River, over toward Mannheim . . . We had a tremendous convoy. I was in a division of some 19,000 men. And there were other divisions before and after us going through there—all on a main road, something like we now call interstates.

We were making tremendous progress. Even though there were Germans in there, we were still going 15, 17, 18 miles a day down the highway. Trucks in three lanes, all three lanes on an interstate. And we were all moving in trucks, most everybody in trucks. And we were moving into their territory for the first time. So we were all enthusiastic and thought we had these bastards whipped.

All of a sudden, I saw for the first time in my life jet airplanes. The Germans had jets before we did. They came roaring down the road. I will say as many as 12 jets came down and sprayed us. I'd never seen one before. Most people had more sense than I did and ran for the woods as fast as they could, as far in as they could, and hunkered down, because those things were spraying down those highways into the trucks.

I got so excited I couldn't believe it, and I stayed out on the side of the road. It was a wonder I wasn't killed. A couple people around me were killed. They were shooting bullets at me and I didn't lie down on the ground, I didn't go to a hole, I didn't hunt for a tree to hide behind. I looked. I couldn't believe those damn jets. I just looked and stared like it was a football game that I couldn't take my eyes off of. And I watched it and they sprayed. For 10-miles ahead of us were trucks, cars and soldiers, hub to hub. . . . Some of the trucks could not move. They blew tires, they blew gas tanks, they broke windshields, they killed drivers.

They went over us as many as six or seven times. They'd come down that road and then they'd go around the circle, 15 or so miles wide. Come back down the 10 miles in front of us and start down the road again. We were all crowded on there so we were an unbelievable target. We were told that we had the Germans routed, and that they were moving away and moving back on the road ahead of us to get to the Rhine. . . .

The most exciting visual experience that I had in the war or since was to see these jets for the first time—unbelievable to me, when I'd really never even heard of them. I thought, *This can't be true. If they got these kind of things, they're going to beat us.* I watched and stayed out there. I was as dumb as you could get. . . . I wasn't running for the woods, because I was so enthralled.

Smith was slightly wounded in the attack.

The next major challenge for Patton's Third Army was crossing the Rhine River. More than a military objective, the Rhine represented the spirit of the German people. Not since 1805, when Napoleon invaded, had an enemy crossed the Rhine in wartime. Once beyond it, the Third Army could thrust a stake into the heart of the Reich.

While the Germans frantically blew up every bridge spanning their beloved Rhine, Allied forces came abreast at the river's edge. Patton's Third Army reached the river near Koblenz on March 7, 1945, and found no bridges intact. According to William Baker of the 989th Engineer Treadway Bridge Company, the river spanned 1,080 feet. It was 1,080 feet of sheer terror for the troops, who had to reach the opposite shore in rowboats.

Al Elliot, a private first class in a mortar company of the 5th Infantry Division, describes crossing the Rhine as his most memorable war experience.

We paddled the Rhine River in a rowboat. Six of us and a mortar. I didn't give it that much thought at the time, but I've thought about it a lot since then. We had hiked through the woods pretty much all night, carrying our mortar. We didn't know really where we were until we got to the edge of the Rhine at about 4 in the morning We knew where we were then, but didn't really think that much about it. Not like they might have at the upper echelons of the Army or the folks back home. To us it was just another river with enemy on the other side.

We threw all of our stuff into a little boat and just started paddling! There was another division crossing at the same time—the 4th Infantry Division, I think. The Germans must have had scouts on the other side and as soon as we got into the boats, they started shelling. A lot of the others never made it—I saw so many boats get hit or flipped. I thought this might be it for us. But we just kept on paddling.

Luck was with us. We made it all the way to the other side. I talked with a guy from the 4th Infantry Division years later. He had been one of the ones flipped in the Rhine. He said he finally got out of the river about a quarter of a mile downstream. He said he was so cold, with no way to get warm, that he got frostbite on his hands and feet, and got out of the ETO a short time later because of it. I'm sure it happened to a lot of guys.

Back to the river crossing. Explosions were happening all around us. You felt the bump in the boat and through the concussion in the air. We were getting splashed by them. It was a moment when you thought you might breathe your last with every breath. You heard screams from other boats as they were hit, but you couldn't see them. Couldn't even tell if they were in front or behind or to the side, because of the acoustics on the water. Through it all, you knew you couldn't do but one thing: Paddle!

And with that paddling, we were able to reach the other side. We didn't lose anyone in my squad. We all made it.

I don't know if we were one of the first boats to reach the other side. It was too dark to tell. The first thing on the other side that I remember seeing was a railroad track that ran right alongside the river. We got up over that railroad track and down the other side and stayed there until the shelling stopped. Finally, some of our planes flew down low there to strafe the German positions. Then we started hiking it out of there.

I remember coming up on the autobahn and seeing 8 or 10 German fighters, Messerschmitts, tucked back into the trees alongside the autobahn. We learned later that they couldn't take off for lack of fuel, but if they could have, it would have meant even more trouble crossing the Rhine.

Under fire in an assault boat, infantrymen of the 89th Division cross the Rhine River on March 26, 1945. Their immediate mission was to create a bridgehead at Oberwessel, Germany, so a pontoon bridge could be erected across. Typical of his unrelenting drive, Patton's objective at the Rhine was to "get as many troops across on as wide a front as possible and keep on attacking." **U.S. Army**

John E. Olson was a first lieutenant in the 4th Armored Division, which had spearheaded much of Patton's blitz through France. At the time of the Rhine River crossing, Olson was a half-track platoon leader in the 53rd Battalion. His battalion was commanded by Lieutenant Colonel Creighton Abrams, a 1938 graduate of West Point, who later went on to become a four-star general and chairman of the Joint Chiefs of Staff. Olson described Abrams as a commander who "ran his units well and kept morale high and was a stern disciplinarian, in the mold of Patton himself." Olson observed both his battalion commander and Patton at the Rhine River.

> When we were ordered to cross the Rhine, we were told the 5th Infantry held 3,000 yards on the other side of the Rhine. If they had 300 feet, it was a lot. The 5th had a lot of casualties from all the German shelling. We were crossing near a town called Oppenheim.
>
> The first time I saw General Patton in person was when the 4th Armored Division was going across on pontoon bridges that the 5th Infantry built. We were near the west bank and Patton came up in a light tank with a 37-millimeter mounted. He came to see the crossing firsthand and, I suppose, to talk with Colonel Creighton Abrams about progress. The Germans fired four or five quick rounds, and he had to go back behind the hill. Even though I was some distance away, I could tell him easily by the ivory-handled pistols as he stood in his vehicle. I don't know, maybe the Germans could tell it was him, too.

Coy Eklund of Lucky Forward was there when Patton himself crossed the Rhine, confirming a story that became part of Patton legend:

> He didn't swim in the Rhine; he did something much more contemptuous in the Rhine. I still have a picture of Patton urinating in the Rhine. Charlie Codman snapped the picture.

◆

Once on the other side of the Rhine, Patton ordered his armor to move quickly overland with the infantry at its heels. The Third Army steamrollered on, crushing everything in its path. In a letter to his wife, dated March 23, 1945, Patton wrote with surprising remorse: "The displaced persons . . . are streaming back utterly forlorn. I saw one woman with a perambulator full of her worldly goods sitting by it on a hill crying, an old man with a wheelbarrow, a woman and five children with a tin cup crying. In hundreds of villages there is not a living thing. . . . Most often houses are heaps of stone. They brought it on themselves, but these poor peasants are not responsible. Am I getting soft?"

The best of the remaining German forces had been decimated on the west side of the Rhine, where Hitler had ordered them to take a stand and not retreat. Now, on the east side of the Rhine, many more prisoners were taken. Left were peasants, townspeople, and defenders not of front-line quality. Olson continues:

Soon after we crossed the Rhine, I thought I had ended the war single-handedly by capturing the entire German general staff (laughs). We approached a village and called for everyone to come out with their hands up. From their cover, out stepped these older men, 50 or 60 years old, wearing brand new uniforms. Generals!

More kept coming. The whole German general staff!

I think they called those guys the *Volksstrom*, something like a home guard. They were wearing uniforms that were brand new because they'd never worn them. They were set outside the villages to defend. They carried rifles but were not really trained.

We would find them in many villages yet to come, but this first set I encountered were the ones I was so sure were generals. Part of my heritage is German—grandparents on my mother's side spoke German at home, so I did know some words. They had told me who they were and that they did not wish trouble.

On the other hand, in one of those villages, I also met a disabled SS trooper, who had lost his leg. Quite a contrast between the fanatic SS trooper and the old men of the home guard. I think even then he would have killed any of us on the spot if he'd been able. By the end of March, you never encountered "Germans" anymore. They were all "Poles, Czechs, and Russians." Only the SS would admit they were German.

Patton's Third Army was not done with river crossings. Another one, the Main River in Bavaria, would prove to be another dangerous challenge, and Olson would carry scars from it for the rest of his life.

When you're that age, you think you will live forever and you don't think of death. Although, sometimes when we got off our half-tracks and had to fight on foot, we were more vulnerable and that brought some fear. That's how I was wounded twice. The first was shrapnel around my face from a shell that hit the ground. The second was when we had just crossed the Main River near an obscure village. My platoon walked across. And I had just gotten across the bridge when the Germans blew up the bridge.

That meant we were across the river alone—me with about 40 men. Another platoon tried to make it across by boat, but couldn't. The Germans held a church and a few other buildings, and they were sniping at the platoon, trying to get across. Since snipers were taking aim, I was careful not to encourage their attention. I tucked my collar insignia under my coat. In combat, you never wanted to show any outward sign that you were an officer and so you carried an M-1 like the rest of the troops, not the .45 pistol or carbine that officers were issued. That would have just singled you out.

A train started coming in and I got orders to stop the train. But I didn't have my half-tracks or anything. Just 40 soldiers on foot and carrying only small arms.

We stopped the train with only machine guns firing at the wheels. I thought it was a troop train, but what it turned out to be was a bunch of real young Germans from an OCS school riding as passengers on the train. However, they were armed.

When the train finally ground to a halt, they all ran out on the other side, using the train cars as protection and they started lobbing light artillery, something like a bazooka that they'd fire up and let fall on us. One hit the ground and shrapnel got me. That was March 25, 1945.

It was as a result of that that I had my second encounter with Patton. I had been taken to a field hospital in Germany. He came to the field hospital to come around and shake everybody's hand. A couple hundred of us laid up there.

He knew all of us there were from his Third Army. He was talking and shaking hands with as many people as he could. I saw him coming down the aisle and I was looking forward to it.

The high-pitched voice was a shock—not at all what I suspected. Kind of a jolt. Something else you noticed right away was that he was what I call "chicken-breasted." His chest kind of protruded and he had spindly legs.

He looked me right in the eye and shook my hand. He asked my outfit and what happened, how I was wounded and he listened as I told him. In a way, he appeared a fatherly figure. I was 20 and he was close to 60 then. I told the folks back home and they were impressed. When I got back home, it was kind of a distinction to have served under Patton.

◆

The old specter of fuel shortage came back to haunt Patton after crossing the Rhine. However, the shortage was brief and not nearly as debilitating as it was at Metz. And it stemmed from different causes, as Stephen Conland of the 5th Quartermaster Battalion explains:

When the Rhine was crossed, rail service ceased again . . . it took time to rebuild the railroad bridges across. Starting about April 1 we moved the bulk of our gasoline by air. As quickly as possible, airstrips were opened up near the front and C-47s flew in rations and gas. A plane can carry about 700 gallons or 140 five-gallon cans.

Chapter Nine

A five-gallon can weighs about 48 pounds. So the math will tell you how we were limited.

Obviously, aircraft aren't the best way to bring in gas. It wasn't only that they couldn't carry as much as by rail. Our biggest problem was that they got stuck in the mud at these airfields, which were really just pastures. We used trucks and chains to pull them out of the mud. It took a little time to build up dumps on the other side of the Rhine, but the armor was able to continue rolling without much of a delay.

The 13th Armored Division came into Patton's fold late in the war, after being assigned to three other U.S. Armies before. The division joined the Third Army on April 21, 1945, in time to steamroller through the Fatherland. Lieutenant Phillip Foraker, a tank platoon leader in the division's 46th Tank Battalion, writes:

General Patton was the only Army commander who personally met with all the officers and noncoms of our division. He told us how to fight on that breakout after the Rhine: We would pull up outside of a German town and if the white flags aren't out we put a round of white phosphorous into the roof of one house. If the flags don't come out we call in the artillery to destroy the town before proceeding. We were to knock out strong points with the tanks and artillery and leave the rest of the job to the infantry following us.

Contrary to armored school doctrine, we were to travel on roads and we were to attack at night. He said we would get good results with fewer casualties.

Our first night attack was memorable. We were organized into battalion-sized combined armed task forces. Our light tank company went out ahead to conduct reconnaissance. I was leading the main attack unit. We saw many explosions on the hills across the valley. Our light tank unit pulled into a small town square and decided to rest and check on everyone.

The lieutenant commanding had his tanks back into streets covering the square. He heard vehicles coming, and signaled his men to turn on all lights at his command once the strange vehicles pulled into the square. No firing until ordered. All went according to plan. The German platoon stopped and dismounted, our lights came on, and they were captured without a shot being fired.

The next morning we found 15 88-mm cannons destroyed and the crews had taken off. Then Patton also told us to ignore tables of organization and equipment and put a half-track behind each unit's lead tank. We were to put three .30-caliber machine guns on each half-track to wipe out German infantry firing *panzerfaust* (a shaped charge fired off a tube loaded with propellant) that could disable or destroy our tanks from the side. Good advice.

General Patton also wanted all officers clearly identified. We found German snipers could also identify us so we covered our insignia of rank with mud, or took them off. The rate of sniper fire at us decreased remarkably. Our men knew who we were.

Another time we were parked on a road in farm country. The company commander called me (I was the sole remaining platoon leader) and directed me to go in a jeep to a nearby town and determine if we should stay there that night. While I was gone the first sergeant was in charge. General Patton drove up. Our men had their steel helmets off and were wearing wool kit caps. The general hated those caps with a passion. He had the first sergeant line the men up at the farm fence and throw those caps as far as they could. He also had some pithy remarks about no officers being with the unit. After the general left those warm wool knit caps magically reappeared under steel helmets.

By May we were approaching the Austrian border—some 60 miles beyond Munich. Our tanks ran out of gas. My orders were to take a half-track and a jeep and proceed to the Inn River. At the river we pulled into a farmyard. A character in civilian clothes—I learned later he had just unilaterally retired as a German captain—wanted to know if we would continue on and fight the Russians. I thought he was out of his mind.

General Patton's advice to us before we started on the breakout saved lives and equipment. He had also told us he wanted us to go home as live victors and to help the German S.O.B. die for his country.

As the Third Army moved through Germany, it captured many of what would eventually total 1,280,688 prisoners of war. Soon after crossing the Rhine, Al Neuharth encountered Patton as the 86th Infantry Division was rounding up prisoners. He writes in *Confessions of an S.O.B*:

I met my first S.O.B. role model at a crossroads near Heidelberg, Germany, in the final weeks of World War II. He threatened to lock me up behind barbed wire.

General George S. Patton Jr. The sometimes bad guy, all-time big winner for the Allied forces.

Our 86th Infantry Division was part of Patton's Third Army. I had made staff sergeant, heading an intelligence and reconnaissance platoon.

Corporal Fran Devine of Wisconsin and I were marching for interrogation. We had stopped to rest at a crossroads.

Chapter Nine

Patton and his driver pulled up in his star-studded jeep. Patton was a nonstop guy. Didn't believe in slowing down or resting. And a master at staging temper tantrums.

The general jumped from his jeep and growled at us:

"Get those fucking Krauts on their feet and moving, or I'll put you behind the same barbed wire they're headed for!"

We snapped to, saluted, and moved on.

Devine grumbled about what an S.O.B. Patton was. I laughed. Of course, he was a borderline S.O.B. But he was a winner. He knew how to move men and win wars. I would have followed him nonstop all the way to Berlin on foot. I hoped I would develop a little of his S.O.B. quality in me someday.

He's still a hero of mine. I've seen the movie *Patton* 11 times.

German prisoners captured by the 90th Infantry Division are marched to the rear in March 1945. Patton writes in his diary on March 24: "Today the Third Army will process the 300,000 prisoners of war taken since August 1. I do not see how [the Germans] can keep it up much longer." **U.S. Army**

Inside Germany, Patton's Third Army was the swiftest of the advancing Allied forces. The tanks of the 4th and 6th Armored Divisions used Hitler's innovative road network, the autobahn, like a raceway to wheel down to the Czech border. As the Third Army approached that border in mid-April, Patton was told to slow his pace, which irritated him. Plus, he was beginning to sense that his troops were being sent on a wild goose chase, away from the real action. Dupré Sassard, assigned to Twelfth Army Group headquarters, remembers Patton's visit to General Omar Bradley.

In early 1945, I was serving as an intelligence briefing officer in General Bradley's 12th Army Group headquarters. The Germans were on the run and the end was near. General Patton's Third Army was sweeping eastward through southern Germany, when General Patton was called back to 12th Army Group headquarters by General Bradley.

We were all in the briefing room when he stormed in, screaming at General Bradley, "Brad, why in hell are you calling me back. I've got the *Boche* on the run and I can surround Berlin and capture the whole German Army if you'll let me go!"

I'll never forget General Bradley's calm reply. "George, these aren't my orders. They come from (General Eisenhower), and they're not his orders either. This is the deal Roosevelt, Churchill, and Stalin made at Yalta, and we have no choice but to obey."

And General Patton *cried!*

Patton's Army continued sweeping through Germany, but veered away from important cities, such as Berlin, and instead headed toward Czechoslovakia. What Maury Laws saw while rolling through Germany surprised him. He had to reconsider the "godless people" of Germany:

Once across the border into Germany, the sight of so many churches struck me. I had never seen so many churches in my life! Each with a little graveyard with a fence around it adjoining the church. It had been a foregone conclusion that Germans were a godless people. That had been pretty well drummed into us in the States. You know, Hitler as their model. And if it hadn't been drummed into you in the States, you reached that conclusion fighting across Europe. But here were churches every where.

Another thing was that you'd find photos of children and wives, and little Bibles—so often Bibles in the breast pockets of dead Germans. I carried a Bible, too. It had a brass cover that I was to carry over my heart for protection. The Germans did that, too. I realized they were human, and just like me. You get close to your Maker in those circumstances—you know, "no atheists in foxholes." I guess the Germans were that way, too. And they, too, believed they were fighting on the side of right.

But none of that would have caused me to hesitate pulling the trigger. It was a matter of survival, and you knew they would shoot you dead if they could. You just begin to feel the insanity of it. You see the craziness. You're put there and the only way out is to survive.

You lose track of what the big picture of the war was about. It wasn't even about "fighting on the side of right" anymore. It was reduced to just surviving another day.

Right after the Bulge, I had changed from Graves Registration to a platoon of scouts. The Army logic was that people coming back from rehab with Purple Hearts should be in that role [of Graves Registration]. So, some of us who had been musicians in the band went right to the front lines. Two were killed immediately.

For some reason, they put me in an I & R platoon (intelligence and reconnaissance). I don't know why; I had no training in it. Here were 26 guys, who ate together, slept together, lived together for three years. They had been close-knit, they knew sign language and practically what the other was thinking before he said anything. So here come me and two others from Graves Registration. There was some mistrust initially, because they didn't know me. But I got on well with them and gained their acceptance eventually.

I discovered that having color deficiency—not colorblindness, but inability to see the red number in the color test—let me see things other people couldn't see. Around dusk, I would lie under cover of woods and watch tanks move around, the Tiger tanks, which were superior to ours at the time. It was a scary thing to see one of those coming at you, and you wanted to know when they were coming. I could see those things moving over the terrain. I was not blinded by camouflage as others with normal vision. That sometimes let me see them first, so the others came to rely on me somewhat for that.

We had two peeps—what we called jeeps—one with a .50-caliber machine gun mounted on the back and the other with a .30-caliber. After a member of the platoon got hit, I became a driver. When that .50-cal was being fired right over your head—oh man. It was always a big surprise because you never knew when the gunner would fire it. Of course, he couldn't say he was about to fire, to warn you. He just fired. One day, a German plane came swooping down toward us, and people all around began firing—including our gunner—and between the mind-numbing blasting of the .50 cal. and the approach of the aircraft I veered left off the road. I jumped out or flew out when we hit the ditch. I caught hell because of that from the platoon sergeant.

More routinely, the gunner would see action up ahead in the woods and he'd open up. I'd never know it was coming, and it would shake the peep and rattle me—scare me to death, because that powerful weapon was just inches away from my ear. It wasn't so bad when I was driving the one with the .30-caliber, because that was mounted on the right front of the thing.

Through the Siegfried Line and Beyond

In the I&R platoon, I never shot and saw someone fall. I'm glad about that. Our job in recon was to stay out of trouble. Not to fight.

◆

As Patton's Third Army progressed through Germany, the monstrous secrets of the Nazis' "final solution" to the "Jewish problem" began to come to light. The first concentration camp liberated was Ohrdruf Nord, near the XX Corps headquarters at Gotha. A short time later, the Third Army liberated Buchenwald, northwest of Weimar. The area had been an idyllic beech forest (the Buchenwald) where the German poet Goethe was said to have gone for inspiration in the early 1800s.

Patton himself toured Ohrdruf and afterward, under his breath, choked out a single comment: "One of the most appalling sights I have ever seen." He dispatched word to Third Army unit commanders that as many soldiers as possible should see the camps, and he issued an order that local German civilians would be forced to tour the camps.

William Jennings, a staff sergeant in the 819th MP Company of the XX Corps, took part in the liberation of Ohrdruf, and carried out the order that forced the civilians to view the unspeakable horror at Buchenwald.

I was in charge of a detail to take 1,000 citizens from Weimar and march them through Buchenwald. They were to see the barracks and the dying and dead. Most of the women refused to look. They put their heads down and walked quickly. They were denying that they knew anything about it.

This was absolutely the most ghastly thing you could ever imagine. The barracks were loaded with living skeletons, a good many beyond saving and who died after liberation. These barracks had four tiers of bunks—not really bunks, more like shelves—and the men would lie with heads toward the aisle. We walked through and some were so weak they couldn't move their arms. All they could do was follow you with their eyes. For some, that's all the strength they had.

At first I was shocked and I became, like most of the guys, just livid—furious at the Germans in the first place as our cause for being there. No one, *no one* in their wildest imagination thought they could be so totally inhumane.

Even though I'd seen this before, it's not the kind of thing you can get used to. A few days before, I had been with the 4th Armored, doing traffic control and prisoner control, when they liberated Ohrdruf—possibly the first one that Americans liberated. At that time, Patton, Eisenhower, and our general, Walker of the XX Corps, came to look at this awful, sorry, mess. I was near them during the walk-through.

The very first sight we had were bodies lying all around the ground with bullet holes in them; they had been evidently the "healthy ones," well enough to be out in the compound—all machine gunned where they stood by the guards when they realized we were approaching to liberate the camps. But they had been routinely killing hundreds of people each week and burning them in ovens. I remember at the end of each barracks there was a storage pit where they'd stack up the bodies of the people who died the night before. All around the grounds were big wagons with corpses lying on them.

Somewhere in Germany I had liberated a 35-millimeter camera and I took some pictures in Ohrdruf. Years later I met up with a 4th Armored vet who also had some photos, so we exchanged. His were even more gruesome than mine. One showing a pair of inmates taking a dead man to the ovens—using tongs to drag him by the head. Awful. Unbelievably awful. Another showed a German camp guard with a hole through him, must have been 2-1/2 inches in diameter. I asked what happened to him. He said simply, "Somebody shot him." With a hole that size, it had to be more than a rifle.

I was 22 when I saw those camps in 1945, and none of the carnage I saw in combat, nothing I've ever seen anywhere—even in my wildest nightmare while sleeping—has matched the horror of those camps.

Moving forward with the Third Army, nurse Eileen Biersteker went into a camp in Austria.

We were the first nurses in one of the concentration camps. This one was near Ebensee, Austria. I don't know if that was the name of the concentration camp or not. The SS troops had just left this place that day.

It was just such an awful place to see. It was the worst thing I've ever seen in my life—the bodies lined up by the crematorium is an image that has stayed with me especially. I have pictures of the crematorium, and about 500 dead bodies lined up beside the crematorium ready to be put in. And sometimes there would be just arms and legs there.

It was more horrible than anything we'd seen. We would go into the places where they were given to sleep, and some would just be lying in the bed—dead ones alongside other live ones. They had four to a bed. Men who were just skin and bone, with rags wrapped up on their feet. Sores all over their bodies.

Our boys gave the inmates some of their K rations, and their systems couldn't handle it. They would just fall over.

We nurses were in there for only about an hour before General Patton ordered all nurses out of concentration camps immediately. That's the way they said it: "General Patton has ordered all of us out of the concentration camp," so I can't say if it was a general order or just for us at that one. Maybe it was so terrible he didn't want us in there. I guess we were happy to leave. We had no idea before that day what went on in the camps.

That night, they quartered us in this town of Ebensee, and we had all our bedrolls downstairs. Everything you owned, you kept in your bedroll, of course. The next morning when we came down, the inmates had moved through the town and everything was just stripped. The inmates were so desperate. They were rounded back up again. We stayed in Ebensee about a week, and watched as the Americans made the citizens take all these dead bodies on horse-drawn carts, march behind them with picks and shovels, and bury the dead bodies outside the town. You'd see all these carts going through the town with the bodies. That was another horrible sight.

You don't know if the citizens were aware what was going on in that camp or not. They say they didn't know. But you had to wonder. We felt anger to them. But any time we had contact with the citizens, they were very polite and friendly to us. I can still see the image of the bodies lined up by crematorium, but can't say I have nightmares about it. We saw so much.

V-E Day, May 8, 1945, brought a mixture of emotions for some of Patton's troops. The intense joy of victory was tainted as the full scope of Nazi horrors was revealed. At about the same time Nazi Germany capitulated, other divisions discovered more concentration camps, including Mauthausen, liberated by the 11th Armored Division. Coincident with the liberation of the camps, Major Martin D. Miller was appointed commander of the 11th Armored Division's 492nd Armored Field Artillery Battalion, after his commander fell ill and returned to the States. At the same time, Miller suddenly found himself also in charge of 10,000 emaciated refugees liberated from Mauthausen.

Miller resorted to doing whatever was needed to feed his new charges, which landed him in hot water. He has shared his story in many classrooms.

Chapter Nine

We hadn't known about Mauthausen concentration camp. We didn't receive any information on it ahead of time to prepare us. We had two observation planes in the air and one of them had radioed that he found this big installation. He said, "It must be a fertilizer plant. The stench is something awful." Then the 11th Armored Division went in and found out what it was—a death camp like none of us had ever seen. Our unit didn't have anything to do with the actual liberation and freeing of the prisoners. We were approaching from across the river at the time.

Patton wanted the soldiers of the Third Army to see a concentration camp. So we crossed the river and went there, as did the rest of the 11th Armored Division who hadn't been up front when the camp was liberated.

The camp was a mess. Bodies were lying all around, starting to decay. It was warm because this was May—right around May 8, the day the war in Europe ended. That memory is commingled with the elation of V-E Day. On one hand, there was unbelievable happiness and relief, and on the other a sickened feeling so deep in your gut when you saw what had happened to these people.

The crematorium had run out of fuel, so they had just laid the bodies out in the open. There's nothing worse than the odor of decaying human flesh. We had to recruit local Austrians at gunpoint to come dig mass graves. It wasn't difficult to do. They were willing to come, at gunpoint.

I was very happy to get out of the camp. We weren't told a lot about where these people came from. We thought they were mostly Jews, but we found out that actually the population of Mauthausen was only 30 percent Jews and the rest were political prisoners.

While we were awaiting further orders, the powers that be had decided on the occupation areas. The British came . . . from the north to occupy the north of the Danube. The Americans were to occupy the south of the Danube. A British officer in the occupation forces to the north ordered the prisoners from Mauthausen to be ferried across the river to the American side—10,000 of them—in small boats. With the prisoners came Red Cross workers. Not American Red Cross, but from England, Belgium, Holland and Spain.

The Red Cross workers who could speak English came to me and said, "These people need food." So, suddenly we needed food to feed 10,000, not just the 450 guys in my battalion. I called Third Army G-4 supply for food to feed them. No food came.

One of my sergeants who could speak pretty good German found out in talking with an Austrian train engineer that a British food train would be coming down the tracks just south of the river, on our side. I decided it was only right to take food destined for [north of the Danube], and feed the refugees.

So, I positioned two M4 tanks on the tracks in a place they could be seen well in advance, enabling it to stop in time. I had one of my lieutenants keep watch for the train, so we could go down to get the food when the train came. When it did, I sent about 15 men to get the food and load it onto trucks to bring back for the displaced Mauthausen inmates. The only people on the train were the engineer and brakeman—no guards. The engineer gave no resistance. He didn't care. We took enough food to last a month, because we didn't know how long they'd be there and needing food. It was German Army food, similar, I suppose, to our K rations in the Cracker Jack box. Unfortunately, it was very potent food compared to what they were used to eating. So the Red Cross workers had to ration this food very carefully, so the people wouldn't get sick.

I made a mistake in my method of stopping the train. I neglected to obliterate the insignia on the two M4 tanks I'd parked on the tracks. The 11-triangle-492AFA marking. The Austrian engineer took note of it and reported it to the Brits. The British complained to Eisenhower. And within a week, I received a reprimand with General Patton's name signed to it.

I sent it back unsigned with a note explaining what I did and why. I got a call from General Geoffrey Keyes at Third Army head-quarters, saying General Patton was sending him and two other generals to inspect the area and to find out why I hijacked the train. General Keyes, one of his staff, was in charge of hospitals.

My guards were keeping watch on the area to keep all these people together, separated from the rest because many of them had typhus. Before the generals came, I asked to meet with some of the refugees who could speak pretty good English. As a group, the refugees were in pretty bad shape, but I wanted to be sure General Keyes *would* know they were in bad shape. I told the English-speaking refugees that the generals were coming and that we needed to put on a good show for them. They asked what I meant by that.

"See that farm house over there?" I said, "It has a second-story window. Have one of your guys with a sore belly get up there and holler. And have some of those who can't walk very well along this path," where I knew the generals would be walking.

One of the refugees said, "Oh, you don't want a show, you want a *demonstración*."

"Call it what you want," I said, "but do it."

Chapter Nine

And they did. They put on a marvelous *demonstración*. After about 15 minutes, the senior general said, "Major, your reprimand is lifted." Two days later, food came from G-4.

Miller's battalion stayed encamped by the Danube with the refugees for two weeks. Then 492nd Armored Field Artillery moved on to occupation duty in Bad Ischl, Austria.

◆

Patton's intensity and passion often made him an open book. But at times, he was able to mask true feelings with a natural flare for acting—a bravura that several of his troops have labeled "his showmanship." The actor in him could even speak with conviction about an unlikely continuation of his combat career in the Pacific Theater. Perhaps it was merely wistful rhetoric, or a tactic to avoid admitting that combat glories were coming to an end. At any rate, in the first week of May 1945, when the Third Army had pushed down into Czechoslovakia and freed Pilsen just before the Armistice, Patton met for a final briefing with his faithful headquarters staff. Robert S. Allen of the S-2 staff recounts:

Patton came in trim and brisk and nodded his usual "good morning." With him was Willie, whom he slapped on the rump and pointed to the floor. Willie eyed Patton for a moment, then lay down obediently. The briefing began immediately . . . and followed the regular routine and, as usual, was smart and thorough.

When the PRO [public relations officer] finished, the chief of staff started to rise. Patton restrained him by putting his hand on the chief's knee. Everyone in the room tensed. Patton sat quietly for a few moments, then walked to the war map and faced the staff.

He stood there tall, straight as an arrow, in his tight-fitting, tailored battle jacket with gleaming brass buttons and 16 silver stars, eight each on his shoulders and shirt collar, knife-creased trousers, and high-polished battle boots. Around his waist was the hand-tooled leather belt with ornate brass buckle and an open holster with a .38-caliber automatic, its black plastic butt inlaid on each side with three white stars.

Then in his slightly squeaky voice, he said quietly:

"This will be our last operation briefing in Europe. I hope and pray that it will be our privilege to resume these briefings in another theater that still is unfinished business in this war. I know you are as eager to get there as I am. But you know the situation. However, one thing I can promise you. If I go, you will go.

"I say that because the unsurpassed record of this headquarters is your work. It has been a magnificent and historic job from start to finish. You made history in a manner that is a glory to you and to our country. There probably is no Army commander who did less work than I did. You did it all, and the imperishable record of Third Army is due largely to your unstinting and outstanding efforts. I thank you from the depths of my heart for all you have done."

That was all. He again stood silent for a few minutes looking at the staff, and they at him. Then he nodded to the chief of staff, and snapped his fingers at Willie, and started for the door at the end of the long room. As the staff started to its feet, Patton said, "Keep your seats."

As he left the room, he remarked to the aide by his side, "The best end for an old campaigner is a bullet at the last minute of the last battle."

Eight months later to the day, Patton was fatally injured.

Chapter 10

Aftermath

Patton's Army had run Germany through with a spearhead of armor, and continued on into Czechoslovakia. As Patton prepared to pounce on Prague on May 8, 1945, Nazi Germany surrendered.

With hostilities ended, some of Patton's soldiers settled into occupation duties in Germany. Others had acquired enough precious service points to muster out and go home. Still others prepared to go to the South Pacific to fight the Imperial Japanese. Patton yearned to continue the fight with them, but General Douglas MacArthur chose the less colorful Courtney Hodges to join him in the Pacific Theater. Now a four-star general, Patton instead was appointed military governor of Bavaria.

In the first few days of uneasy peace, the Third Army was located just opposite its Russian occupation counterpart on the Danube. When a high-ranking Russian officer came to Patton's headquarters with "demands," it prompted a double-barreled response from Patton, as Paul Harkins describes in *When the Third Cracked Europe*:

> Shortly after May 9, General Patton was sitting quietly one afternoon in his office at Bad Tolz, in southern Germany, smoking a good cigar and working on his notes, when his chief of staff, General Hobart Gay, entered and said, "General, there's a Russian brigadier general out in my office who says he has instructions to speak to you personally."
>
> "What the hell does the son-of-a-bitch want?"
>
> Gay said, "Well, I only have part of the story, but it's about river craft on the Danube."
>
> Patton replied, "Bring the bastard in, and you and Harkins come with him."

Aftermath

The Russian general started his story. It seems that during the frantic last days of the war, many of the German boatmen on the Danube, hearing of both the approach of the Russian and American Armies, decided to take their chances with the Americans rather than the Russians. They moved their craft, forthwith, to the American Zone and dropped anchor. The Russians heard of this and demanded their return. The Germans refused to go back to the Russian Zone.

In his summary to General Patton, the Russian brigadier said, "General Patton, March (Polkovnik) Tolbukhin of the 4th Russian Guards Army demands that you, General Patton, return these craft to Russian control."

The atmosphere in the general's office exploded. General Patton reached in a desk drawer, slammed his pistol on his desk, stood up in a rage and shrilled, "Gay, goddammit! Get this son-of-a-bitch out of here! Who in hell let him in? Don't let any more of the Russian bastards into this headquarters. Harkins! Alert the 4th and 11th Armored and 65th Division for an attack to the east."

General Gay escorted the Russian general out; [I] alerted the divisions. The Russian general was shaking and white as a sheet. Gay and [I] reentered General Patton's office. The general was sitting at his desk—the pistol back in its drawer, the cigar was lit again. He looked up with a smile and said, "How was that?"

"Sometimes you have to put on an act, and I'm not going to let any Russian marshal, general, or private tell me what I have to do. Harkins, call off the alert of the divisions. That's the last we'll hear from those bastards."

It was. The boats remained under American control.

◆

In June, Patton returned to the States for a short stay that was just long enough for his mouth to get him in trouble again. This time he spoke out against denazification policies, which promptly drew salvos of criticisms in a war-weary world. To top it off, the press broke a story about his appointment of ex-Nazis to high administrative positions in Germany. Likening it to political parties in America, he rebutted: "It is just like republicans and democrats." And stretching to new heights of political incorrectness, he even suggested that Britain and America should rearm the Germans and make them part of a continuing Anglo-American force against the Russians. After public outcry, Patton was relegated to command of a paper army, the

Chapter Ten

Fifteenth Army, charged with "studying military operations in north-western Europe."

Patton's defenders recognized his reckless lack of discretion, but still spoke up for him. Colonel Bradford G. Chynoweth, a friend of 37 years, spoke for many of his contemporaries:

> Once more, I find myself in accord with George Patton. He was severely censured because, after World War II he wanted to give amnesty to former Nazis. He pointed out that they had to be one thing or another in Germany. He made the tactless remark that "it is just like republicans and democrats back home." Poor old George! His telegram to me, after my [promotion] board could apply even more to him. "You are a hell of a good soldier with a hell of a big mouth!" George was a better soldier than I ever could have been, and he also had a very active vocal apparatus.

Before leaving the States to return to an assignment in Germany, Patton paid a visit to Walter Reed Army Hospital in Washington, where he saw not only his former soldiers but his second daughter, Ruth Ellen Totten. She shares a story with Harry Semmes for his *Portrait of Patton* about the visit:

> During 1944–1945 while my husband was in the Pentagon, I was a Red Cross aide at Walter Reed and helped in occupational therapy. I ended up in the double amputee ward for enlisted men. I was Mrs. Totten to everyone out there and didn't mention my maiden name, thinking that I might embarrass some of the men. One day I was helping out in the heart ward and an old Third Cavalry sergeant spotted me. We had a wonderful talk about the old days. I thought no more about it but next time I got back to my own ward there was a certain stiffness, and finally one of the patients who had been there longer asked me why I hadn't told them. Out of an empty head I babbled, "How would these headlines have looked, Wounded Private Slaps General's Daughter?" That broke the ice and we were all friends again.
>
> When Daddy came back in 1945 on that quick tour, I asked him to come to my ward on the day he visited Walter Reed. He loathed visiting hospitals but he said he would, and he got in there with Mother, two doctors, and myself. I had worked there so long I didn't realize how pitiful my patients looked. There was not a man in there over thirty-five and everyone was missing all or part of at least two limbs. Daddy marched in looking magnificent and stood right in the middle of the ward. There was a throbbing silence and then he began to bawl, hauled out his handkerchief, mopped his eyes and said,

Aftermath

"Men—all I can say is, if I had been a better general, most of you wouldn't be here." Then he marched out. There wasn't a dry eye in the ward.

The Patton family, June 1945: son George IV, the general, wife Beatrice, daughters Ruth Ellen and Bee. **Patton Museum**

◆

Patton returned to Germany for the new assignment, which located him in Bad Nauheim. In August, a very young sergeant named Horace Woodring became the general's personal driver. Probably no one was with Patton more in the second half of 1945. In a personal interview, Woodring talks about how he came to be Patton's driver and the road adventures that followed:

I was with him seven days a week for those last months. Right after I became his driver, he didn't talk with me for probably the first week. But I knew I was doing all right, or I would have been out of the car walking. I never had a chance to talk with the previous driver, who headed back to the States to get out of the Army. Never met him, but wished I could have. So I just drove like I *thought* Patton would want me to drive.

I was coming over a hill one day at high speed. A dog ran out in the street—a German shepherd—and I ran over that dog. I didn't bat an eye. Patton just said, "You ruthless son of a bitch." And he grinned. He couldn't believe that I did that without batting an eye. I guess that impressed him, because after that I could do no wrong.

Chapter Ten

People wondered how someone so young as me could have been chosen as his driver. I had driven a truck, a gravel truck in Kentucky, since I was 15. I was 17 when I went into the Army, in June 1944.

I had gone to chauffeur's school at Fort McClellan and then infantry training. I was put in the infantry and was on the boat at Christmas (1944) and went from one "repo depot" to another, but was never in the Third Army.

I got my feet froze in the infantry. All I had was the old leather combat boots. I got to the point that I couldn't walk anymore, so I got sent to the hospital. I got to thinking there must have been others who got their feet froze, and I was reading an article last year that said 15,000 got their feet froze. After that, I got sent to a motor pool. I became General [Leonard] Gerow's driver in early 1945. After that [in August], I became General Patton's driver.

I remember the first time I saw Patton. I was taking General Gerow to a meeting with Ike. Suddenly, here comes Patton—the horns were blowing and everything. Seeing him for the first time brought chill-bumps. We all knew what he had accomplished, but people either loved him or hated him.

Every day was memorable with General Patton. We always traveled at a high rate of speed, [because] he never had time for travel. Most of the time we took the 1938 Cadillac limo. It could go close to a hundred miles per hour wide open. And we did that whenever we [were] on the autobahn. Whenever we were on the open road, he'd say, "Let's go!" And that meant go wide open.

I remember we were going into Frankfurt one morning. There was a trolley track separating the boulevard there. About a half-mile from a main intersection, our side of the road became totally blocked with Army convoys. Patton never wanted to sit and wait. So I looked around, realized I couldn't go down the sidewalk because of so much rubble from the blown-out buildings. Then I noticed a bomb crater on the trolley track and there the fence was down just past it. I could see nothing on the trolley tracks between there and the MP, about a quarter-mile down. So I just swung onto the trolley track. It was quite bouncy. I started blowing the air horn and the MP looked up and started blocking traffic for us to pass. I blasted on through and I turned around to see Patton laughing to beat hell. It was the kind of thing he really liked.

The air horns were already installed on that car when I came, so I didn't put them in, but I had to make damn sure they were blowing all the time! The compressors would wear out [because of so much use]. So I had three of them—one in the shop, a spare one in the car, and one on the car hooked up. If I could tell the one hooked up was failing, I'd install the spare, so they would always be working well. After the war, I had those horns for years. I took the horns, the flag, and the star plate, and sent them home [after the accident]. For a few years I had the horns on my own car, but in 1953 we had a garage fire at my home in Kentucky and they were destroyed. I gave the star plate to the Patton Museum and I still have the flag.

We had conversations. He cursed with every breath. He used to call me every name he could think of. Nothing serious, you know. That's just the way he talked. I'd pull some trick and he'd say how stupid I was. But he would always laugh. It was always good natured and in fun.

His dog Willie would sometimes go along. I knew Willie real well. In *Patton* the movie, Willie was portrayed as kind of a coward in one scene. Not true. He was a pit bull, and wasn't afraid of anything. In fact, he would have eaten another dog alive if they'd gotten close to him. That's the way Patton liked it. Patton probably turned over in his grave when they portrayed Willie as a coward.

We were going to Brussels for a decoration ceremony. We stopped at the border to Belgium, where the MPs had set up an escort for us. It was four Harley bikes in front of us going about 40. Patton said, "Get 'em going, get 'em going!" I hit the air horns and the MP sergeant looked back. I waved him on. So they sped up to about 50. Patton said, "Get those sons of bitches out of the way!" So I blow the horn and he looks back again and I wave him off this time. They pull over and we took off. I knew where we were going. He had no time for an escort. It was fun being part of all that. I really liked the old man.

Everyday was a trip somewhere. He enjoyed the trips. He was to be the guest of the king of Denmark and the prime minister of Sweden. He spent a week in Denmark and a week in Sweden, and I went along as part of his personal staff. He took us along with no duties, in his private plane, and also by train. The day before we were going to go, we were going to work and this little German car came across the street at us. In trying to avoid a collision with him, I clipped a post and knocked it down. It didn't damage much. We stopped though, and the other driver made a big mistake of stopping, too.

Patton gets out of the car, walks over to the other car, reaches in and grabs this guy out and says, "Shoot this son of a bitch."

The guy happened to have only one arm. "Nah, nah, nah," Patton said and shoved him toward Colonel Smith, his aide. "Lock the son of a bitch up, and throw away the key." He turned to me and said, "Take me to work."

Chapter Ten

That night I was taking Patton somewhere. He had had a drink of I.W. Harper—that's what he drank—and he turned to me said, "Woodring, when you get back tonight, get that poor Kraut turned loose. Maybe I shot that arm off myself." So he had a heart—probably bigger than he was. He had a huge heart. And he loved his soldiers.

◆

On Monday, December 10, 1945, Patton was to leave Europe for a permanent transfer to the United States. It would be his first Christmas at home in three years with his wife, Beatrice, and his two daughters and son. Patton had little to do the morning of Sunday, December 9, so generals Hap Gay and Geoffrey Keyes suggested that he hunt pheasant in the local woods surrounding Mannheim. The fateful day is recounted by the two other men who were there—Gay, his wartime chief of staff, and Woodring, his driver. First, a snippet from Gay's oral history:

General Patton was going to fly over to London on Monday . . . and then come back to the United States on his own mark. This was a Sunday. He was a little bit upset, nervous, over the happenings before this [continuing public criticism] and so, Colonel Harkins and I persuaded him to go pheasant shooting and he said, "All right."

The driver, General Patton, and I were going down the valley. We came to a railroad track and there was this train crossing it. We waited and waited and, finally, it moved on. We went on. We hadn't gone 100 yards when a truck coming down facing towards us—the driver happened to look up to see where he was supposed to turn off, and he turned off in front of us.

We weren't going, in my opinion, over 15 miles an hour. After the slight crash, General Patton said to me, "Are you hurt?"

I said, "No, not a bit."

He said to the driver, "Are you hurt?"

Woodring, the driver, said, "No, not a bit."

He said to me, "I believe I am paralyzed. Take and rub my arms and shoulders and rub them hard." I did. He said, "Damn it, *rub* them."

I knew then there was something wrong because he couldn't feel it, and just then a man came along in a jeep and got out. He was a doctor so he took charge and took General Patton on in to General Geoffrey Keyes' headquarters, where he died a few days later.

No premeditation, I'm sure, because nobody knew two hours before it happened that we were going. Nobody knew the location we were going to. We were even telling the driver where to go as we went.

Aftermath

Horace Woodring fills in details.

The day was December 9, 1945. Sunday morning. I was told we would be going on a pheasant-hunting trip. Patton was a big hunter, tremendous shot. The orderly was sent over to tell me he was ready to go early that morning.

Sergeant Meeks, his orderly, woke me up to say, "They're going hunting, so get ready. You'll leave in a short while." I lived right across the street in house from his house. I lived there in a nice home, along with Sergeant Meeks and Sergeant Lee, his cook.

General Keyes had spent the night, but had just left. In the area where he planned to hunt was between Mannheim and Heidelberg. Pretty good run down the autobahn.

He wanted to stop and look at an old castle. There was snow on the ground, pretty high up. I stayed in the car—it was real cold. He came back and got back in, but in the front seat with me, so he could use the heater vent to dry his boots which got a lot of snow on them.

Just before we got off the autobahn, we had to stop at the checkpoint. And at the checkpoint, the hunting advisor, Sergeant Spruce, was waiting there for us. He had already taken the dog out and was there with it. The dog got real cold—short-haired pointer, so Patton got out to talk with Sergeant Spruce and then got back in as did the dog. The dog got down on the floor board. And we headed out with Sergeant Spruce ahead of us in a vehicle.

A couple miles down the road we got separated, because Sergeant Spruce got past the train crossing, but a train came and separated us. We stopped until the train passed, then started out again.

General Patton was talking with Gay. Just after the railroad track was an Army quartermaster dump, where there were wrecked jeeps and tanks and trucks. They were talking about all the blown-up material. Patton liked to look ahead, to be aware where we were going.

In the movie *The Last Days of Patton*, they showed a bunch of burnt-out buildings with lots of people around. Really, there was none of that around. And no one in the area. Not anyone behind or in front. Nothing moving except the truck [coming toward us]—probably a half-mile down.

The driver of the truck suddenly decides to turn into the entrance to this factory or whatever it was, and in doing that he ran right into the front of my car. I never had a chance to even hit the brakes. It hit on his right front fender and bumper. His bumper being quite a bit higher than ours, it pretty well mangled our car— side and front.

Chapter Ten

Patton's 1938 Cadillac limousine staff car after the collision with an errant American 2-1/2-ton truck. Patton's driver, Horace Woodring, explains: "His bumper being quite a bit higher than ours, it pretty well mangled our car—side and front. Patton flew forward and hit the windowsill of the limo's partition that separated the driver from the back. His forehead caught that windowsill, just above the eyebrows. It peeled the skin back so it hung like a flap."
Horace Woodring

It happened so fast that I didn't have time to react at all. I was trying to get to the brakes, but it was so quick I didn't have an opportunity to do anything.

Patton was in the very back on the right-hand side. People who have told this story always said he like to sit on the edge of his seat, but contrary to that he rarely *ever* sat on the edge of his seat. On impact, he flew forward and hit the windowsill of the limo's partition that separated the driver from the back. That window was down as always. His forehead caught that windowsill, just above the eyebrows. It peeled the skin back so it hung like a flap.

General Gay was thrown forward, too, but he was much smaller than General Patton. When we came to a halt, they were thrown back again into their seat, and he ended up under General Patton.

I got out and opened the back door, and the hunting dog bolted out. When I first looked, it was total shock. I could see Patton's skull, from when the windowsill peeled it back. I could see bone. The first words out of General Patton's mouth were, "Is everybody all right?" Believe it or not, he was always concerned about his fellow man.

Of course, by then, he was bleeding bad. He was laying across General Gay. And General Gay asked me to help him get General Patton off of him. Patton said, "Hap"—he always called him Hap—"I can't seem to move."

General Gay picked up Patton's arm and asked if he could feel that. Patton said he couldn't. Patton was not able to move himself, and he was quite disturbed that he wasn't able to move. I slid my arms under him and helped lift so Gay could get out from under.

The first vehicle on the scene happened to be an Army ambulance. That was within two or three minutes [of the crash at 11:45 a.m.]. It just happened to be passing by. Not all reports and stories say that, but that's what happened. Next came a car with an Army doctor, full bird colonel I believe.

They patched him up, put him in the ambulance and took him to Heidelberg.

Woodring's judgment was never doubted. The driver of the truck would have been questioned, except that Patton himself ordered a halt to even a routine investigation. MP files relating to the accident were destroyed. Woodring continues:

It was Sunday morning and these guys were recovering from the night before. They couldn't believe they had hit General Patton. They couldn't believe it had happened. I talked with the driver and other guys from the truck to say they better settle down, because they hit General Patton's car and it was serious. I'm sure it struck the fear of God into them.

Patton stated later, "Let no one be responsible for the accident." That cleared the other driver.

Seeing the wound was not traumatic for me. I had seen combat. But this was an unusual wound. In the movie *The Last Days of Patton*, they had shown the wound right on the top part of the head, but that's not the way it was. It was just above the eyebrows and peeled back the skin. Of course, he sustained a broken neck—a separation of the spinal cord. I was not injured and neither was General Gay.

I did not speak with General Patton after that. Once they took him to the hospital, the only ones allowed in to see him were high-ranking officers and family. I met his wife, Beatrice, when she flew into Frankfurt with Dr. [formerly Colonel R. Glen] Spurling. They flew over from the States. General Gay had told me that General Patton had asked that I pick them up from the airport to take them to the hospital. So I used General Gay's staff car to do that.

Mrs. Patton was a small person, but a fiery person—very much like him in that way. She knew I had been driving General Patton, but she didn't ask me about the accident.

Later came the accounts that have said we were being followed by a lieutenant, an MP who saw the wreck. But that wasn't possible. He wasn't at the wreck and couldn't have seen it happen. Completely erroneous.

Chapter Ten

I have a letter that I received from General Gay in 1979. He had seen me on the Mike Douglas show, where I told what happened and that it *was* an accident. It contradicted the story that some others had told, but I have the letter which, to me, is priceless, because he said I'd told it just like it had happened [see letter below]. After the wreck, none of 'em had told it the way it happened.

The TV talk show, which aired in 1979, suggested the car wreck might not be an accident. Hap Gay saw it and wrote Woodring a letter of affirmation:

Feb. 16, 1979
Dear Woodring:

My writing was always terrible but now due to loss of eyesight it is even worse. I do however want you to know that you were great on the TV.

Of course, it was purely accidental. In fact, as you know, the trip was not planned until late that morning, and the next day he was flying to London.

My best,
(signed) Hap Gay

Stitches around the flap of skin on his forehead and a bandage across his nose repaired the superficial injuries, but the dislocation of his third and fourth cervical vertebrae—essentially a fractured spine—could not be so easily repaired.

As Patton lay paralyzed in the Army hospital at Heidelberg, Eisenhower wasted no time in writing to his friend:

Gen. George S. Patton Jr.
Commanding General
15th U.S. Army
APO 408, U.S. Army

10 December 1945

Dear George:

You can imagine what a shock it was to me to hear of your serious accident. At first I heard it on the basis of rumor and simply did not believe it, thinking it was again a story such as the one that came out only a couple months ago. I immediately wired Frankfurt and learned to my great distress that it was true.

Aftermath

My Secretary General Staff, Colonel Bowen, knows Ruth Ellen very well and we used that channel to notify Big Bee and then Surles [Beatrice and Dr. Spurling] went out personally. I gave orders that everything possible was to be done, including the very fastest transportation for Big Bee in the event that she was in position to go to Germany. Last evening, just before she took off, she called me but there was nothing I could think of to send on that I have not already said to you in my telegram. Actually, I awoke out of a sound nap and probably was not functioning too well.

By coincidence, only the day before, on Saturday, I had directed that you be contacted to determine whether you wanted a particular job that appeared to be opening up here in the States. The real purpose of this note is simply to assure you that you will always have a job and not to worry about this accident closing out any of them for your selection.

As you know, it is always difficult for me to express my true sentiments when I am deeply moved. I can only assure you again that you are never out of my thoughts and that my hopes and prayers are tied up in your speedy recovery. If anything at all occurs to you where I might be of some real help, don't hesitate a second to let an aide forward the message to me.

The whole Country shares my sentiments. The President, the Secretary of War and the whole public have been notified of your accident and without exception all are praying for your complete and speedy recovery.

With my affectionate and warm regard,

As ever,
(signed) Dwight D. Eisenhower

With the best medical care possible and his wife by his side (often reading history to him), Patton hung on. But his breathing became increasingly labored and irregular. On the afternoon of December 21, 1945, he passed away in his sleep.

Major General Albert W. Kenner was chief surgeon for Service Forces, European Theater. He wrote two letters to medical colleagues after Patton's death. The first was to Colonel R. B Hill, surgeon, Chanor Base Section, dated December 27, 1945:

Poor Georgie passed out on me, as you know by this, but he certainly received everything in the way of medical care. Two days before his demise, he had a shower emboli that hit his right chest and he started to fill up with his own sputum. We managed to get that pretty well under control, only to see him die very suddenly as a result of another showering down of emboli. As a matter of fact, he went out like a light and certainly suffered no pain. The service lost its best field commander and I lost a damn good friend.

A half-track serves as the hearse for a funeral procession for Patton through the dark streets of Heidelberg, Germany, on December 23, 1945. Master Sergeant William George Meeks, Patton's long-time orderly, is at left. A special train took the body from Heidelberg to Patton's final resting place at Hamm, Luxembourg. **Patton Museum**

The second was to Colonel J. B. Coates Jr., a doctor in the medical section of the Third Army, dated January 4, 1946:

I am sorry we had to lose General Patton but, at best, had he pulled through, he would have been paralyzed from the waist down, and he was too grand an old soldier for that sort of life.

◆

Aftermath

Patton himself had spoken matter-of-factly about death, according to Harry H. Semmes. He recounts a flashback under the heading "Incidents Tell the Man" in *Portrait of Patton:*

Some distant relative died and the Patton family was sadly discussing it. The general heard the family talking and came in and said, "What is so strange or unusual about dying? You just walk back out the same door you came in. When you came in, you had no complaints about where you'd come from."

Patton had also made this remark repeatedly: "The proper end for the professional soldier is a quick death inflicted by the last bullet of the last battle." Patton envisioned perhaps a misty sort of warrior's heaven (Valhalla), where the faithful fallen of his Armies stood together awaiting him amidst the volleys of a 21-gun salute. Chester B. Hansen of Bradley's staff alludes to this in a diary entry of December 8, 1944— exactly a year and one day before Patton's mishap:

Patton believes earnestly in warrior's Valhalla. He honestly thinks it is to the glory of a man to die in the service of his country. Admittedly, there is no better way to die if die one must.

Patton's assistant G-2, Robert S. Allen, died in 1981. His widow, Adeline, in a letter to the author, writes about friendships maintained during the decades after the war and "Third Army heaven" where all the old soldiers must be:

I'm afraid most of Patton's staff is now gone, but they kept in constant touch with Colonel Allen [in the years following the war]. . . . I remember their visits' impact on Bob Allen. He could be having one of his red-headed tirades over some bureaucrat, but as soon as an Army friend called or walked in, his voice would turn to honey-coated greetings, and all was well again.

When Colonel Allen asked me to marry him, I talked to Colonel Hal Forde, who commanded XIX TAC air bombings over Germany, and he thought it was a fine idea. We kept in touch by mail for several years and during that time, he wrote of his wife's death, and then he, too, went to what must be Third Army heaven, because Patton's men were a solid team!

Patton was buried at Hamm, Luxembourg, on Christmas Eve Day 1945. The General Patton Memorial Museum first opened its doors on July 7, 1995, at nearby Ettelbruck. Citizens of Luxembourg still consider him their liberator.

Patton's grave at Hamm, Luxembourg. Patton was initially buried within the immaculate rows of soldiers killed in action primarily during the Battle of the Bulge, but a high volume of visitors prompted the grave to be moved within the cemetery to the front and center, nearest the entrance. Directly behind the grave is a small chapel dedicated to Patton and his men, whom Luxembourg's citizens credit with liberating their country.

Patton is one of the rare individuals who attained legendary status while still alive, according to a *New York Times* editorial. If Patton were a legend in life, the legend has grown since his death.

◆

From the perspective of many decades later, Patton veterans reflect on their leader, the war, its aftermath, and how the experience shaped them: George Davis, 8th Infantry Division, says:

I got to visit Patton's grave three or four years ago. I took a vacation to Europe and went to Luxembourg. Stepping up to the grave was a weird feeling. It was a sad place because so many of the boys are there—several hundred graves. I was with a group, but none of them had been in the service. I was the only one who had been there and knew what it was all about. Several people took pictures of me by that grave.

Seeing the grave made me think of him in life. I could see Patton in my mind as clear as the first time I saw him at St. Lô. He was in his command car, a Dodge car with the top off, standing on the front seat and holding on to that windshield. His two pistols on his hips. He stood so straight—the picture of the perfect soldier. It was inspiring to us. We thought, *Here's a leader—up here with us and he's not afraid. If he can do it, I can do it.*

It was something you kept with you forever after that. And I also thought of those many others in life—the boys lying there since World War II. I looked at some graves but didn't have time to look more closely. If I'd had time, I know I could have found boys I actually knew. We lost a lot of boys in that area. I'd like to go back and spend three or four days to go through the cemetery. I thought about how they died as such young men. It made tears come. And I thought I could have been right there with them. But I went on to marry and had one son and one daughter.

Patton was one of the best generals there was. He got the job done and didn't beat around the bush to do it. That's the kind of general the men wanted to fight for. He was a leader, pulling us from the front, not pushing from the rear. He talked about an army being like cooked spaghetti: You had to pull it, not push it. He had to make some hard decisions, some that put many boys in the graves at Hamm, but in the long run, it probably saved lives.

Chaplain George W. Knapp of the 4th Infantry Division remembers seeing Patton near the war's end:

The battalion was rolling through a town in our vehicles. The chaplains were in their jeeps along with medics and others. We were told to pull off to the side of the road and stop. Soon, here comes Patton. Anybody could recognize him, standing up as straight as a stick in a jeep. The jeep had a special bar that was attached for him to hold on to, because all Third Army jeeps had their windshields folded down with canvas spread over them so that the lights would not reflect off of them.

I was pleased that I was able to see him, but disappointed that there was no acknowledgment or talk from him. If I would have talked with him then—or if I could talk with him today—I'd congratulate him for his great leadership. The war was all but done at that point, and he certainly had a hand in winning it. It would have been nice to have given him credit for the good work he had done.

In occupied Germany, Patton encountered many who had served with him inside and outside his command. William E. Kepner had been commander of Eighth Air Force Fighter Command, which provided valuable air support for Patton on the drive through Europe. Meeting him only briefly before, Kepner finally had the chance to talk face to face under more casual circumstances:

I met Patton several times. He was a striking looking fellow and had a high voice and I'd seen him and watched him play polo in

World War I when I was executive officer of Headquarters Troops, Occupation Forces in Koblenz.

In the fall of 1945, he invited everyone over to Nuremberg. They were all dressed up and boots shined like a fresh egg, helmets shined and wore their belts exactly so and side arms. Patton was supposed to be there to host the lunch for about 20 of us.

We got a message to go ahead and eat. He couldn't make it. He was to come in on a plane and the weather was too bad. So we went ahead and ate. Afterwards, we were to watch a polo match, so the chief of staff said, "Let's go on out to the stadium before the games start."

We went out and there must have been 200 officers—major and lieutenant generals. He had invited a lot of us. Everyone of them was spic and span except me. I had a flat Air Force hat and yellow trench coat. I furnished ground support not only to Patton but to Hodges, Simpson, and the rest of them.

I wasn't particularly awed by George Patton. I'd run into him a time or two and he'd cursed me out at long range about the fact he couldn't get gasoline and I should bring some in on my airplanes. And I did.

Everybody was talking right and left and all of a sudden there was silence. We looked down and there was Patton. He was tapping his quirt on his boot.

"Keep on talking, don't stop for me," Patton said. "I'm just looking you over to see how many look like officers and there's damn few of you." He looked around, saw me and pointed his quirt and motioned me to come on down. I was just standing there sort of grinning. The fellow beside me said, "Are you going to catch hell."

I said, "What do you mean, catch hell?"

"The uniform."

"I make my own uniform and I'll be the first one to tell George Patton that." And I walked down.

He had a friendly grin and I said, "You're a hell of a host. You invite me over here, I furnish you air support, and you don't even show up for lunch."

"Well, this pilot of mine said the weather was too bad and didn't want to fly. Too risky."

I said, "That's right! You listen to that pilot and you'll live longer. Don't tell him when to fly."

"I won't."

We chatted for a while and I said, "I'd like to know how you get away with this idea of not complying with orders."

Patton said, "Oh, I comply with orders."

Aftermath

I said, "Well, there's an order here that soldiers will not associate—fraternize—with the Germans. And you got all kinds of it down the road from my headquarters."

"Oh, I don't have any of that."

"I'll find you 20 witnesses within two hours that will swear they've seen your men in these places."

Patton said, "I didn't say any anything about it except I put out an order that 'no man of the Third Army will appear in the presence of Germans at any time, at any place, unless he has on his boots, has a belt, has on a helmet, and everything will be shined up spic and span and stay that way.' Now you know damned well you can't do any fraternizing dressed like that."

I said, "You win."

He started laughing and I did too, and the crowd came down. They had waited for me to break the ice and were shaking hands and saying, "Glad to see you, General." I liked the guy. He was a great guy. Just phenomenal, really, but he created a lot of trouble.

Patton was a fellow that really got out and did things. He went through holes when we were bombing German lines in Normandy. Some of the Armies were unable to get through there for five to six hours. In the meantime, the terrific shock experienced by bombs dropping all around them could have passed on, and the Germans were back, quick witted and ready to fight . . . the Army had a pretty tough time many times going through after the Germans closed the holes.

We always were very happy when we were bombing ahead of Patton, because within a half an hour, and sometimes less time, he cut through the hole and when he came through he didn't find much resistance.

He got out of traps when they had him trapped. He saw to it that they didn't delay and he was a wonderful tactician. I think he's the Stonewall Jackson of that particular war. He got in more trouble than Stonewall Jackson ever did—at least history didn't give Jackson credit for that much trouble. But Patton was a fellow who did things and I suspect General Eisenhower, at times, wished he didn't have to go down and soothe some guy's feelings for what Patton had done. But I also think General Eisenhower must have thought that it was all worthwhile because, after all, Patton was the guy that broke out into an open line and opened things up. That kind of guy is hard to find. Patton was that way and I think he was an extraordinary man.

Kepner's thoughts about exploiting holes are reinforced by German Major General Richard Schimpf, who was captured while in command of the German Third Paratroop Division. His opponent's perspective was preserved and probably translated by Robert S. Allen of Lucky Forward.

> We always confidently relied on Allied hesitancy to exploit successes to give us the time to withdraw and regroup in order to slow up the next thrust. But with your General Patton, it was different. He was very aggressive in exploiting a penetration. His breakthrough at Avranches was an outstanding example of this. So was his phenomenal campaign in the Palatinate.

Maury Laws, 26th Infantry Division, recalls:

> I encountered Patton a second time, right after the war. [The first had been when he was lost in the Moncourt Woods—see chapter 6.] It was in Czechoslovakia. We were at a riding school, and Royal Lipizan horses had been brought there to do a performance for him.
>
> We happened to be billeted near there. And the word came down that Patton was coming that day. So a couple hundred of GIs were brought in for this, too. I remember thinking I didn't want to be there, and I know a lot of others thought the same. The higher ups of my regiment were "putting on the dog." Patton had come with an entourage and sat in seating set up like a reviewing stand to watch this performance. Being around a general like Patton made you nervous. There was a certain reverence there. He was a great man.
>
> They played recordings of Mozart and the horses did their thing. They moved this way, that way, crossing, and so on. All through the performance I concentrated on the music—how the arranger had written the strings, the violins. It impressed me.
>
> I myself had made a deal with God back on the battlefield. *If I get through this thing*, I pledged, *I'd do nothing but music—really commit myself fully and settle for nothing less.*

Laws lived up to his promise. He went on to become a nationally known musician—director, composer, and arranger—lending his musical genius to classics of the big screen and television, including *The Hobbit, Frosty the Snowman*, and many others.

Martin Blumenson, a Third Army historical officer near the end of the war and who later became Patton's biographer, comments:

> The first time I saw him was as he went by in a jeep near the end of the war. I also saw him being decorated in a ceremony with the French. I thought, *Here is a great soldier*. I think Patton was certainly the most brilliant general on the battlefield during World War II. (I can't say beyond that, though he was pretty good in World War I.) There

was a greatness about him. Anyone who came into contact with him, even someone who came into contact so briefly as I did, could recognize that essential greatness. That charisma. That *whatever* it was he had. You just felt confident and pleased that he was commanding things in your area. The fact that you were working for him meant a great deal.

I remember I was in Paris around Christmastime. There were about six of us sitting around a table having sandwiches and a drink. Friends of mine—young people like me, nobody important. All of us expatriates, so to speak, in Paris after the war. And we were told that Patton had died. And all of us there who had been in the Third Army almost cried when we heard the news. It was a very gloomy afternoon that we spent at that table.

For troops not retained in the occupation forces or mustered out at home, the Pacific Theater awaited them. Victory in Europe didn't mean a ticket back home—it meant finishing off Imperial Japan. After seeing months of combat with the 86th Infantry Division, Staff Sergeant Al Neuharth prepared for more. After a brief celebration back home, he went to the Pacific, but returned after a long oceanic voyage none the worse for the wear.

After V-E Day, our 86th Division and the 84th were the first two to return from Europe. We were hailed in a victory parade down Fifth Avenue in New York. After 30-day furloughs at home for "rest and recuperation," we were the first to be redeployed to the Pacific, where the war was still on.

We were lucky. We were on board troopships en route to the Philippines when the atomic bomb was dropped on Hiroshima. For the Japanese it was a disaster. For us it was a blessing.

On my trip back from the Philippines to California, our troopship looked like a gambling casino. Everybody wanted to score a big hit before being discharged from the Army.

Tom Rosser had taught me to play poker when things were slow in the butcher shop in Alpena [South Dakota]. It became one of my favorite pastimes. Poker pays off for the business of bluffing. A game with a practical purpose. When to hold, when to fold. How big a risk to stake.

I had saved nearly $200 from my sergeant's salary. I decided I'd go home either broke or with a nice bundle. A thousand dollars was my magic goal.

In nine days and nights of poker playing, I parlayed the $200 into $1,100. It was my first big gamble and I won. The poker winnings paid for the used 18-foot house trailer that became home for my bride, Loretta, and me after we were married in June 1946.

Good fortune continued for Neuharth. The stakes became much higher, as he went on to found *USA Today*, one of America's most widely read newspapers.

Another Third Army soldier who would become recognized nationally is Chesterfield Smith of the 94th Infantry Division. Smith is a lawyer who became famous for, among other things, his stand that "no man is above the law" during the Nixon Watergate scandal. Smith acknowledges the influence of World War II on his life and, even after decades spent inside the circles of the world's most powerful people, he remains awed by Patton.

I was adoring. Amazed. He was all the books say about him. He was arrogant, demanding, magnificent. Everybody adored him, even though sometimes they couldn't stand him.

He came up to division at least twice. I was a first lieutenant and a captain then. It was in France or could have been Luxembourg. It was kind of a rally. He talked about what we had done and what we were going to do. Our troops were doing well. He could sell himself. It was like, "By God, here's a man who'd do it right. He wasn't scared of anything and didn't want you to be."

We had to censor the mail for our troops. I had about 140 troops. We had to look at the mail and almost every letter I saw go home to wives and children and friends, but especially wives, would start off with the most unbelievable compliments and bragging like "I'm a Patton man." They were all so proud. They wanted to be a fighter because of him. They wanted to win that damn war because of him. And they'd all put it in their letters.

Things Patton did are very important to a war. The leadership he furnished made people risk their lives for their country. Made people try to do [more], even though by playing it safe they might have had a better chance of getting home and living a long time. He influenced people. Really I'm still amazed what Patton did.

Sometimes people that'd write those letters saying how wonderful Patton is would go outside and bitch about him to each other. Didn't like him. They'd say, "He's not looking out for us. He's giving us too much risk." But when they'd write home, they'd brag, brag, brag. They'd say, "I'm a Patton man!" I heard a lot of people who questioned Patton that were serving under him—like, "That bastard is going to kill us. He doesn't care a damn thing about us. He just wants to win the war and be in a book or something." But when they would write home, they'd brag endlessly. It's just kind of the way people are. I think, frankly, they all admired him every way as a soldier. Maybe they were thinking, *I don't have to be myself with this good of a soldier. Yes, I could do quartermaster work, moving supplies. But I should be up here dodging bullets. Patton wants me to dodge bullets.*

In the closing weeks of the war, Smith was assigned command of a region in the Ruhr Valley, the great industrial center of Germany. Even though fighting continued in the east, all shooting had stopped in the Ruhr Valley. And it was Smith's responsibility to restore order by working with the equivalent of a county manager. "He reported to me, just like I did to my colonel and general," he explains. "We tried to keep the railroads running, the roads open, the telephones working. We tried to make that a stable place."

He mustered out of the Army as a major in late 1945, after starting as a private called to active duty when the National Guard was mobilized in 1940. He returned to his native Florida to earn his law degree with financial help from the GI Bill. He went on to become president of the American Bar Association (his term began in the midst of Watergate) and his lifelong commitment to law and courageous causes merit his moniker of "Citizen Smith."

◆

Ivory-handled pistols, shiny star-studded helmet, sharp tongue, and teeth-gritted resolve. This is the Patton the world knew. It was the side he had wanted known. But what lay behind the blood-and-guts exterior—beneath what some here have called "theatrical" and "showmanship"—when he was away from the combat troops for whom the persona was carefully crafted? A cadre of insiders saw Patton daily and interacted with him as part of his staff, or as his peers and superiors. Coy Eklund of Lucky Forward's G-1 section saw Patton regularly. Not one to glorify Patton or their working relationship, Eklund speaks frankly:

> We didn't love Patton. We weren't buddy-buddy with him. We avoided him as much as we could. If I saw him coming toward me and I could make a tactful move in another direction, I sure did.
>
> You couldn't be comfortable around him. He was profane almost every other word. I think that even his peers were not comfortable

around him. But I think they admired him. *We* respected and admired and believed in him.

It's not easy to present a balanced picture of Patton. When the *Patton* movie was made, we worried that he would be depicted as an oversized hero or an extreme egomaniac. In the end, it turned out to be quite fairly balanced. Although George C. Scott never imitated his voice or his shuffle. Patton did not stride, never moved quickly. He *shuffled*. He was hurt during World War I, shot in the hip, and never did get totally comfortable after that. There was quite a bit made of reincarnation in the movie. He didn't do much talking about it, but he believed it. He believed he was in the Battle of Carthage. Just a little private idiosyncrasy.

Eklund returned to civilian life at war's end and entered the insurance industry, eventually becoming CEO of the Equitable Life Assurance Society of the United States.

Of all those who knew Patton well and wrote about him, Robert S. Allen expresses some of the most eloquent and perceptive thoughts. Allen's observations are recorded with the discerning eye of a professional journalist, which he was before serving as a lieutenant colonel in Lucky Forward's G-2 section.

The chief of staff, section chiefs, and other senior officers were important. But not all-important. Under Patton, only one man ruled the roost—Patton.

Literally, as well as theoretically, everyone worked for him.

That initial impression never changed. It remained as true the last day as the first.

This trait is a significant key to Patton's little-known and less understood, underlying character.

Throughout his life he completely dominated every unit he commanded. Yet in dominating, he did not domineer. Patton always led men. He did not rule them.

This vital distinction explains many things about him.

It explains why the troops called him "Georgie." Why his men and units always were the most soldierly, the most efficient, the most aggressive, and cockiest. Why he always got so much out of them. Why he had peerless staffs, and developed four outstanding corps and many division and lower-unit commanders. Why, although he was inherently aloof and reserved, and in combat violent and ruthless, hundreds of thousands of men served under him with boastful pride and truculent devotion.

As is often the case with men of Patton's type, there was wide variances between popular conception and the real individual.

Aftermath

With Patton, much of the former was deliberate pictorialization: a conscious headlining of certain aspects for a specific purpose. In this he had the active assistance of the press, particularly its "Blood and Guts" tagline.

The phrase was extracted from a colorful training-camp speech. The war was only a few months old. Training is tough on trainees, but it doesn't make front-page copy. A picturesque United States military figure was urgently needed. Patton had color, to spare. Also, he was very willing to be portrayed as a fire-eating scourge. It was part of his battle paraphernalia. So the gory label was hung on him and it stuck—in the public mind.

Patton was not idolized by his men. He wasn't that type. Naturally reserved and combative, he was not a hail fellow well met. He had social friends and professional admirers, some of the latter, notably other generals, reluctantly so. But outside of his immediate family, Patton had no intimates.

There was nothing stuffy or pompous about him. He had a salty sense of humor and mingled easily and freely. But at the same time, he always maintained a certain intangible but definite distance between himself and others. To his staff who lived and worked with him, and to the troops who saw him constantly, he was "the general" formally, "Georgie" privately.

Combativeness was Patton's dominant characteristic. But he was more than merely an instinctive fighting man—he was a fighting man engaged in the profession of arms.

To Patton, war was a passionate pursuit, a pursuit as coherent and profoundly satisfying as music is to a composer and painting to an artist. War made sense to Patton, and he lived it, thought it, and worked at it, ardently and unceasingly, every day of his life from earliest youth to death.

He did not become a soldier by accident or to earn a livelihood. He was five years old when he informed his parents he intended to become "a great general." When he learned to read, the first book he bought was a history of decisive battles. In school he was always organizing sham battles. On his honeymoon in France, he took his young bride to historic battlefields and fortresses. Later when stationed in Hawaii, he and his wife and young children would stage assault landings while on sailing trips. Even playing his beloved polo and fox hunting, he played at war.

Waging war was Patton's vocation and avocation. All his life he consciously and purposely molded and trained himself to fight. Nothing else really mattered to him. It is significant that the Germans and Russians rated him as the foremost allied combat commander.

Patton's personal life was the direct antithesis of the popular conception of him. Independently wealthy, he lived well but quietly. He had only one love affair in his life. He met his wife when both were in their teens and married her after graduating from West Point. She was at his bedside when he died.

Harry H. Semmes, who served under Patton in both World War I and II, writes this under a heading of "Religion" in his *Portrait of Patton*:

From his adolescence, he had always read the Bible, particularly the life of Christ and the wars of the Old Testament. He knew by heart the order of morning prayer of the Episcopal Church. His thoughts, as demonstrated daily to those close to him, repeatedly indicated that his life was dominated by a feeling of dependence on God. Unless this is borne in mind, it might seem that Patton had the *Gott mit uns* [literally, "God with us"] complex of the German Kaiser of World War I. This was not true, for he turned to God for comfort in adversity and to give thanks in success. General Patton was an unusual mixture of a profane and highly religious man. The Pattons had a cook during one of his tours of duty at Fort Myer, Virginia, when, as a colonel, he commanded the famous 3d Cavalry Regiment. He had to leave on one occasion for several weeks on maneuvers. On his return, the cook said, "It sure is nice to have the Colonel goddamming around the house again."

Paul D. Harkins, serving as deputy chief of operations for the Third Army, observed Patton's curious relationships with Bradley and Eisenhower.

Eisenhower, Bradley, and Patton were good friends. I think that General Patton was senior to both of them, but that didn't bother him. He liked to fight. He'd rather fight than eat.

After Sicily, General Eisenhower had really just gotten command of the whole theater. The Sicilian operation was one of the big ones and we came out of it pretty well. One staff officer visiting from Washington said, "Somebody had made the remark that General Eisenhower was *making* Patton." The staff officer said, "No, General Patton is making Ike."

General Bradley was under Patton in Sicily, but then he was over him in Europe. They got along fine. Bradley's staff was not as involved in operations, as far as keeping the supply coming from the rear and things like that, although they were in the overall operational planning, but not in the specifics. When you get down to the

Army and down to the corps and down to the division, you are getting in to the operations a little bit more. Bradley visited us frequently and they seemed to get along fine.

Considering all the potential for conflict, Patton and General Omar
N. Bradley had a remarkably good relationship throughout the war.
Bradley tells of the turnabout in reporting relationship from his point
of view, during the early phase of the Battle of France, in *A Soldier's Story*:

My own feelings on George were mixed. He had not been my
choice for Army command and I was still wary of the grace with
which he would accept our reversal in roles. For George was six years
my senior and had been my Army commander when I fought II Corps
in the Sicilian campaign. I was apprehensive in having George join
my command, for I feared that too much of my time would probably
be spent in curbing his impetuous habits. But at the same time I
knew that with Patton there would be no need for my whipping
Third Army to keep it on the move. We had only to keep him pointed
in the direction we wanted to go.

George soon caused me to repent these uncharitable reserva-
tions, for he not only bore me no ill will but he trooped for 12th
Army Group with unbounded loyalty and eagerness. Shortly after
the war an officer from Third Army recalled the rancor with which
Patton had frequently excoriated his senior commanders. "And yet
in all those outbursts," he said, "I never heard the general speak an
unkind word of you."

Before many more months had passed, the *new* Patton had
totally obliterated my unwarranted apprehensions; we formed
as amiable and contented a team as existed in the senior command. No longer the martinet that had sometimes strutted in
Sicily, George had now become a judicious, reasonable, and lik-
able commander.

Several months later when George outlined a prospective
scheme of maneuver, I showed him several faults in it. Instead of
replying huffily as he might have a year before, George merely crin-
kled his eyes and chuckled. "You're right, Brad," he said.
"Goddammit, you're always right."

Long-time Bradley staffer Chester B. Hansen writes in his diary
about how perceptions of Patton changed through time at higher
headquarters.

December 8, 1944: I have revised an earlier attitude. With Bradley
to control and guide him, with Gaffey to hold down his administration,

Chapter Ten

Patton provides the leadership and aggressiveness needed to make an army an aggressive and going concern. Patton has daring, he has a great personal ambition to do spectacular things, largely to reassert himself in the eyes of the public, although his publicity appears to have been adequate on that score.

There is no doubt that he is capable. But he is more of a sledge-hammer than a skillful commander. He has more punch than he has knowledge of tactics. He is a brave commander but he is not a brilliant one. His greatest feat consists of his kicking corps and division commanders in the tail whenever they get bogged down. For the impetus on an advance must come from the top and be kicked all the way to the bottom.

Patton's long-time friend and peer, Major General John P. Lucas, would disagree with Hansen's assertion about the need for control and guidance to balance Patton. Lucas came as an observer to Mostaganem, Tunisia, when preparations were under way for the invasion. In his private journal for June 1943, Lucas writes about the way Patton handled the planning, and about their relationship on a personal level:

George's plans were well drawn up and seemed very complete. He strives to give the impression of doing things in an impulsive and "on the spur of the moment" manner but back of all his actions in war is very careful staff planning and much thought. We have been close friends for years and the remark I have heard made so often—that he needs a balance wheel with him to keep him on the right track—I know is unjust and untrue. He makes his share of mistakes but so do all the rest of us. He will never make the most common and deadly mistake of all—inaction.

Spent last night with George. We discussed many subjects. He always gives me a lift. A timid man by nature who has the strength of character and determination to overcome it. I consider him our greatest soldier. He will be great because he has the moral guts to take a chance when weaker souls pull back.

When asked what influenced him most in his future endeavors, Colonel Paul D. Harkins (who would retire as a major general) replies:

Working with General Patton probably influenced me most. He was an ardent student of history and he was a student of others' mistakes. He said, "You don't study history just learn the dates. You study history to learn what to do right and what to do wrong." The idea of anybody who wants to be as good as he was, had to pay the price, and do a lot of studying. You don't get anything in life unless you pay the price, one way or the other. We were going up to the SPH after the Bulge and I went with him. We were on the way back. He stopped in the Maginot Line, which is where the French were in their defensive attitudes. They had quite a setup there . . . the turrets would come up and the gun would shoot and the turrets go down. The soldiers lived right underneath and the ammunition was also down there. They had clubs and everything else, all built underground. General Patton said, "This is man's monument to stupidity." He said, "The enemy knows where you are and they'll just leave you there."

One time we were at the crossing of the river at Avranches, General Grow and his 6th Armored Division had just gotten to the river. He bivouacked on our side. General Patton and I went down and General Patton said, "You get your division across there tonight." General Grow was going to let them rest. General Patton said, "Well, if you study history," he said, "I can give you five examples where people stopped on this side of the river and the bridge wasn't there in the morning. Now I'm going to get two or three divisions across there tonight and then we can take a rest." I asked him why he made Grow do that and he said, "You don't study history to just know the dates. No, you got to find out what happened. What made the success and what made the failure."

I think working with General Patton taught me how to be a commander. I could never be a General Patton. When the Lord made him, He threw away the mold.

───────────◆───────────

When Patton veterans talk about what they learned from their experiences, some talk with hushed reverence about the great events they took part in and how those events shaped them. Lewis Ingalls, who was in the field artillery, says:

The experience makes you grow up. Having been in the Army and in the war, it hardens you to some things and softens you to others. You have a better understanding of life.

It helped me set priorities. Especially the experience of command. My whole business, a sawmill and logging operation, I ran like the Army.

Nothing in this world struck me like when I saw the Statue of Liberty. I almost cried. I swore I'd never set foot out of here once I got home.

Chapter Ten

Through the trials of life, Carl Ulsaker, 95th Infantry Division, has sometimes compared life at its worst—the hellish scene of Ensdorf, Germany, where he had seen carnage beyond imagination:

Certainly, it was a relief to escape the hell of life in Ensdorf; on the other hand, it was disappointing to have to give up ground won with so much difficulty and the sacrifice of so many good men. Even as I recall the events of that day long ago, it nags me to think Tyler, Mazur, Getz, and the others gave their lives for such little purpose. I can say that the successful survival of two weeks in Ensdorf did one good thing for me: it provided me early in life with the nadir of my existence, enabling me to cope calmly with all subsequent crises; for nothing I have since faced has proved to be worse than that experience.

Gerald Nelson, 7th Armored Division, relied on a prayer to get him through.

Talk about praying. I used to pray the 23rd Psalm—"Yea, though I walk through the valley of the shadow of death . . ." I'd pray that a lot during combat. But I'd pray only half of it. I'd say, "I fear no evil because thou art with me. Thy rod and thy staff comfort me." But I'd stop there. The rest goes on like the future: "Thou preparest a table before me in the presence of my enemies; thou anointest my head with oil, my cup runneth over . . ." That's all in the future, and I stopped before that thought. All I could pray for was courage for the here and now—that I'd be able to do my job. Somehow, I couldn't say the rest until I was safe back home.

With far-reaching impact, the war experience has affected Patton veterans more than any other life event. Eileen (Courtney) Biersteker, 65th Field Hospital, looks back across six decades in amazement and gratitude:

I think about how vast this was. How we moved from England to France, into Belgium and on through Germany. All the way from Cherbourg to Austria.

We were happy to be doing what we were doing, and to this day I am happy to have been a part of that. The guys didn't forget us. A friend in Milwaukee was listening one night during the war and heard a soldier interviewed who said, "I would like to see Lieutenant Courtney again, the one who took care of me." Our boys were always so happy to see an American nurse. The way we operated was such that we would take care of them for three or four days and then move on, so we never knew the outcome of them at all. I didn't remember this person. We saw so many.

Aftermath

I came back after the war and married someone who had been in the Army from the beginning to the end of the war, but he'd never left the States. I had brought back a German helmet. My little son would be playing out in the backyard wearing this helmet. And the neighbor lady asked, "Did your father bring that back?" He said, "No, my mother did."

We had been on a truck and asked the truck driver to stop when we saw a bunch of helmets laying in a ditch. And we all jumped out and got one. But oh, were we reprimanded for that, because the Germans knew what souvenir seekers we were, and they would put land mines under things like that.

We still have the helmet. I also still have the silk hankies made by the nuns of Bastogne, who used parachutes of the 101st Airborne to make them and even wrote "Nuts!" on them, like General [Anthony] McAuliffe said to the Germans there.

I was very happy I could be of service, that the Lord made me a nurse to go over there and give some help. All my life it shaped me. I'm a very caring person, did a lot of volunteer work since. Continued nursing after that. Went to Marquette for public nursing. What I saw in World War II was so entirely different than the hospital, where there are such sterile conditions. After that, I guess I was unshakable.

I was over there when Patton was injured and died. We all felt very bad. It was the very general feeling throughout the American forces that he should go that way.

Spoken through a wry smile, W. King Pound of the 4th Armored Division remembers how dedication to Patton almost cost him a job opportunity after the war:

The second time I encountered Patton was when he spoke to us as a unit soon after we got to France. He was up on a hill and the P.A. system was terrible. It was a drumbeat message and he had a few choice words, which he was famous for—words that didn't endear him to the chaplains at all.

Funny thing, after the war, I applied to a Catholic newspaper. It was 1951 and I was interviewed by a monsignor for the archdiocese and I noticed on his lapel a pin for the 82nd Airborne.

I had known a number of men who hated Patton, like one of the guys in our tank platoon who swears he would have killed him on sight. So I said, "Well, you either hated Patton or you loved him. I loved him." The monsignor was obviously of the other camp. The monsignor thought he was a gross, base man. I damn near didn't get the job because of that.

Chapter Ten

◆

What if Patton had lived on after the war? Horace Woodring, Patton's driver, has thought a lot about Patton through the events of passing decades since World War II, prompted by ties with the Patton family and a certain namesake:

    I think the Vietnam War would have driven him up the wall. Korea, too. He would have wanted to go in there and win. There's lots of things that would have bothered him. He in no way wanted to be involved in politics. I heard him say to his aide that he was very close with President Roosevelt. But when Roosevelt died, he said, "Uh-oh, now I'm in trouble. Yeah, Truman was a captain under me and I gave him the biggest ass-chewing anybody ever got, and I'm sure he hasn't forgotten about it."

    General John Waters was married to Patton's number two daughter. He comes to Detroit once a year and I see him. I did meet the oldest daughter. We went to a TV show on the tour for the movie. I was informed that General Patton's daughter, Mrs. Totten, would be on the show—a local version of *Good Morning America*. She said afterward, "I didn't give a damn about the show, I just wanted to meet you." She reminded me so much of him in her actions and her speech, although she didn't cuss. In fact, the cohost asked Mrs. Totten how the family handled all the cussing her dad was known for: "Did he cuss at the breakfast table?" She answered, "He cussed only in Latin."

    I thought very highly of General Patton. I had just reenlisted four days prior to the accident. He had wanted me to work for him in civilian life, but to stay in the Army one more year to work for him there. He had planned to retire in a year. Of course, that all ended with the accident, so I just stayed overseas that year. He was my idol.

Horace Woodring named his son John Patton Woodring.
Daniel Kennedy, Lucky Forward's engineering section, speculates on where Patton would be if he were living now.

    If Patton were in the civilian world today, he'd be one of the best professors of business administration or a big-time company president. When you figure that, once we were operational in the Third Army we had 350,000 troops and several times had 400,000, that was quite a feat to manage. Think about supplying them with everything—food, ammunition, clothing, and everything they needed. And to move as fast as we did across Europe. That took some technique.

Aftermath

He'd do well in the business world. There they don't have near as many to worry about. Leading 400,000. Think about it.

His gaze fixed on his advancing troops, Patton presides over fighting around El Guettar on March 30, 1943. A few months earlier, as he stood poised on the brink of his destiny, he pondered in his diary: "I can't decide logically if I am a man of destiny or a lucky fool, but I think I am destined. I feel that my claim to greatness hangs on an ability to lead and inspire."
Patton Museum

Peter P. Joseph, 503rd Military Police Battalion, reflects on his identification with Patton that has continued since the war:

We served with him until war's end in May and then became occupation troops in Bavaria, with General Patton as military governor of Bavaria. When he was finally relieved of his command of the Third Army around the end of September 1945 or the first of October, I don't believe many of us were aware of this. His military career has shown him to be the country's greatest general, destined to die on the battlefield where he spent so much time, only to have his death result from an accident instead. He had stated before that war was his destiny—"In peace I am useless." So maybe what seemed to be an untimely death was meant to be. He will always be remembered by me and, I'm sure, my colleagues of the 503rd Military Police Battalion, as having been a real soldier, committed to the task he was given, and fulfilling it to the end. I am proud to have served in this great Army and with our MP unit, and am pleased to have had such a great man as our commander. Books have been written, stories have been told, and his legacy will live on in the annals of history.

Sources of Quotations

Chapter 1: Training for "A Nice Juicy War"

Page	
12	Hooper. Memoir.
13	Luttrell. Letter to the author.
13–14	Luman. Letter to the author.
14–15	Semmes, *Portrait of Patton* (New York: Appleton-Century-Crofts, Inc., 1955), p.14.
17	Harkins. Oral history, the U.S. Army Military History Institute (USAMHI), Carlisle Barracks, Pennsylvania.
17–18	Hooper. Memoir.
18–19	Rosato. Memoir.

Page	
19–20	Sassard. Letter to the author.
20	Luttrell. Letter to the author.
20–22	Moncrief. Interview with the author.
22	Erbes. Memoir.
23–24	Chiriaco. E-mail to the author.
24	Gish. Interview with the author.
24	Moncrief. Interview with the author.
24	Gish. Interview with the author.
24–26	Markovitz. Interview with the author.
26–27	Gish. Interview with the author.
27	Wolczyk. Letters to the author.

Chapter 2: Dueling in the Desert

Page	
30–32	Watters. Memoir.
32–34	Burt. Interview with the author.
34–36	Erbes. Memoir.
36–37	Gay. Oral history, USAMHI.
37–39	Kunz. Interview with the author.
39	Watters. Memoir.
40	Davidson. Memoir.
40–41	Erbes. Memoir.
41–42	Watters. Memoir.
42	Erbes. Memoir.
42–43	Codman. *Drive* (Boston: Little, Brown and Company, 1957), p. 45–47.
43–44	Davidson. Memoir.
44–45	N. Allen. Wartime diary.
45	N. Allen. Letter to the author.
46	Oakley. Interview with the author.
46	Kness. Interview with the author.
46	Evans. Interview with the author.
47	Hansen. Wartime diary, USAMHI.
47	Skogsberg. Memoir.

Page	
48	Haas. Interview with the author.
48–49	Oakley. Interview with the author.
49	Davidson. Memoir.
50	Codman. *Drive*, p. 87.
50–51	Goldsmith. Brief written account found at USAMHI.
51–52	Evans. Interview with the author.
52–54	Oakley. Interview with the author.
54–55	Skogsberg. Memoir.
55	Skogsberg. Interview with the author.
56	Skogsberg. Memoir.
56	Bessman. Brief written account found at USAMHI.
57	Skogsberg. Memoir.
57–58	Kunz. Interview with the author.
59	Luman. Letter to the author.
59	Skogsberg. Memoir.
60	Farrell. Interview with the author.
60–61	Moorman. Letter to the author.

Chapter 3: Racing Across Sicily

Page	
63–64	Fleser. Interview with the author.
64–65	Kunz. Memoir.
65	Kunz. Interview with the author.
66–67	Lucas. Wartime diary, USAMHI.
67–69	Irish. Memoir.

Page	
70	Fleser. Interview with the author.
70–71	Skogsberg. Memoir.
71	Lucas. Wartime diary, USAMHI.
72	Gay. Oral history, USAMHI.
73–75	Sims. Interview with the author.

Page	
75	Erbes. Memoir.
76	Burt. Brief personal account found at USAMHI.
76–77	Fleser. Interview with the author.
77–78	Luman. Interview with the author.
78–79	Sims. Interview with the author.
80–81	Erbes. Memoir.
81	Kunz. Interview with the author.
81–82	Farrell. Interview with the author.
82–83	Davidson. Memoir.
83	Lucas. Wartime diary, USAMHI.
83–84	Evans. Interview with the author.
84–85	Kunz. Interview with the author.
85	Lucas. Wartime diary, USAMHI.
85	Kunz. Interview with the author.
86	Lucas. Wartime diary, USAMHI.
86	Kunz. Interview with the author.

Page	
87–88	Codman. *Drive*, p. 111.
88	Medical officer's report, USAMHI.
89	Sheaffer. Interview with the author.
89–90	Eisenhower. *At Ease: Stories I Tell to Friends* (New York: Doubleday, 1967), p. 270.
90–91	Conway. Brief account found at USAMHI.
91	Luttrell. Letter to the author.
91	Codman. *Drive*.
91–92	Harkins. Oral history, USAMHI.
92	Lucas. Wartime diary, USAMHI.
92–93	Codman. *Drive*, p. 114–115.
93–94	Davidson. Memoir.
94	Farrell. Interview with the author.
95	Eisenhower. *At Ease: Stories I Tell to Friends*, p. 269.

Chapter 4: Preparing in Britain

Page	
96–97	Hose. Interview with the author.
97	Eklund. Interview with the author.
97–98	R. Allen. *Lucky Forward* (New York: The Vanguard Press, 1947), p. 16–17.
98–99	Hose. Interview with the author.
100–101	Joseph. Letter to the author.
101–103	Hose. Interview with the author.
103	Pajerski. Interview with the author.
103–104	Eklund. Interview with the author.
104	Joseph. Letter to the author.
104–106	Pajerski. Interview with the author.
106	Unrath. Memoir.

Page	
107	Thomas. Interview with the author.
107	Gish. Interview with the author.
107–108	Robbins. Letter to the author.
108–109	Thomas. Interview with the author.
109–110	"Operations Sub-section, G-3, Plan for Operations in the Field," USAMHI.
110–112	Unrath. Memoir.
112–113	Eisenhower. *At Ease: Stories I Tell to Friends*, p. 279.
113	Ibid., p. 269–270.
113	Hose. Letter to the author.

Chapter 5: Rampaging Through France

Page	
114–116	Ulsaker. Memoir.
116–117	Green. Memoir.
118	Hose. Interview with the author.
119	Reimers. Wartime diary, USAMHI.
119–120	Bradley. *A Soldier's Story* (New York: Henry Holt and Company, Inc., 1951), p. 357–358.
120–121	Pound. Interview with the author.
121–122	M. Davis. Interview with the author.
122	G. Davis. Interview with the author.
123	Joseph. Interview with the author.
123–124	Pound. Interview with the author.
124	Joseph. Interview with the author.
125	Pound. Interview with the author.
125–126	G. Davis. Interview with the author.

Page	
126–128	Baker. Interview with the author.
128–130	Schladerman. Memoir.
131	G. Davis. Interview with the author.
132–136	Flaten. Oral history, Wisconsin Veterans Museum, Madison.
136–138	Gish. Interview with the author.
138–144	Gill. Oral history, Wisconsin Veterans Museum, Madison.
144	Tousignant. Letter to the author.
144–145	Robbins. Letter to the author.
145	M. Davis. Interview with the author.
146–148	Reimers. Wartime diary, USAMHI.
148	Kennedy. Interview with the author.
148	R. Allen. *Lucky Forward*, p. 129.
149–150	Kepner. Oral history, USAMHI.

Chapter 6: Stalled at the Moselle

Chapter 7: On the Hunt Again

Chapter 8: Battling the Bulge

Chapter 9: Through the Siegfried Line and Beyond

Chapter 10: Aftermath

Selected Bibliography

Allen, Robert S. *Lucky Forward*. New York: The Vanguard Press, 1947.

Blumenson, Martin. *The Patton Papers, 1940–1945*. Boston: Houghton Mifflin Company, 1974.

—, *Patton: The Man Behind the Legend, 1885–1945*. New York: William Morrow and Company, Inc., 1985.

Bradley, Omar S. *A Soldier's Story*. New York: Henry Holt & Co., 1951.

Codman, Charles R. *Drive*. Boston: Little, Brown & Co., 1957.

Eisenhower, Dwight D. *At Ease: Stories I Tell My Friends*. New York: Doubleday, a division of Random House, Inc., 1967.

Farago, Ladislas. *Patton: Ordeal and Triumph*. New York: Dell Publishing Company, 1963.

Harkins, Paul D. *When the Third Cracked Europe*. Springfield, Virginia: Army Times Publishing Company, 1969.

Patton, George S. Jr. *War As I Knew It*. Boston: Houghton Mifflin Company, 1947.

Semmes, Harry H. *Portrait of Patton*. New York: Appleton-Century-Crofts, 1955.

Index